# The 1922 Committee

Manchester University Press

# The 1922 Committee

Power behind the scenes

Philip Norton

MANCHESTER UNIVERSITY PRESS

Published by Manchester University Press
Oxford Road, Manchester M13 9PL
www.manchesteruniversitypress.co.uk

British Library Cataloguing-in-Publication Data
A catalogue record for this book is available from the British Library

ISBN 978 1 5261 7330 0 hardback

First published 2023

The publisher has no responsibility for the persistence or accuracy of URLs for
any external or third-party internet websites referred to in this book, and does
not guarantee that any content on such websites is, or will remain, accurate or
appropriate.

Typeset by Newgen Publishing UK

# Contents

v

# Contents

# Preface: what is 'the 1922'?

There are some questions that probably should not be attempted, or even asked, in pub quizzes. 'What is the 1922 Committee?' is a prime candidate. The name crops up in the British media, especially during periods of political crisis. It is mentioned in some texts and political memoirs. The problem is that attempts to explain what it is frequently get it wrong. Even its own executive committee has on occasion mistaken the date of its formation. 'It is a political body set up in 1922.' Incorrect. 'It's the name for the Parliamentary Conservative Party.' Strictly speaking, no. 'It is a group of Tory MPs set up to keep the party leadership on its toes.' Incorrect. 'It is a cabal' (according to a Tory party activist in 2022). Er, no.

What media reports of the 1922 Committee do convey is that it is an 'influential' or 'powerful' body. Every so often, it appears prominently in media stories, not least when there is conflict or a leadership crisis in the British Conservative Party. At times, it has been seen as the body that has forced ministers out of office. A number of senior ministers under the governments of Margaret Thatcher and John Major fell foul of the 1922 Committee and resigned. However, its greatest impact has been seen in both making and destroying Conservative leaders. In the twenty-first century, it is not so much the making as the slaying of party leaders that has rendered it a powerful body. In the three years from 2019 to 2022, the UK had three prime ministers who resigned, each doing so after being visited in No. 10 Downing Street by the chairman of the 1922 Committee,[1] Sir Graham Brady. None was removed by the electorate. Each had been the subject of Conservative MPs writing to Brady, calling for a vote of no confidence. Brady was a regular presence on television screens. In determining the fate of Conservative prime ministers, the 1922 Committee clearly matters.

However, it was not ever thus. The 1922 Committee has had an eventful, but uneven, history. It is in large part shrouded in mystery, reported, albeit sporadically, in media stories, but rarely the subject of sustained scholarly study. Its role in Conservative leadership elections, and in inducing ministerial resignations, is what renders it the focus of media attention, but it had no such role for the first few decades of its existence. It has, though, had some notable consequences for British politics. Those consequences are varied and significant.

Its name is a misnomer. Over the decades, many writers have indeed assumed that it was founded in 1922 and some have ascribed its origins to a meeting of Conservative MPs at the Carlton Club in October 1922 that brought down the Liberal–Conservative Coalition led by Liberal Prime Minister David Lloyd George.[2] The claim was still being made in 2022.[3] Even the officers of the 1922 Committee have at times been confused as to the year of its creation and its origins. In 1971, one of the joint secretaries suggested writing a history to mark the 1922's half-century the following year.[4] It was pointed out that it was a year too early. The Committee clearly lacked an institutional memory, as in 1992 the officers were contemplating holding a 70th anniversary event until it was pointed out it was not 70 years of age.[5]

The 1922 Committee was not founded in 1922 and it is a not a committee. As we shall see, it was founded in 1923, formed by some MPs newly elected in the general election of November 1922, and was nothing to do with the Carlton Club meeting of the previous year. The motivation for its formation was not political, but practical: it was to enable new MPs to make sense of their surroundings.

# Preface: what is 'the 1922'?

It evolved from being a body of newly elected MPs – the class of 1922 – to one encompassing all Conservative private members. It is the closest there is to being the Parliamentary Conservative Party, but it is not a creature of the party, nor is it the whole parliamentary party – it excludes the party leader (always) and ministers when in government. It was not formed by the party leadership, but by the members themselves, resulting in a body that enjoys autonomy within the Conservative Party.

Scholarly analyses of the 1922 Committee have been notable for their rarity. With the exception of the historian Stuart Ball, few have studied its history. The dearth of scholarly attention has meant that the 1922 is a powerful political body hiding in plain sight. This volume seeks to fill a notable gap. It has been written to mark the centenary of 'the 1922'. In 2013, I wrote a booklet to mark its 90th anniversary.[6] This is a greatly extended and updated version of that work. It retains the same basic framework, but with a much greater emphasis on the impact of the Committee, drawing out its consequences for the political system. It constitutes only the second book written exclusively about the 1922 Committee. The first, by one of its joint secretaries, Philip Goodhart, was published in 1973 to mark its 50th anniversary.

In writing this book, I have benefitted enormously from the support and co-operation of the current chairman of the Committee, Sir Graham Brady, and of other officers as well as of a wide range of past and present Conservative MPs. As explained in Chapter 1, I have benefitted greatly – indeed, the work would not have been possible without it – from access to the minutes of the Committee.

I am also indebted to Manchester University Press for the care and attention they have given not only to the editorial process, but also to the production process. One incentive for accepting the contract to publish the volume with MUP was the quality demonstrated in publishing *Governing Britain*,[7] showing that books can be published in hardcover, with excellent print quality, at a price that students can afford. I am also grateful for the valuable and enthusiastic comments of the anonymous referee, whose feedback has been enormously helpful.

Although I have benefitted greatly from the knowledge and insights of a wide range of parliamentarians, as well as fellow scholars, I alone am responsible for what follows. I welcome comments from readers.

*Philip Norton*
University of Hull

# Chapter 1

# Setting the scene: parliamentary parties in perspective

Political parties are fundamental to legislatures. They mould behaviour. It is impossible to discuss political activity in legislative chambers and committee rooms without reference to party. Candidates normally stand under a party label and are elected because of that label and once in the legislature their lives are shaped by party.

Since the emergence of organised mass-membership political parties in the nineteenth century, parties have been at the heart of normative assessments of parliaments, the growth of party seen as facilitating the transfer of power from the legislature to the executive. The scholar-politician Lord Bryce in 1921 identified the multiplication of parties as one of the 'chronic ailments' undermining representative assemblies. He titled one of his chapters 'The decline of legislatures' and the term entered the scholarly lexicon.[1] 'Writing just after the First World War, Bryce at once summarised the view of an entire generation of observers of representative institutions and provided a dogma for a new generation of disillusioned democrats.'[2] In the UK, there was a perception of a fall from the 'golden age' of Parliament, or, as Bernard Crick put it, of 'an ideal image of the past'.[3]

Subjective assessments aside, government of a nation is party government. Parties contest elections for the purpose of achieving a sufficient number of seats to form a government or to be able to form part of a governing coalition. The relationship between government and the legislature is determined in most cases by party. Anthony King, in a seminal article on executive–legislative relations, identified five modes of the relationship: the opposition, intra-party, inter-party, cross-party and non-party modes.[4] They all derive from, and are meaningless without reference to, party. Members normally sit in party groups and vote loyally as their leaders dictate. Deviations from the party stance are the exception and not the rule.[5] In the UK House of Commons, when members are permitted free votes, unencumbered by a party line, the best predictor of voting behaviour is party.[6] In the House of Lords, where parties have few means of imposing discipline on members, peers display high levels of party loyalty in votes.[7] High levels of unity, as well as deviations from the party line, have been the subject of scholarly analyses. Various sophisticated models have been devised to explain party cohesion.[8]

Yet what is notable about this growing body of scholarship is what is missing. The literature addresses primarily observable, recorded and quantifiable behaviour. Speeches and questions asked can be subjected to rigorous qualitative and quantitative analysis. Votes, especially in legislatures utilising roll-call voting, can be analysed and assessed, employing techniques to test theories of legislative voting behaviour.[9] Yet political parties, or party groups, do not operate solely in the chamber and committee rooms. They typically have a distinct organisational structure within the legislature. Party members do not simply come in as individuals and vote as the party dictates. They form part of a formally recognised, and organised, party group. Party groups normally have to be recognised as such by the chamber authorities, or rules, in order to be allocated resources. The party or party group will usually have a formal structure, with leadership positions and whips. They may have their own dedicated space. In the US Congress, for example, each party in each House has its own room, known as a cloakroom, where members can meet, discuss legislative strategy and prepare Floor strategy.[10] Party members may meet, or caucus, on a regular basis and have their own secretariat, separate from the formal leadership. In some legislatures, the vote of the caucus binds members to support the decision in the chamber. When the Parliamentary Labour Party (PLP) was formed in the British Parliament in 1906, the party's constitution required Labour MPs to abide by decisions of the parliamentary party in carrying the aims of the constitution.[11] As party leader Clement Attlee later observed, the party 'insists … on majority rule'.[12]

Relative to the mass of scholarship on party behaviour in the chamber and committee rooms, that within the party organisation is neglected. That this should be so is explicable in that such behaviour is not normally observable and measurable. Party caucuses are usually held behind closed doors. Members of a party may prefer to mix with one another informally or to utilise the party infrastructure to discuss matters independent of party leaders or in order to convey their views privately to the leadership. Members can give vent to views they may not wish to be made public. 'The idea of keeping the proceedings private is simply that the party does not wish to advertise publicly its internal strains and stresses.'[13] What happens in the private confines of a party caucus may determine members' behaviour in public. Behaviour in the chamber may be explicable only by what has happened in private party deliberations. Yet while the former is much studied, the latter is largely ignored.

There is some English-language literature on party organisation in particular legislatures, as on the US Congress,[14] but little that compares legislatures. The most substantial comparative work is *Parliamentary Party Groups in European Democracies*, edited by Knut Heidar and Ruud Koole, published in 2000.[15] The contributions to that work provide valuable analyses of party groups in Western legislatures. The focus, though, is often the relationship with other political actors, such as the extra-parliamentary party, and the rules and powers of the party group, not least in enforcing discipline. A more recent analysis by Schindler and Kannenberg also focuses on the formal rules – the standing orders – of party groups and the extent to which groups enjoy autonomy from the party leadership.[16] To what extent does the party leadership determine the decisions of the party group? Members may have to sign up to accept party discipline. This is a common feature of analyses of the link between parties and parliamentary voting behaviour: the extent of intra-party democracy and its impact on candidate and leadership selection typically form the basis for explaining levels of party cohesion.[17]

There are few analyses of what actually happens *within* the party groups when they hold their regular meetings. The limited literature is summarised by Saalfeld and Strøm in their overview of political parties and legislators in *The Oxford Handbook of Legislative Studies*. As they observe, 'The "black box" of intra-party preference heterogeneity, organization, and decision-making (and its importance for legislative outcomes) has rarely been opened up.'[18]

Our purpose here is to prise open the 'black box' and look at the consequences of party organisation within the legislature. We do so through a case study of the party group in the British House of Commons known as the 1922 Committee. 'The 1922' may go through periods of not receiving much media coverage, but when there are tensions in the Conservative Party, especially at times of a leadership crisis or a Conservative minister coming under attack for a policy or behaviour, the 1922 comes under the media spotlight. It is described as 'powerful' or 'influential' and, in terms of removing the party leader, as a kingmaker. Yet this powerful body is much misunderstood – its name alone giving rise to false assumptions – and little studied. As noted in the preface, few scholarly analyses have been published. Other than studies by the historian Stuart Ball[19] and this writer,[20] the only substantial work has been by a secretary of the 1922, Philip Goodhart, to mark the 1922's 50th anniversary in 1973.[21] This work seeks to fill a notable gap and comprises both a history of the 1922 during the first century of its existence and an assessment of its consequences.

## The power of the 1922

Power is a term much used in political discourse, but it is a concept that has different meanings. Steven Lukes advanced three views: in essence, the pluralist, elitist and institutional.[22] The first is concerned with who achieves a desired outcome once an issue is on the agenda, the second is concerned with who determines what gets on the agenda, and the third is concerned with the structures and processes that determine how an issue is resolved. The first tends to be the view utilised by most studies of political decision making. Each has a utility for analysing the consequences of the 1922 Committee for British politics.

The pluralist view is concerned with observable outcomes when there is a dispute over what to do. Has A achieved the outcome desired in getting B to do that which otherwise B would not do? It may be achieved through coercion, B believing that they have no practical capacity to resist, or through persuasion, B having a choice but exercising it in favour of A. In the context of the 1922, the Committee is powerful when there is a dispute and it achieves an outcome desired by most of its members.

An elitist view of power is concerned not with how issues are resolved once they are on the agenda, but with how they are kept off the agenda.[23] Issues may be kept off by shared attitudes of those who set the agenda not wanting something discussed,[24] or by anticipated reaction, that is, wanting a matter considered but anticipating it will engender opposition and possible defeat. It may not be worth the effort. An issue may be kept off the agenda if a leader or minister believes that MPs won't support it and, in order to avoid conflict in the chamber or with the 1922 Committee, does not pursue a policy. The problem with non-decision-making is that it is not usually observable and quantifiable. There may be occasions when some information is gleaned that anticipated reaction has deterred a minister from proceeding with a particular policy, but on other occasions there may be no record of it.

The institutional view of power is not concerned with the substance of a dispute, but rather the process by which it is resolved. Institutions are not neutral in their effect. Their structures and rules can affect outcomes in a way that differs from what would happen if they had different structures and rules or if they did not exist at all.[25] MPs' behaviour in the House of Commons is shaped by detailed rules, interpreted and enforced by a presiding officer. Members' behaviour may change as rules change. Leadership of parties is determined by a set of rules that may be amended over time. The rules may differ between parties. Had the British Labour Party in 2015 had the same rules as the Conservative Party for electing a leader, Jeremy Corbyn would almost certainly not have become leader of the party. Had the Conservative Party retained its pre-1965 process of selecting a leader by 'emergence', Margaret Thatcher by her own admission would not have become party leader in 1975.[26]

Not offering a definition of power can result in analysts talking past one another. The 1922 may not regularly challenge successfully policies favoured by the leadership; from a pluralist perspective, it is thus not very powerful. However, when it comes to electing the leader of the Conservative Party, it is the 1922 that determines the rules and timetable. Those seeking to be leader have no option but to work within the rules set by the 1922. Thus, from an institutional perspective, the 1922 matters and it matters greatly.

## A functional approach

These views of power are not mutually exclusive. Each allows us to examine a body from a particular perspective to understand its effect on the political system. They provide a framework to explore the consequences of the 1922, which, following Robert Packenham, we term functions of the 1922.[27] As Packenham noted, those who write about legislatures assume that that they have consequence for the political system; as such, all those who study legislatures are, explicitly or implicitly, functionalists.[28] Packenham spent time observing a legislature in action and teased out consequences it had for the political system. He was examining a body that had little or no impact on public policy – it was a legislature operating in a nation under military control – but nonetheless fulfilled tasks, such as acting as a safety valve for tensions generated by the political system. As he recorded of the legislature, 'even if it had no decision-making power whatsoever, the other functions which it performs would be significant'.[29] Research of legislatures in other non-democratic nations has led to a similar conclusion.[30]

A functional approach provides a basis for scholars to assess the impact of party groups in legislatures. This approach does not rest on a theory of party groups, but rather, following Packenham, offers a checklist for scholars to utilise in assessing the behaviour of party groups in legislative chambers.[31] Are these functions replicated in other legislatures? Do they have the same significance? Even where, as is variously the case, party groups are not autonomous of the party leadership, do they have consequences for the political system? This is essentially a starting point for making sense of party groups in their legislative environment and comparing consequences provides the basis for seeing commonalities, and differences, and generating theories to explain them.

## Methodology

This study of the 1922 Committee utilises a range of methodologies. The principal approach is anthropological. As Emma Crewe, herself an anthropologist, wrote in her study of the House of Commons, 'Parliament has everything an anthropologist loves,' including conflicts, rituals and hierarchies.[32] 'The Westminster Parliament is famous, changing and misunderstood; perpetually in the news but always mysterious.'[33] The 1922 Committee can well be claimed to fall within the mysterious, certainly for the scholar, given that it operates primarily in private space. The challenge is essentially getting behind the scenes and immersing oneself in the life of the community.

For that purpose, this study utilises the most common form of anthropological study, namely that of participant observation. It is 'a way of knowing *from the inside*'.[34] It entails observing while participating in the rituals and other events of the specific community. 'There is no contradiction ... between participation and observation: rather, the one depends on the other.'[35] As a Conservative peer, I have had the opportunity to attend the weekly meetings of the 1922 Committee and have done so regularly since entering Parliament in 1998. It is a case of not just observing the natives, but also being one of them. I have drawn on my notes of meetings, made contemporaneously. Discerning readers will see the odd reference in the text that demonstrates my occasional engagement going beyond passive attendance.

An anthropological approach also has one other distinguishing feature. 'To do anthropological research well, you have to have an open mind and to approach conversations, observation and encounters with a willingness to learn.'[36] This study is therefore not couched within a particular theoretical approach: there is a basic framework in terms of power, but no testable hypotheses. Different behavioural theories have helped inform my observation, but none has formed an exclusive basis of analysis.

As part of an anthropological study, participant observation is complemented, and for the early history of the 1922 substituted, by textual analysis. This encompasses archival research, drawing on the minutes and other records of the Committee held in the Bodleian Library, Oxford, as well as other primary material, such as that held in the Thatcher Archive at Churchill College, Cambridge, and newspaper articles available through *The Times* Archive and the British Newspaper Archive. It also encompasses

my own archives, comprising records of interviews and correspondence with MPs who sat in various twentieth-century parliaments, undertaken in the early 1970s as part of research on
Conservative parliamentary behaviour. Utilising these sources is
necessary to analyse the historical development of the 1922. There
is no one still alive who can recount events in the first few decades of its existence. Diaries and memoirs of parliamentarians can
provide information beyond that given in the formal minutes, not
least in providing insights, identifying the impact of the speaker,
and giving a sense of the mood of the meeting. Memoirs may also
offer useful reflections on the nature and utility of '22 meetings.
They can have value in terms of what is not said, with a dearth of
references suggesting that the '22 has not impacted greatly on the
political life of the writer.

Archival research extends to media reports of the 1922 throughout its history. This encompasses regional and local newspapers,
not least for the early decades when they were an important source
of information for citizens. Media stories can be useful for reflecting the importance of an issue. Some members may leak what
has happened in meetings of the 1922, though their interpretation
is likely to be partial and can be at odds with the interpretation
offered by others who were present. Lobby correspondents 'are
experts at reading between the lines and writing very plausible
stories – usually with a considerable basis of truth',[37] though on
occasion the information is garbled or simply incorrect. Michael
Spicer, chairman of the 1922 Committee, recorded in his diary on
28 June 2001: '*Evening Standard* says I was overridden on the timing decisions [of the party leadership election] by '22 Executive
committee – not true.'[38] Media reports have been utilised to reflect
when activity of the 1922 is deemed to merit attention. At times
of high tension within the party, as when a leader is under pressure or a leadership election is under way, the corridor outside the
committee room where the 1922 is meeting is usually crowded by
journalists, 'waiting', in the words of one MP, 'to ensnare unwary

backbenchers'.[39] Members may have difficulty navigating their way into the room. News bulletins and the next day's newspapers will cover the meeting. At other times in recent years, there is at most a lone journalist hoping to catch a snippet from departing members.

For recent decades, I have also drawn on interviews with MPs and former members. These include those who have served as officers and others who are regular attenders, as well as members who are infrequent attenders. Recent decades have seen senior and sometimes not so senior politicians publish their memoirs or diaries. A good number have proved a valuable source for reports of activity in the 1922. Some make no mention of it, which, as already noted, may reflect the fact that it does not figure significantly on their radar, with these politicians preferring to devote their time to other political activities.

The book is divided into three parts. The first recounts the history of the Committee, based on three critical junctures. Various events determined the birth and development of the 1922. In the early years, its continuance was by no means guaranteed. Nor was it initially a powerful force in the Conservative Party. That it became so was a consequence of events in the 1930s exogenous to the Committee. Controversy over the traditional means of selecting the party leader led to it becoming a key actor in determining who became leader and, in most cases, prime minister. Had events worked out differently – had there not been a chief whip sympathetic to the purpose of the 1922 when it came into being, had there not been a national coalition government formed in 1940, and had there been an obvious and undisputed successor to Harold Macmillan as party leader in 1963 – the 1922 is not likely to have the consequences it does today.

The second part details the organisation and leadership of the 1922. Media and scholarly attention is often confined to the weekly meetings of the Committee, but the 1922 is much more than the gathering each week of Tory backbenchers. For a good part of its history, it was complemented, and often overshadowed, by back-bench subject committees. The powerhouse of the 1922 is its executive committee. It has been led by a notable line-up of chairmen, some serving very short terms in office while others have served for a decade or more. Some have been notably influential, while others have had little or no impact.

The third part identifies the consequences of the 1922. By meeting and acting in a particular way, the 1922 shapes the behaviour of MPs that has consequences for the political system. For some commentators, and even for some Tory MPs, the consequences are seen as limited, the 1922 being viewed as little more than a talking shop, with little or no impact on decision making. As already mentioned, some Tory politicians have written memoirs in which the 1922 either doesn't figure or gets only a passing reference. It hardly gets a mention, for example, in Margaret Thatcher's *The Downing Street Years*. (When she does mention it, it is to misstate the reasons for its formation.)[40] Even MPs who attend meetings can be dismissive. Tory MP Julian Critchley variously wrote about its activities. He drew attention to Walder's Law of the 1922, devised in the 1960s by David Walder, MP for High Peak, which was: 'the first three people to speak from the floor on any matter whatsoever were invariably mad'.[41] As Critchley recorded, 'David was right; I cannot remember who they all were … but Major Morrison's injunction [asking for matters arising] did seem to encourage the dim and the dotty to hold forth, and at some length.'[42]

However, as Critchley recognised, there was more to it than that. The 1922, he acknowledged, could make a difference. 'The individual backbencher', he wrote, 'does not count for much … but the '22 does matter; the anger of two hundred or so back-benchers when focused upon a man or an issue can destroy the reputation of a minister … or force a resignation …; it can also gravely weaken the standing of the Prime Minister of the day.'[43] In so writing, he effectively acknowledged the importance of institution – the 1922 provides a structured framework for the expression of that anger – and the multi-functional nature of the body, impacting on the careers of ministers and on policies. The effect on policies may be direct, focused on the particular issue, or indirect: if a minister is forced from office, his or her successor may pursue different policies, or, if having faced a hostile meeting, may be deterred in future – the anticipated reaction dimension – from undertaking a policy that may encounter hostility from the '22.

The principal consequences are those of facilitating socialisation as well as enabling MPs to establish themselves and be heard, meetings of the '22 serving as a platform, sounding board and safety valve, as well as enabling backbenchers to put a warning shot across a minister's bows. The Committee also serves as a trade union for backbench interests (in essence, for Tory MPs as MPs) and as a means of maintaining a distinct party voice, especially important when the party is not alone in government. It can influence public policy, challenge ministers and choose – and remove – the party leader. It is the last two of these that tend especially to be contentious and attract the headlines, even though it may be the others that are carried out on a more persistent basis.

By providing a means for Tory MPs to meet together on a regular basis within a structured framework to discuss issues, with an agenda and officers, the 1922 also contributes to the institutionalisation of the House of Commons. Meetings of the '22, like meetings of the Parliamentary Labour Party, provide a particular dimension to how MPs use space within Parliament. Their most visible activity is in public space – what goes on formally in the chamber and committee rooms, where what happens is scheduled and recorded publicly – but they also utilise informal space and private space. Informal space is where MPs gather without any agenda, rules or presiding offices, such as dining and tea rooms, as well as the corridors and division lobbies.[44] Private space is where they gather away from publicly visible and recorded activity, but where behaviour is governed by rules, an agenda and with a presiding officer. As with formal proceedings and discourse in informal space, meetings of the 1922 help facilitate the autonomy of the legislature, differentiating it from the wider environment as well as enhancing its capacity to limit the influence of external forces, such as the party leadership.[45] It may help integrate members into the institution, facilitate a mode of behaviour, as well as clearly contribute to the complexity of the institution.[46] As with informal space, the use of private space contributes to the utility of the legislature.[47]

The list of functions is not definitive – it derives from my observation and analysis – nor exhaustive. Others may discern consequences not covered here and may offer different interpretations to those offered here. It is designed to facilitate an understanding of the difference the 1922 has made to the life of Parliament and British politics. The functions have accumulated over time, some fulfilled on a continuous basis and some sporadically. Parts I and II of the book describe what the 1922 has done, and how it has been organised, during the first century of its existence. Part III explains why it matters.

**Part I**

# History

## Chapter 2

# Modest beginnings: the origins of the 1922

The Conservative Party evolved from the Tory Party in the 1830s[1] and by the end of the century was the 'in' party in British politics.[2] The party in Parliament was notable for its cohesion and for its top-down control. In so far as there was an organisation, it consisted primarily of the whips and the party leaders.[3] There were occasional meetings of Conservative MPs, but these were summoned by the leader primarily for the purpose, as Aspinall put it, of 'laying down the law'.[4] There was no mechanism for backbenchers to engage with the party leadership. One member of the 1918–22 Parliament, interviewed many years ago by this writer, recalled that one was expected to accept 'unquestionably' the domination of the leadership.[5]

The absence of a means of regular dialogue between backbenchers and the party leaders was to cause tensions, in the first decade of the twentieth century over tariff reform and in the third over the coalition with the Liberals under Prime Minister Lloyd George. Dissatisfaction with the latter culminated in a meeting at the Carlton Club in October 1922 at which Tory MPs voted, against the advice of party leaders, to fight the next election as an independent party, in effect to bring the coalition with the Liberals to an end. This precipitated the resignation of the party leader, Sir Austen Chamberlain, and a general election.

The meeting of Tory MPs at the Carlton Club is variously claimed to be the cause of some MPs getting together subsequently to form a body – the 1922 Committee – that was to become for all intents and purpose the parliamentary Conservative Party.[6] However, there is no causal relationship between the meeting at the Carlton Club and the formation of the 1922 Committee. The '1922' was not formed as a 'ginger group' to enable some MPs to act as critics of the leadership, nor was it formed to prevent a repetition of the clash that had occurred between leaders and the led. There is no evidence of those who formed it being influenced by the events of the previous year to which, in any event, they were not a party. The proximity of the formation of the '22 to the Carlton Club meeting is coincidental, not consequential.[7]

The motivation for the creation of the '22 was more immediate. The prompt was the absence of any induction process for newly elected MPs. Once elected to the House of Commons, MPs turned up at the Palace of Westminster and were expected to find their own way around the parliamentary estate and learn what to do by observation and talking to other more experienced members.[8] For some members, not least those with no prior parliamentary knowledge or engagement, the practices, procedures and norms could be baffling.[9]

The general election of November 1922 saw the return of a Conservative government and 111 new Conservative MPs. One of them, Gervais Rentoul, a 38-year-old barrister, returned as MP for Lowestoft – he had put himself forward as candidate after seeing a newspaper advertisement (see Chapter 8) – decided that there may be a case for forming a party group for the guidance of those like himself who were new to the House: 'After consulting a few colleagues who were chafing, as I was, against the feeling of ineffectiveness and bewilderment, an invitation was issued to all the new comers to meet in one of the committee rooms and discuss what could be done about it.'[10] The response, he reported, was enthusiastic. This was the beginning of the 1922 Committee. In short, as *The Times* was later to report, it was formed by 'new members who were somewhat dismayed at their ignorance of Parliamentary practice and procedure'.[11]

Since its founding, there have three significant stages in its history: the early years (1923–40), when it emerged principally, though not exclusively, as a body for information sharing; the maturing stage (1940–65), when it became a body influencing both policy and ministerial careers; and the senior stage (1965 to date), when it acquired the power to determine the leadership of the Conservative Party.[12] Each was made possible by a critical event: the decision of Gervais Rentoul in 1923 to initiate a self-help group of new MPs; the advent of a national government in 1940 following the fall of the Chamberlain government; and the controversy in 1963 over the methods used for selecting a new Conservative leader.

## Getting started

Rentoul invited other members of the 1922 intake to a meeting on 18 April 1923. Those present elected Rentoul as chairman and then adjourned until 23 April. At this second meeting, the principles of the body were agreed and officers and an executive committee elected. It came into being 'for the purpose of mutual co-operation and assistance in dealing with political and parliamentary questions, and in order to enable new Members to take a more active interest and part in Parliamentary life'.[13] The Conservative Private Members (1922) Committee – which came to be known popularly as the 1922 Committee – was born.

However, in fulfilling its tasks it was dependent on the goodwill of the new MPs as well as party leaders. It decided to meet weekly when the House was sitting, but the form of the meetings was to be shaped by the actions of leading figures in the party and by political developments. The Chief Whip, Colonel Leslie Wilson, was invited to attend a meeting, which he did on 30 April. He 'expressed his approval of the objects of the committee … and his belief in the usefulness of the group' and 'after some words of advice and caution' outlined some of the work of the House and offered his assistance, and that of his colleagues, at any time.[14]

Not all in authority shared Wilson's benign view of this new body. Rentoul recorded that other party leaders regarded it as rather a nuisance. 'It is always so much easier to deal with either supporters or opponents individually than collectively. The "Whips" feared it might become a "cave", an opportunity for the ventilation of criticism, which it would be better should not exist.'[15]

Wilson's view prevailed and in June he suggested the Committee organise a rota of speakers in the chamber to keep debate going where necessary between 8.00 p.m. and 9.30 p.m. The following month, Wilson wrote to express his appreciation of the work of the Committee, his letter being received 'by members with satisfaction'.[16] The same meeting passed a motion congratulating Wilson on his appointment as Governor of Bombay. His successor as Chief Whip, Bolton Eyres-Monsell, also saw the value of the Committee and, as Stuart Ball recorded, took it under his wing, 'without which it would have been as ephemeral as so many other unofficial cliques'.[17] Usefully for the 1922, Eyres-Monsell remained in post until 1931.

Although the membership was initially open only to newly elected members, it was able to draw on the advice and support of more senior figures, who – reflecting the motivation for the establishment of the group – 'endeavoured to instruct the new members on matters of parliamentary procedure and general policy'.[18] By the end of the session, some 20 to 30 such members were co-operating in its work. The Committee also set up nine sub-committees to consider different areas of public policy – reports were variously presented at the weekly meetings – and began inviting guests to address it. The first, reflecting the purpose of the Committee, was a long-serving MP, Sir Frederick Banbury, on parliamentary procedure. He was followed by the Chief Whip and the party chairman, Francis Jackson. Members then heard from ministers: Air

# Modest beginnings

Secretary Sir Samuel Hoare, the Under-Secretary for the Colonies William Ormsby-Gore, and Minister of Transport Wilfred Ashley, all addressing meetings in July. The Committee was just getting into its stride when a general election intervened.

In October 1923, Prime Minister Stanley Baldwin decided to go to the country. The 1922 had been in existence for six months, but in that time had managed to develop a notable infrastructure and engage the interests of not just new MPs, but also some longer-serving members. Its value was recognised by the party leader and whips. At the end of the session, Baldwin sent a personal letter of thanks. Eyres-Monsell maintained the co-operation of the whips.

The general election, held in December 1923, saw the Conservative ranks depleted and a Labour government take office. In the new Parliament, the decision was taken for the 1922 Committee to re-form. There was a feeling that Baldwin had rushed the election and not adequately consulted party members. At a special meeting, which former members were invited to attend, two motions were passed, one supporting Baldwin's leadership, the other calling for party organisation to be placed 'upon a democratic basis', with closer contact between leaders and the rank-and-file.[19] It was agreed to seek a meeting with Baldwin.[20] Two days later, the '22 considered a report from a sub-committee that analysed the reasons for the election defeat, ascribing it to not everyone understanding the policy of protection, the unpopularity of rent restrictions, poor organisation in the constituencies, a rushed election, and a failure to meet the social needs of the industrial community.[21] The report was agreed and was to be sent to the Chief Whip and party chairman, saying that it represented the views of 65 present members of the Committee and 40 former members.

A deputation met with Baldwin, former leader Sir Austen Chamberlain, and Eyres-Monsell, and put the case for regular meetings of the party's MPs to be chaired by the leader, or a deputy appointed by him, so that the policy of the party could be explained and members could have the opportunity to raise questions of importance.[22] They 'complained of being left too much in the dark regarding the purposes and policy of the Government'.[23] Baldwin demurred, as he felt details of such meetings would be leaked to the press. Chamberlain felt it may also encourage schisms in the party. 'To this', recalled Rentoul, 'we retorted that it might be the means of preventing schisms developing.'[24] Chamberlain – who had resigned as party leader, having lost the trust of backbenchers – also argued that the party must trust its leaders. One member of the delegation, Sir Douglas Newton, pointed out that the deputation represented 25 per cent of the parliamentary party and were unanimous in putting the proposal forward.[25] However, Baldwin, while sympathising, noted that many similar bodies to the 1922 had been set up in previous years and had in a short time disappeared.

Rentoul reported to the Committee the disappointing outcome. He was then deputed by the meeting to seek a meeting with the Chief Whip to request that a whip be present at meetings to explain legislation for the current week and to answer any questions. At the next meeting, on 10 March 1924, he was able to report that the Chief Whip had agreed.[26] As Rentoul recalled in 1940, 'This practice still prevails, and is undoubtedly one of the most useful means of keeping Party leaders in touch with rank-and-file opinion.'[27]

Two other developments helped determine the form the 1922 was to take. One was the decision to expand membership, initially to other MPs newly elected in 1923 as well as some senior members, and in the next Parliament to all Conservative private members (see Chapter 6). The other followed the decision of the party leadership at the start of 1924 to establish backbench committees to cover different areas of policy (see Chapter 7). These displaced the need for 1922 sub-committees, but agreement was reached that, subject to the approval of the chairman, each committee could report on its activities to meetings of the 1922. Reports from committees became a regular item of business. Indeed, the reports occupied most of the meetings for the rest of the short 1924 Parliament.

Although the Committee was not an official party body, agreement was reached with the party's Principal Agent at the start of 1925 for an official from Central Office to act as secretary and Mr J. Green, of the Central Unionist Office, was appointed to the post. The practice was also resumed of inviting ministers to address it – it heard from the Home Secretary (on Communist agitation and propaganda) in May 1925, the Minister of Labour the following month, and the month after that the Financial Secretary to the Treasury. Fifty-one members turned up to listen to the Home Secretary. It also held meetings to discuss specific issues. In 1925 there was a flurry of activity over a Private Member's Bill to reform trade union law. It took an appeal from the Prime Minister for the '22 to decide not to press ahead with the measure.[28] In 1926, a discussion on the TV Levy Bill attracted 77 members. The broadcasting of debates also became an issue, considered by the Committee in 1927 and again the following year.

For the rest of the decade, it discussed a range of issues, variously – notably at odds with what became its later practice – taking votes and passing resolutions. It engaged with ministers over a number of contentious issues. It had some sporadic influence, as in 1926 over a proposed government grant of £200,000 for civil service sports grounds. A meeting of the 1922, attended by 115 members, decided that this was not an opportune time to make such a grant, given the need for economy.[29] The issue aroused considerable controversy. The *Manchester Evening News* reported that members were 'receiving a great number of letters on the subject, and many who have been in their constituencies during the weekend tell of the indignation aroused up and down the country by the grant'.[30] A deputation of six members was appointed to see the Prime Minister, but Baldwin indicated that as he had already had a full report from the whip who attended the 1922 meeting it was not necessary to receive the delegation. The activities of the 1922 attracted widespread media attention, not least at a local level.[31] On 1 March 1926, Rentoul was able to report that 'the grant would not be proposed this year'.[32] In March 1929, the Home Secretary, Sir William Joynson-Hicks, attended a meeting of the '22 'at which recent criticisms of the Home Secretary and the Shop Hours Bill were considered'.[33] He 'dealt at length' with the criticisms.

The growing engagement of the 1922 with issues and ministers was reflected in Rentoul's observation that during the ten years after it was formed, 'it developed into a real parliamentary force, and the recognized means of crystallizing rank-and-file opinion. So much so that in 1927, when the government was about to introduce its Trades Union Bill, the Committee was invited to place its considered views before a committee of the Cabinet.'[34] In 1928, it was credited with persuading the government to withdraw a kerosene tax.[35] In 1930, the '22 also became a forum for growing discontent over naval reductions and decided to register a protest against the proposals.[36]

In 1928, Rentoul issued a circular referring to the usefulness of the Committee 'as a means of ascertaining and representing rank and file opinion and as a "clearing house" for information on matters of common importance to Members of our Party'.[37] He was writing at what was a high point for the impact of the '22. As Ball recorded, 'The Parliament of 1924–9 proved to be the golden age of the 1922 Committee during the inter-war years, and a diminution of its activities became apparent after the general election of May 1929.'[38]

It suffered from what it didn't discuss as well as what it did. It was peripheral to debate on the major issues dividing the party. Its lack of impact was apparent in the 1930s when it was not a significant force in the crisis over Baldwin's leadership,[39] nor in the debates on the key issues of the decade, including protectionism, Indian home rule and appeasement. It heard from speakers on the issues, but it was not a site of conflict between critical backbenchers and party leaders. It discussed the White Paper on Indian Constitutional Reform at a packed meeting (200 MPs attended, 25 spoke) in March 1933 and further discussed India – a joint meeting with the India Committee – the following February. Winston Churchill attracted a large audience in 1936 – about 150 MPs – when he spoke on rearmament.[40] As we shall see, the Committee variously discussed the situation in Europe. However, critics of the government utilised other means to pursue their disagreement with policy. Churchill – who, as Neville Chamberlain noted, 'has no following of any importance' – primarily used the public platform.[41] He did speak at the India Committee, where critics of the government's policy tended to assemble,[42] but India was not an issue preoccupying the '22. As Goodhart recorded, 'This did not mean that the Parliamentary Party failed to discuss the subject, but it did mean that the bitter argument was carried on in the specialist committees and not in the 1922 Committee itself.'[43]

When the Committee did turn its attention to a major policy, it attracted serious criticism. The outcome was to diminish its standing and return it essentially to being, in Ball's words, 'an information service for MPs'.[44]

The economic crisis of 1931 generated significant debate in the 1922. In 1932, it established an Economy Committee to address the crisis and come up with proposals for 'drastic public economy'.[45] The Committee worked through five sub-committees, each working, as Rentoul conceded, in 'watertight compartments', and under considerable time pressures.[46] Some members of other parties who supported the national government were co-opted onto them. The sub-committees offered particular recommendations for economies, amounting in aggregate to more than £100 million. The recommendations, 140 in all, were drawn together in a report that proved controversial,[47] fuelled by the fact that it was not discussed in the 1922, but published after Rentoul had consulted the sub-committee chairmen and some senior members. He justified the decision not to consult on the grounds that secrecy was impossible.[48] The decision encountered opposition. 'MPs who sit for dockyard constituencies found themselves supporting reductions which would put half the remaining dockers and shipyard hands out of work ... Revolt was organised. Lord Cranborne was furiously active.'[49]

At a meeting on 14 November 1932, attended by about 125 members, Lord Cranborne, the MP for South Dorset, objected to publication and moved that it should be neither circulated nor published. Views for and against were rehearsed.

> The Chairman then stated in reply to a specific query, that he had allowed discussion on the motion ... in the hope that a free expression of opinion might finally satisfy the Committee that the course which had been agreed upon by the Chairmen of the Sub-Committees was the only practical procedure. As, however, the differences of opinion seemed so acute, he felt he had no alternative but to rule the motion out of order.[50]

The controversy spilled out into the public domain. Some members publicly dissociated themselves from the report. Eight, led by J. Sandeman Allen, the MP for Birkenhead West, wrote to *The Times* stressing that the responsibility for the contents for each sub-committee report lay solely with the members producing it.[51]

The controversy dented the reputation of the 1922 and the report had no impact on government policy. It did not even attract a wide audience, most copies remaining unsold (5,000 copies were printed, but only 1,391 sold).[52] Rentoul made a personal statement to the 1922 on 28 November. There is no formal record of what he said, but the *Leeds Mercury* carried a brief note saying that he argued that secrecy was impossible and that the report indicated that the 1922 Committee was not committed in any way to the proposals it contained. Although the story (which reads as if it emanated from Rentoul) stated 'Sir Gervais Rentoul's explanation was accepted by the meeting as satisfactory',[53] there is nothing on the record to suggest it was and it did not assuage critics, who held a meeting and decided to run a candidate against him for the chairmanship.[54] The following month, about 200 members attended the annual general meeting, at which W. S. Morrison, the MP for Cirencester and Tewkesbury, challenged Rentoul for the chairmanship. Rentoul was voted out of office by a decisive margin: he lost by 117 votes to 76.

## Limited impact

The failure to engage effectively with the core issues of the day led to the Committee focusing on listening to speakers. In opposition, it heard from a number of guests from outside Parliament. On 3 February 1930, Mr Jones of the United Steel Companies, Sheffield, spoke on coal marketing schemes, and in April, it heard from Dr Weizmann, head of the Jewish Agency for Palestine on the situation in Palestine. In the following Parliament, when the party was back in government, speakers included the chairman of Lloyds Bank, the commissioner of the Salvation Army, the chairman of the Federation of British Industries, and the director-general of the BBC (Sir John Reith). However, what was notable was the shift in emphasis from domestic issues to what was happening on the international stage. The Committee heard from speakers on developments in the Middle East – Dr Weizmann's talk was part of this – and later on about what was happening in Europe as well as in India.

Among the various speakers on developments in Europe were Captain Malcolm Bullock, the MP for Waterloo, in March 1932 on the situation in Germany; Field Marshall Lord Milne in May 1935 – when 90 MPs attended – on imperial defence; Secretary of State for Air Lord Swinton in February 1937 on air defences; and Captain Liddell-Hart in December that year on the military situation. As events in Europe became more ominous, the Committee in May 1938, after hearing from Colonel Sir Edward Grigg, MP for Altrincham, decided to send a deputation to the Prime

Minister. Later that month, it listened to Mr Smolka, London correspondent of *Prager Tagblatt*, on the situation in Czechoslovakia. In October 1939, the Foreign Secretary, Lord Halifax, spoke at a meeting that attracted an audience of 200 members.

Members found it helpful to hear from speakers as to what was happening. However, although useful activity, the Committee was nonetheless not making a mark in the party. The meetings attracting three-figure numbers were the exception. The turnout was generally respectable, but showed signs of declining over the decade. The average attendance in 1934 was just over 80 and in 1938 it was 60.

In terms of engaging the interests and commitments of members, it was overshadowed by unofficial groups set up by MPs to advance particular causes or strands of thought within the party. Baldwin had been correct in noting that such groups were variously formed and that they generally had a limited existence.[55] Once their goal was achieved, they had no reason to continue. However, although some attracted few followers, others engaged the energy of MPs and sometimes on a widespread basis. In the late 1920s, the Empire Industries Association (EIA), favouring protection, was especially active and by 1930 was claiming widespread support among Conservative MPs. The India Defence League, opposing Baldwin's policy on India, claimed the support of 80 MPs in 1935.[56] Many of those supporting protection and the retention of India in the Empire, among other things, formed an informal group known as the 'Diehards', who were essentially opposed to change, wanting to uphold the standards of a past generation.[57] There was a less radical right-of-centre group that called itself the Boys' Brigade and a small progressive group of Tory MPs dubbed the YMCA.[58] Although these groups did not usually achieve their goals, they absorbed the commitment of many backbenchers and on some issues, notably protection and India, caused considerable problems for the government.

## Modest beginnings

In Fleming's study of how the Conservative right sought to influence policy through bodies such as the EIA, the 1922 is rarely mentioned.[59] The '22 was also overshadowed by the backbench subject committees. These were permanent and, as we shall see in Chapter 7, absorbed the energies of members. As Sir Austen Chamberlain reported, 'When I have said, "But why are there so few fellows on our benches", I have been told, "Our committee on India is meeting", or something of that kind.'[60] The committees met regularly and were valuable sources of political intelligence for the leadership. On occasion, deputations to ministers were sent by the committees. There is some evidence of influencing government policy, not least in terms of deterring ministers from proceeding with a particular policy. Although the committees could and did make reports to the 1922, they operated independently of it. If anything, the '22 at times piggy-backed on the popularity of the committees, occasionally organising joint meetings with them.

The 1922 was not an arena in which major battles were fought, nor was it a critical friend of those in power. In June 1930, at a meeting at Caxton Hall at which Baldwin had defended himself against attack by press barons, a motion supporting the leader was moved by Rentoul.[61] Although backbench support for Baldwin wavered in the period of opposition, the '22 did not serve as a body through which this manifested itself. Support for the leader was most pronounced under Baldwin's successor. Samuel Hoare recalled that whenever Neville Chamberlain addressed meetings of the 1922, and explained his line of policy, 'he invariably received an overwhelming vote of confidence'.[62] In the autumn of 1938, he explained what he was doing to reach agreement with Mussolini and Hitler. 'I was at the meeting and I well remember the cheers that greeted his speech. In 1939 there were similar demonstrations of support.'[63] As another MP recalled, when Chamberlain spoke to the 1922 on 28 March, he 'had a riotous reception and was cheered and cheered'.[64] *The Times* reported that 'None of his audience came away with any feeling but one of thankfulness that Mr. Chamberlain was at the head of affairs in these difficult times.'[65]

The Committee, unlike some of the backbench committees, also lacked active leadership. After Rentoul's departure, the 1922 had three chairmen in eight years (with the elderly Sir Annesley Somerville serving briefly as acting chairman in 1939), none having the effect of raising the Committee's profile.

The Committee, as Ball recorded, was in danger of becoming 'almost a lecture club',[66] with no clear sense of direction and no discernible impact on the work and direction of government. Sir Ivor Jennings wrote that 'its importance has been exaggerated', noting that: 'The 1922 Committee is more like a glorified political discussion group, though its meetings are usually more interesting and therefore more popular than the debates in the House.'[67] It had never had a regular or major impact on government actions and it was now diminishing in its capacity to shape events. Illustrative of its lack of impact was when the delegation went to see the Prime Minister following the address by Sir Edward Grigg making the case for a national register for national service. It received, reported *The Times*, 'a frank and courteous negative'.[68]

The most telling evidence of the 1922's failure to make a notable mark on British politics during the first 17 years of its existence is to be found in the autobiography of its founder. Although in his book, *Sometimes I Think*, published in 1940, Rentoul details the motivation for, and development of, the 1922, it is not a work about the 1922. His coverage occupies two chapters out of 40, one of which is devoted to explaining what happened over the Economy Committee report. In his autobiography, *This Is My Case*, published in 1944, he offers his reflections on Parliament and parliamentary life, but mentions the 1922 only once and then only to justify his role in the controversy over the Economy Committee, for which, as chairman, 'I was the target for a good deal of disagreeable criticism and had to bear a large measure of personal responsibility for its inevitable unpopularity in certain quarters: indeed, this unpopularity was so great that in the end the whole economy campaign largely fizzled out.'[69]

The limited space given to the 1922 may reflect his feelings after being voted out of office, but one might have expected him to highlight the Committee's successes under his founding tutelage. Instead, he appeared to take as much if not more pride in his work in the law, leaving the Commons in 1934 to become stipendiary Metropolitan Magistrate for West London. Yet his coverage of the 1922 in *Sometimes I Think* constitutes the only significant writing on the Committee in its formative years. Otherwise, it only achieved mentions in newspapers when occasional crises arose. It was not a body notably to the fore in the major political events of the time.

Perhaps the most optimistic assessment of the utility of the '22 was offered by Sir Charles Ponsonby, who became joint secretary in the 1938–9 session. He described the 1922 as a 'useful body of backbenchers': 'Here, by exchange of ideas', he wrote, 'it is possible to learn what is going on in the constituencies throughout the country, what the feeling is upon a subject which has suddenly sprung into importance.'[70] He also argued that it was a forum in which internal differences could be aired (and possibly adjusted) and a minister, or the Prime Minister, could attend to explain a pressing problem or what was happening in their departments and receive criticism or ask for assistance. What his account fails to recount is that such occasions were rare. The emphasis was on being better informed. Unlike in the 1920s, it was not on an upward trajectory in terms of developing a role as an influential force within the Conservative Party.

This was all to change as a result of international developments. 'Lacking a clear role and with its leading figures either promoted to office or nearing the end of their parliamentary careers, it is likely', wrote Ball, 'that the Committee would have dwindled away if the outbreak of war had not rescued it.'[71] The onset of war and, crucially, the formation of a coalition government, transformed its fortunes.

# Chapter 3

# Speaking truth to power: in war and peace

The period of national government from 1940 to 1945 transformed the fortunes of the 1922 Committee. The Committee played no role in the downfall of the Chamberlain government of 1940. It did not meet following the emergency recall of Parliament in September 1938 or before the crucial Norway debate in May 1940. Some members clearly harboured doubts about one of Chamberlain's confidants, head of the civil service Sir Horace Wilson. John Colville, the Prime Minister's private secretary, recorded in his diary: 'The 1922 Committee have shown great animosity against Horace Wilson and he will probably have to retire upstairs in any case.'[1] But there is no evidence of the '22 affecting the course of events. The opposition had a greater, indeed decisive, influence. A combination of the Commons' vote on 7 May 1940 and the refusal of the opposition to serve in a national government under Chamberlain brought his premiership to an end. The '22 was peripheral to what was taking place, but the events were crucial in creating conditions for it to flourish. They brought it out of its adolescent stage.

The formation of a national government, all parties united in prosecuting the war, had the effect of putting the 1922 in a new, and pivotal, position. This was for two reasons. With the end of public adversarial conflict between the parties, it was the 1922 that served to maintain the integrity of the Conservative voice in dealing with ministers. Much of the organisation of the Conservative Party was suspended. The 1922 Committee continued to meet and was effectively the only authentic Conservative voice.

At the same time, although the government was vested with formidable powers,[2] it had to maintain a united front. All members were supporters of the government, but, as Stephen King-Hall noted, 'since all members are supporters of the Government so all members are potential critics of the Government'.[3] Opposition publicly expressed could undermine its position. It was thus highly sensitive to opinion within the House. It had to keep members in all parts of the House on side.[4] The party organisations – the 1922 and the Parliamentary Labour Party – provided structured means of doing so away from the floor of the House. In the confines of the meetings, dissatisfaction could be heard and tackled to avoid it being made public. There was a particular challenge to the new Prime Minister given that there had long been a 'simmering dislike' of him in the 1922.[5] Conservative MPs were essentially Chamberlain supporters; the chairman of the 1922, William Spens, had written to Chamberlain following his resignation telling him he had the confidence of 'moderate Conservative opinion, in the House, in the Party and in the country'.[6] The secretary of the 1922, Maurice Hely-Hutchinson, told R. A. Butler that three-quarters of the party were willing to put Chamberlain back in power.[7] A meeting of the 1922 at which sending a congratulatory message to Churchill was discussed was described as 'stormy'.[8] Churchill was highly sensitive to his initial political weakness.

Wartime saw the 1922 become a significant political actor. Ministers, including those drawn from the Labour Party, regularly addressed meetings. There was also one other significant development that facilitated the 1922 filling a new role during this period and that was the election of a new chairman, Alec Erskine Hill (he changed his name to Alec Erskine-Hill in 1943), the MP for Edinburgh North, who was to prove an energetic chairman during his four-year tenure.

The shift in the significance of the role of the 1922 is reflected in media coverage of its activities. *The Times* had covered various activities of the '22 in the years immediately after its formation, but its coverage diminished in the 1930s. It increased sharply in 1942. Such coverage was facilitated by the fact that the 1922 executive had agreed in 1940 to release short reports of its activities of important proceedings for the duration of the war,[9] but that fact alone does not explain the spike in media coverage. The 1922 proved a source of media interest on a scale that was not to be repeated until the 1970s. Perceptions of the impact of the '22 were also to find reflection in various letters and articles. In 1942, the Conservative MP for South Cardiff, Arthur Evans, wrote to *The Times* suggesting that Conservative MPs should be able to join Labour MPs in sitting on the opposition front bench. 'Thus would the voice of Conservative back benchers be heard to proper effect, and the public would not get the erroneous impression that Tory M.P.s only express themselves – and get things done – through the medium of that much abused and sadly misunderstood 1922 Committee.'[10]

The significance of the '22 is also reflected in the published diaries of Conservative MP 'Chips' Channon, the Member for Southend, from 1935. The first of the three volumes edited by Simon Heffer, covering the period up to 1938, is notable for the dearth of references to the 1922. There is a single mention, covering the banquet given for Chamberlain in 1937.[11] The second volume, covering the period 1938–43,[12] contains regular references (35 in all), with Channon apparently attending regularly, whereas before he either did not attend or, if he did, deigned not to regard the gatherings as worthy of note. Coverage continues in the third volume, covering the years 1943 to 1957.[13] He recorded the attendance of ministers and the quality of their speeches and how they were received; his coverage of Churchill's appearances reflected the enhanced status of the '22 as well as the mixed feelings of members about his performance.

The change in the terms of trade between the 1922 and the party leadership is reflected also in an early tussle with Churchill. At the end of 1940, Churchill, as head of a national government, indicated that he was minded to ask Cabinet ministers not to address the 1922. This, not surprisingly, was not well received by the executive of the 1922. It resisted and after its new chairman, Erskine Hill, met the new Chief Whip, James Stuart, it was agreed that the existing procedure of ministers addressing the 1922 would continue, but that an 'all-party' meeting should be held occasionally. Goodhart refers to this as the Chief Whip meeting the Committee 'more than half-way'.[14] It was not so much a compromise as a climb-down. It can be seen as pivotal in the development of the 1922. Had it conceded, losing its capacity to engage directly with ministers, the Committee's history would likely have been very different.

Churchill came to acknowledge the importance of the '22. He received a deputation which welcomed him as leader and 'expressed the hope that, to the extent that a war-time Prime Minister who is head of an all-party Government is able to do so, he would keep himself in close touch with his Conservative supporters and their views'.[15] *The Times* reported that 'the members of the deputation were left in no doubt that the desired relations between leader and back-benchers will be established'.[16] The following March, the '22 organised a lunch for Churchill. About 150 MPs attended. 'The Prime Minister was given a great reception.'[17]

Erskine Hill, as we shall see in Chapter 12, was active in ensuring the 1922 was heard by ministers. Stories appeared suggesting he exercised influence in relation to ministers. The decision in 1942 of Lord Beaverbrook to resign as Minister of Production, according to a report in the *Edinburgh Evening News*, 'followed conversation the then Minister of Production had with the [1922] Committee's Chairman'.[18] Also in 1942, at the height of the crisis that year, Erskine Hill was reported to have sounded out Lord Woolton, the Minister for Food, about succeeding Churchill.[19] These events may well derive from Erskine Hill's inflated sense of his role as chairman of the 1922, but they are indicative of how the occupant saw his role, inconceivable in the period before 1940. The fact they appeared in the press also indicates a media interest not apparent before the war.

The 1922 met regularly. During 1942, an attendance running into three figures was the norm. The turnouts are especially remarkable given the number of MPs engaged in war service. (By early 1941, 116 were serving in the forces and a further 200 were engaged on government service of one form or another.)[20] The '22 served as a forum in which members could raise issues to which they could not give voice in the chamber. One regular concern was the extent to which Labour was benefitting more than the Conservatives from the new situation. The most important topic was, hardly surprisingly, the conduct of the war.

The extent to which the Labour Party was benefitting unduly from the new situation was a continuing issue of frustration, Labour getting credit for the actions of the government of which it was a part, while some backbench Labour MPs were able to act as critics of the conduct of the war. The same could be said of the Conservative Party, which also had some backbenchers willing to challenge the government publicly, but within the 1922 there was a feeling that the party was being out-manoeuvred by what the members invariably referred to as the Socialist Party. One of the joint secretaries of the '22, J. F. Crowder, told a meeting in Finchley that 'Conservative members are getting very restive and are very tired of all the Left Wing propaganda, especially that generated by the BBC.'[21] Labour ministers attending meetings, however, appeared generally to be well received. Attlee in 1941 'made a favourable impression'.[22]

The 1922 continued to voice anxieties over the perceived extent to which government proposals were being driven by a Socialist agenda. A coal-rationing scheme ran into significant objections. Members stressed the need to increase coal production rather than the government's proposed rationing scheme and advocated an alternative that did not involve coupons or a large administrative staff. About 130 members attended a meeting that lasted for two hours in which they expressed their objections.[23] There was a further meeting the following week, the day before the House was due to debate the scheme. At another well-attended meeting, 'Members were emphatic in their objection to any scheme of fuel rationing involving the use of coupons, on a points system or otherwise'.[24] Six days later, it was announced, to the surprise of MPs and the dismay of some Labour members, that the scheme would be postponed.[25] According to one MP, 'The Conservative Party, through its powerful unofficial 1922 Committee and in other ways, opposed the scheme, and the Government had eventually to abandon it.'[26] A Catering Wages Bill in 1943 also encountered opposition – 116 Conservative MPs voted against it on Second Reading[27] – as did a Requisitioned Land and War Works Bill early in 1945.[28] When the former came up for its Third Reading, the minister moving it said that he would 'freely agree that the searching examination to which the Bill has been put in Committee has improved the Measure, as, indeed, my right hon. Friend has demonstrated by the number of Amendments he has either moved or accepted'.[29] When the latter Bill had its Second Reading, the Chancellor promised so many concessions that one backbencher, who had put his name to an amendment to reject the Bill, wondered what there was left to object to, other than the title.[30]

Ministers had to work hard to keep MPs on side, especially during the early years of the war when criticisms were voiced following major failure, such as setbacks in North Africa and Greece in 1941 and the fall of Singapore the following year. Although the government won support publicly in the chamber, in the confines of the 1922 there were calls for a restructuring of the government. Churchill's handling of the situation, and his carrying of the defence portfolio in addition to being Prime Minister, came in for criticism. His Parliamentary Private Secretary (PPS), George Harvie-Watt, gave the Prime Minister 'all the gossip and growlings' from the House. In Harvie-Watt's view, feelings were running so high that 'the Government must be reorganised, otherwise Churchill would be forced to resign by the march of events'.[31] There was a major restructuring of the government in February 1942.[32]

The importance of keeping abreast of backbench opinion through the '22 was reflected in the fact that Harvie-Watt became a regular attender at meetings.[33] As he recalled, 'since it was my duty to keep my ears to the ground, I learned a lot about reactions to Government policies and actions'.[34] He reported backbench sentiment to Churchill, as when Sir Stafford Cripps, as Leader of the House, aroused intense resentment after telling off MPs for poor attendance during a debate on India.[35] It is indicative of the changed status of the 1922 that Harvie-Watt described it as 'the most powerful committee in the House'.[36]

The link between ministers and the '22 was also strengthened when the Committee decided in 1943 to admit ministers to membership. 'This inclusion was a sign of the Committee's growing status and confidence, for it was intended to create a more direct means of influencing the leadership – not to become subservient to them.'[37] It also demonstrated the unique nature of the '22.

Throughout the war, the private space of Westminster remained much used. According to Anne Scott-James, writing in *The Picture Post* at the end of 1942, there were over 200 members working in committee rooms when Stafford Cripps, as Leader of the House, criticised members for the low attendance.[38] How the figure of 200 was ascertained is unclear, but the report conveys the varied activity of MPs. There continued to be groups set up to advocate a particular cause, some geared to the conduct of the war (such as the Watching Committee) and some looking ahead to peacetime (such as the Tory Reform Group), and subject committees continued to be active, but the 1922 was *the* body able to speak for Tory MPs. The government could not afford to lose the support of its backbenchers.

## Speaking truth to power

At the end of the war, the Committee's status was much enhanced from its pre-war position in the party. It was now clearly a permanent body and one that the leadership could not afford to ignore. This status is reflected in the fact that outside speakers were no longer a notable feature of meetings. It became very much a party gathering, backbenchers coming together to hear from, and engage with, a leading figure in the party.

## Policy and influence

The 1945 general election proved disastrous for the Conservative Party. The parliamentary party was essentially halved in number. Among the casualties were the chairman of the 1922, Jock McEwen, and his predecessor, Alec Erskine-Hill. However, the new Parliament and Churchill's leadership created conditions that further enhanced the position of the 1922. The Committee reverted to its original role in helping new Conservative MPs understand and adapt to the workings of the House of Commons. Meetings of new MPs were organised so that they could be briefed on procedure by senior members. The '22 provided a forum in which tactics could be discussed and the troops could be rallied to challenge the new government. Churchill's somewhat absentee leadership created both a problem and an opportunity.

There were concerns as to Churchill's capacity to lead the party in opposition. 'Although he made it plain that he had no intention of retiring, it soon became clear that he had equally little intention of actively leading any opposition.'[39] He was not greatly interested in domestic policy or in the rigours of spending time on the opposition front bench. 'Winston', confided Cuthbert Headlam in his diary, 'is relying solely on his war record – he is seldom in the House – and when he comes into the Smoking Room he does not mix with his party, only with his own little clique… .'[40] One backbencher, Robert (Bob) Boothby, told Churchill he should retire.[41] Another backbencher told Harold Nicolson that there was a feeling among young backbenchers that Churchill was 'too old'.[42] There were media reports of speculation as to a successor.[43] Churchill failed to dispel criticisms effectively. He addressed the '22 on 21 August 1945 and, according to 'Chips' Channon, 'seemed totally unprepared, indifferent and deaf, and failed to stir the crowded audience'.[44]

In 1946, disquiet about Churchill's leadership was raised in meetings of the 1922.[45] Churchill, according to one MP, listened to the critics, 'but was so moving in replying to them that they were almost all reduced to tears. His line was that he was the servant of the party and that he would stand down any time the party wished him to do so, and against such a disarming reply the opposition melted away'.[46] Disquiet nonetheless continued to be expressed throughout the Parliament, including by members of the front bench (some of whom met privately in 1947 to discuss recommending that he should retire),[47] but as Churchill was determined to stay, there was not the commitment to remove him. Instead, criticism was levelled at party performance. When Churchill attended a meeting of the 1922 in March 1949, members attacked the strategy adopted by the front bench. They did so at some length: the meeting lasted about two hours. Churchill 'listened patiently to a good deal of criticism and then told us how optimistic he was about the result of the coming GE ... people were rather critical and disgruntled and not at all impressed by his optimism'.[48] Channon, although he felt Churchill silenced his critics, conceded that he was 'losing his hold on the party and is undoubtedly ageing'.[49] There was no promise of a policy restatement.[50]

The 1922, as well as grassroots members at the party conference, pressed Churchill to produce a statement on party policy. The chairman, Sir Arnold Gridley, had written to him putting forward 'nine points of Conservative policy' suggested by members of the executive.[51] Churchill responded to the pressure by setting up a committee to define Conservative attitudes towards industry. The committee, comprising four frontbenchers and four backbenchers, produced a report entitled 'The Industrial Charter'. It wanted to remove unnecessary regulatory burdens, but also envisaged co-operation between government and industry, full employment and a workers' charter. The charter conveyed the party's willingness to adapt to post-war conditions.

The task of generating policy in other sectors, and parliamentary tactics, was also left to others.[52] Churchill was not greatly interested and told the '22 in 1947 that the party should not say too much about what it would do when in power and must make no promises that it could not fulfil.[53] Anthony Eden was essentially left to lead the party in the Commons, R. A. (Rab) Butler was primarily responsible for developing policies[54] (the 1950 party manifesto 'was largely Rab's handiwork'),[55] while Lord Woolton oversaw a major restructuring of party organisation. An Advisory Committee on Policy and Political Education became in 1949 the Advisory Committee on Policy, its membership chosen by the parliamentary party and the voluntary wing of the party, the National Union. Policy sub-committees worked up detailed recommendations. Within the House, the backbench committees were reorganised and expanded.

By 1950, the Conservative Party was a very different body to that facing the electors in 1945. It ran the Labour Party a close second in the 1950 general election, the government's narrow majority creating opportunities for members of the '22 to harry it through late-night sittings and occasional snap votes. Although there was a recognition that the Parliament could not last long, dissatisfaction with Churchill's leadership continued to simmer: '"Winston M[ust] G[o]" is already being whispered,' wrote one MP. 'He certainly lacks political judgement, as I have always asserted.'[56] Churchill attended meetings to address concerns about tactics. At a packed meeting in January 1951, he advocated working with the Liberals to ensure Labour was defeated at the next election, a stance heavily criticised by Derek Walker-Smith and John Boyd-Carpenter. 'Churchill was obviously affected by their outburst. At one point he wiped away a tear which was beginning to run down his face and after a brief half-hearted reply, he left.'[57] He returned on 14 June. At the meeting, attended by 160 members, there was a lengthy discussion about the party's tactics in the debate on that year's Finance Bill. (The previous week, members had expressed dissatisfaction that the party had not voted against increases in income tax.)[58] Boothby argued the case for compelling the government to remain at full strength while only part of the opposition's strength was used, the remainder being reserved for surprise attacks. 'Mr Churchill said our first object was to turn out the Government and the other to obtain proper time for discussion. He considered Mr Boothby's plan more easily said than done.'[59] However, Boothby's proposal would be most carefully considered. He also congratulated members on the manner in which they had kept together and maintained arguments at such a high level. However, his talk, according to Channon, was long and meandering; 'for the first time we were conscious of his age as he made little sense, but he was still captivating'.[60] Two weeks later he returned to the Committee, this time to 'say a few words on the situation in Persia'.[61]

Questions of policy were dealt with by Butler. He attended the 1922 on 9 May 1951 and 'replied to a considerable number of questions and dealt with many suggestions from Members on matters of party policy'.[62] Dissatisfaction with the leadership continued to be expressed, but it was put to one side when the harassing of the Labour government bore fruit and Prime Minister Clement Attlee sought an election in October 1951. It produced a Conservative victory with Churchill returning to No. 10. It also produced a new and invigorated era of influence for the 1922 Committee.

During the period of Churchill's domestic premiership (1951–5), the 1922 emerged as a powerful body, both in pluralist and institutional terms. In the wake of the election, it reverted to its initial role – there was a new intake of Conservative MPs requiring guidance – but it also had other consequences. It exerted influence over public policy, it provided an arena for MPs as MPs (rather than as Tory MPs) to express their preferences, and for the first time we see the 1922 demonstrably responsible for a ministerial resignation. Its significance was acknowledged by the leadership, the Prime Minister not only attending to address it on an end-of-term basis, but appearing in order to address major concerns on issues of public policy. It benefitted from a combination of members willing to press for policy changes and from a government that was not driven by a clear vision. As Robin Harris noted, the incoming government was faced with a choice between holding power and using power. 'Churchill chose simply to hold it.'[63] There were times when the leadership not so much led as responded to backbench pressure.

The new chairman of the '22, Derek Walker-Smith, held meetings with Churchill, accompanied on occasion by the executive. In 1952, it was agreed that the whips could attend meetings of the '22 as observers, enhancing the capacity of government to get a feeling for backbench opinion. That opinion soon began to express itself. Pressure from members resulted in getting the government to do that which otherwise it would not have done.

A small group of backbenchers, led by Charles Orr-Ewing, John Rodgers and John Profumo, lobbied hard to end the BBC's broadcasting monopoly and started to attract support from other members of the '22, both on grounds of principle (favouring competition) and perceptions of BBC bias. At a meeting of the '22 on 28 February 1952, Lord Salisbury, for the government, resisted. Ministers saw no popular demand for change. However, by the time of the meeting, proponents of reform were able to claim about 95 per cent of Tory MPs were concerned over continuing the BBC's monopoly.[64] Eventually, after a deputation chosen by the '22 executive went to see party chairman Lord Woolton, the government conceded the case. Churchill came out in support of the 1922's position. Under pressure from backbenchers, Churchill also came to the 1922 in April 1952 to announce that steel and road haulage would be denationalised as soon as possible.[65] Ministers had to work hard to head off demands in the '22 for an inquiry into the National Coal Board and to rescind cuts in the pensions of retired officers in the armed services. To counter the latter, both the Chancellor of the Exchequer and Foreign Secretary turned up to explain the Cabinet's reasoning.[66]

Churchill in December 1953 sought to use his address to the annual luncheon of the 1922 to reduce tensions over negotiations for Britain to withdraw from the Suez Canal zone. 'Churchill's personal appeal to the 1922 Committee had succeeded in quelling some dissent on Egypt but the Suez Group remained defiant in debate.'[67]

In 1954, the 1922 was exercised both by a political crisis and by a recommended pay rise for MPs. There was a scandal over the government's failure to offer the former owner of land at Crichel Down, taken over for use in wartime, the opportunity to buy the land back. The Minister of Agriculture, Thomas Dugdale, was attacked both for the way the issue was handled and the policy. Realising that he had lost the confidence of the '22, he resigned (see Chapter 12). Members of the '22 were divided over the government's attempts to resist a pay rise for MPs and instead provide for some subsistence allowances (see Chapter 10). The issue proved so contentious that the Prime Minister, Chancellor of the Exchequer and Foreign Secretary turned up to hear members' concerns, with the PM and Chancellor returning to a subsequent meeting, joined by the Leader of the House. After a vote in the House on the proposals, the 1922 executive met with the Prime Minister. The issue divided the '22 and took up more time than any other issue that year.

Churchill was clearly reaching the end of his premiership. Channon recorded his increasingly poor performances before the '22. In April 1952 he spoke for over an hour and was received rapturously, but 'for the first time there was some disquiet in the important Committee and whilst he was treated with affectionate

44

respect – the awe had gone';[68] three months later, 'a lamentable performance: the old lion was discursive, long-winded, at times inaudible and only once funny'.[69] Churchill finally retired in 1955, to be succeeded by his long-time heir apparent, Sir Anthony Eden.

However influential the '22 had proved under Churchill's premiership, it was to acquire even greater significance under Eden. Eden proved a poor leader,[70] but it was his policy following the nationalisation of the Suez Canal Company by President Nasser of Egypt that was to divide the House and end his premiership. British military intervention was ended by American opposition. During the crisis, the 1922 held six packed meetings, with usually about 250 MPs present. A phalanx of ministers, including the Prime Minister, attended to explain the government's actions. Eden made a statement on 13 September 1956. 'Many members addressed the Committee. The Prime Minister replied to the more important points before leaving the Foreign Secretary to reply to the remaining matters.'[71] The Foreign Secretary, Selwyn Lloyd, returned the following month. Butler, as Leader of the House, and Harold Macmillan, the Chancellor, spoke on 22 November, in an attempt to keep the party together.[72] There was a packed meeting on 6 December ahead of a vote in the House.

Although generally supportive, the '22 heard critical voices. When Eden spoke to the '22 in December, an official statement said that he was 'loudly cheered' – Channon thought that he had a 'considerable triumph'[73] – though, according to the *Belfast Telegraph*, 'The Prime Minister had a "cool" reception, a "sympathetic" reception and a "restrained reception"'.[74] Eden gave the impression that he was not planning to give up office. In the event, his doctors decided otherwise. The following month, the '22 was sending a message of congratulations to the new Prime Minister, Harold Macmillan.

What was most remarkable about the '22 during this period was how it became an arena in which potential candidates – or rather one particular candidate – for the leadership used it to pitch for support even though the '22 itself had no formal role in the process. At the meeting on 22 November – what one of those present, Nigel Fisher, recalled as an 'excited, flag-waving meeting of the 1922 Committee'[75] – Macmillan gave what amounted to a bid for the leadership.[76] He spoke for 35 minutes and gave a bravura performance:[77] 'Butler struck the backbenchers as feeble, unconvincing, a "weak sister"; Macmillan was virile, at ease with the new world structure and the American President, eager to define Britain's role in that world.'[78] As Peter Rawlinson, who was also present, noted: 'After this, in the hearts of the parliamentary Party, although not expressed to the Lobby correspondents who hung about waiting to ensnare unwary backbenchers and who so wrongly forecast the succession six weeks later, the leadership question had been all but decided.'[79] It was a decisive meeting: 'the confrontation passed into 1922 folklore'.[80] 'The historic significance of the scene', Channon recorded, 'was evident to most.'[81] The folklore was more important than the reality. The Cabinet was the key player in determining the succession, though the preference of most of its members for Macmillan was reinforced by the chairman of the '22, John Morrison, telephoning the Lord Chancellor to tell him that back-bench opinion strongly supported that view.[82]

Macmillan, having appealed to the 1922 in his quest for the premiership, took trouble to maintain its support. He made regular appearances. He appeared twice shortly after becoming Prime Minister. 'It would be an exaggeration to say that the Prime Minister was always popping in to talk to the 1922 Committee during the first year, but that was the impression he gave.'[83] Macmillan confided to his diary that he generally judged his performances to be successful.[84] He similarly saw his meetings with the executive in a generally positive light.[85] He faced an uphill task in office. In the wake of the Suez debacle and economic problems – the Chancellor, Peter Thorneycroft, resigning in 1958 along with his Treasury ministers – the party was in a difficult position. There was unease in the parliamentary party. Lord Hailsham recalled that senior members of the '22 'were actively or covertly disloyal both to the leader and myself, and spent the next months writing to the leader asking for my removal and talking to the Lobby saying that the leader was no good'.[86] Despite this, Macmillan managed to restore the party's fortunes. Following a 'give away' budget, economic conditions improved. The PM proved a deft parliamentary performer and also spent time mixing with backbenchers.[87] No serious issues came up at '22 meetings. Attendance dropped off in the run-up to the general election that Macmillan called for the autumn of 1959. He had a good campaign. 'Inside and outside the 1922 Committee "Supermac" seemed to reign supreme, and at the General Election on Thursday, 8 October, the Conservative Party increased its majority to 100.'[88]

In the new Parliament, Macmillan attended and spoke at '22 meetings and was generally well received. However, within a couple of years, tensions started to appear. Initially these were on the government's Africa policy, decolonisation being pursued with vigour by Colonial Secretary Iain Macleod, but 'it was never the subject of much enthusiasm among the majority of Conservative MPs'.[89] One new MP recalled being virtually shouted down when he defended Macleod's policy.[90] Macleod then found himself having to defend the Commonwealth Immigration Bill, limiting immigration, which did not go as far as some members wanted, and too far for more liberally minded members. Macleod made clear his distaste for it, but that he regarded it as necessary. He told the '22 that, if it had not been introduced, 'there might have been 250,000 immigrants next year'.[91] Moves to enable peers to renounce their titles elicited little enthusiasm. Attempts to tackle the economic crisis dented the party's popularity. There were critical voices heard at meetings of the '22.

Then in July 1962 came the 'night of the long knives', when Macmillan dismissed a third of his Cabinet, including Chancellor Selwyn Lloyd. This followed John Morrison, the chairman of the 1922, reportedly seeing the Chief Whip to press for a reconstruction of the government.[92] The scale of the changes, however, proved highly controversial. Macmillan sought to justify his actions to the '22 and, although he felt that feeling was moving towards him, he was defensive and left after about 20 minutes for another meeting.[93] The reception he received 'was afterwards described officially as "cordial" … and was unofficially spoken of as frigid'.[94] His sacking of Lloyd was attacked in the backbench Finance Committee: 'speaker after speaker criticised the dropping of the former Chancellor … Some described it as "grossly unjust".'[95] The 1922 also discussed the Vassal affair in 1962 (when minister Tom Galbraith was accused of overly close relations with an official who turned out to be a Russian spy) and the Profumo affair in 1963 (when War Minister John Profumo was accused of an affair with a nightclub hostess who was also involved with the Russian naval attaché). Macmillan's reaction in Profumo's case suggested a prime minister who was out of touch and distant from the unfolding events. Macmillan saw John Morrison, as chairman of the 1922, for a half-hour meeting and arranged to meet him again on the morning of the day the Commons was to debate the case.[96] Two hours before the debate began, the Chief Whip, Martin Redmayne, and Party vice-chairman, Oliver Poole, attended a crisis meeting of the 1922.[97] Macmillan's failure to act on rumours about Profumo, and his admission that he was the last to hear about them, badly undermined his standing. The government survived the Commons' vote, albeit with a reduced majority (27 Tory MPs abstained), but Macmillan's leadership was now under pressure and it was unclear as to whether he would be able to lead the party into the next election. 'He gave the impression of being old and tired and out of touch.'[98] At a meeting of the 1922 the day after the debate, the suggestion by John Hall, the Member for Wycombe, that the vote should not tie the party to accepting the continued leadership of Macmillan, reportedly attracted a loud murmur of support.[99]

According to Ramsden, 'a wave of hysteria swept through the parliamentary party when the officers of the 1922 Committee pressed the case for an immediate succession', apparently favouring jumping a generation and going for the new Chancellor Reginald Maudling.[100] The '22 executive estimated that between 60 and 70 per cent of the party were ready to support Maudling in the event of a vacancy.[101] However, at a meeting of the '22, Derek Walker-Smith 'defused the situation by stating plausibly and confidently that if Macmillan resigned the Queen might not ask another Conservative to form a Government, and there would be a dissolution. The argument was nonsense but it did the trick.'[102] However, Macmillan's performance may have been the trigger for Morrison believing that the time may have come for new leadership.[103]

Macmillan's assessment of his appearances before the '22 tended over time to diverge from how members viewed his performance. As one MP recalled, he 'would attend upon the '22 with difficulty, nervously fingering his Brigade tie. Somehow the old magic did not work as well as it once had, and his mannerisms no longer beguiled'.[104] On 25 July 1963, he spoke to the '22 and said a transition to a new leader had to be smooth, but he would not give up until he knew a new leader would make the party stronger and more united. After the meeting, two senior members of the '22, vice-chairman Charles Mott-Radclyffe and executive committee member Harry Legge-Bourke, discussed the PM's position with Morrison. There was a substantial body of feeling among the executive that, despite Macmillan's strong performance (he judged he had received 'a triumphal vote of confidence'), he 'should go very soon'.[105] All three then appear to have played a critical role in determining who would succeed to the premiership and who would not. The driving force behind the Queen sending for Lord Home to form a government is usually portrayed as Harold Macmillan, deriving from his antipathy to Butler succeeding him, but Morrison proved a key player, creating conditions that formed the basis for Macmillan's recommendation to the Queen.

Morrison was aware of backbench sentiment. Between 80 and 100 MPs were reported to have written to him or the Chief

Whip saying Macmillan should retire before the October party conference.[106] He took soundings and, with Mott-Radclyffe and Legge-Bourke, concluded that Butler was unacceptable, and that the Foreign Secretary, the Earl of Home, should run.[107] They persuaded the initially reluctant peer to let his name go forward. Morrison was visited at his island home by former Chief Whip Edward Heath, who also threw his support behind Home.[108] At the 1963 party conference, members of the executive gathered in a hotel, joined by the Chief Whips from the Commons and the Lords. 'Two of those present supported Maudling and two Hailsham but the remainder were for Home; there was virtual unanimity that Home was the candidate most likely to unite the Party at a moment when recent vicissitudes had created sharp divisions.'[109] They agreed to sound out MPs, asking not only their first and second preferences, but also whether they were particularly opposed to any of the four presumed candidates, a process that was likely to favour Home to whom few were opposed.[110] That was then the approach taken by the Chief Whip in the Commons, Martin Redmayne.

Morrison accompanied Redmayne to visit Macmillan in hospital to present 'their combined report of the feeling' among junior ministers and backbenchers.[111] Butler could have prevented Home becoming PM by refusing to serve under him, but Morrison had earlier told him that 'the chaps won't have you'.[112] (When Butler later consulted members of the 1922 executive, they confirmed Morrison's assessment.) In declining to act, he may have been influenced by what Morrison had told him. Iain Macleod was to condemn Home's succession to the premiership as the work of a 'magic circle', one that, according to one MP, Sir Gerald Nabarro, was 'led, insofar as it was led at all, by Major John Morrison, then Chairman of the 1922 Committee'.[113]

The extent to which Morrison consulted members of the '22 is not known, but he obviously felt confident enough to tell Butler the views of backbenchers. He played a key role away from the public platform. The events also contributed to the '22 acquiring a more formal, and public, role in the selection of future leaders.

Alec Douglas-Home, as Lord Home became, had a short-lived premiership. During it, the only issue that aroused controversy was the measure by the President of the Board of Trade, Edward Heath, to abolish resale price maintenance. Some members opposed it because of the effect it would have on the livelihood of small shopkeepers, but the principal opposition was on grounds of timing. Heath defended his policy at a meeting of the backbench Trade and Industry Committee (see Chapter 7) and the following week at a packed meeting – about 200 MPs attended – of the '22:[114] his argument, according to one member, 'went down like a lead balloon'.[115] The government narrowly avoided defeat when the Bill was debated, an amendment to exempt medicine and drugs being rejected by only one vote.[116]

Within a year of Douglas-Home entering No. 10, the Parliament reached its five-year maximum. The party lost the general election, albeit only narrowly. In opposition, Douglas-Home, conscious of the controversy generated by his 'emergence' as leader, set in train a review of the how the leader was chosen.[117] Although Tory MP Humphry Berkeley claimed credit for initiating an election process, the driving force was the party leader.[118] Berkeley 'was neither responsible for putting reform on the agenda nor influential in shaping the rules that were adopted'.[119] The details were agreed in discussion with the '22 executive, one of the joint secretaries, Peter Emery, playing a key role.[120] Once the review was completed, Douglas-Home announced to the '22 on 25 February 1965 that his successors would be elected by the party's MPs with the chairman of the 1922 being responsible for the conduct of the ballot and 'all matters in relation thereto'. The 1922 now had a new and decisive role in determining who would be leader of the party.

# Chapter 4

# Wielding the sword: the era of electing the leader

Once the new rules for electing the Conservative Party leader were in place, they were soon employed. There had been mutterings about Douglas-Home's leadership – the 1922 executive was divided on his leadership and various figures in the party, including the Chief Whip and party chairman, had advised him to step down[1] – and, although he was not forced out by backbench pressure, he felt it was not worth continuing as leader in opposition for what could be an arduous stint. He attended a meeting of the '22 on 15 July 1965 at which he was expected to challenge his critics, but instead announced he was relinquishing the leadership.[2] The announcement was unexpected and, as Selwyn Lloyd noted, 'received with obvious sadness and sympathy'.[3]

## Heath, Thatcher and Major

The first leader to be elected by Tory MPs under the new procedure was Edward Heath, emerging victorious over two other former Cabinet ministers, Reginald Maudling and Enoch Powell. As leader, Heath set up a series of policy groups – 29 in total were created – in which members of the '22 participated.[4] Although almost 200 MPs and peers were involved in the process,[5] there were complaints they were only allotted a half share in the operation and 'efforts had to be made to keep them satisfied'.[6] Officers of the relevant backbench committees were included on, or later co-opted to, most groups and regular reports were made to the 1922 executive.[7]

Under Heath, the party spent five years in opposition, with the emphasis on detailed policy preparation, before he led the party to an unexpected election victory in 1970. However, throughout his time as leader, both in opposition and government, he never achieved a close relationship with the very body that had been responsible for him being leader. He was more comfortable in dealing with policy than people. He did not utilise informal space to mix with backbenchers – he was notably distant – nor did he use the private space afforded by the '22 to engage with supporters.[8] Even his colleagues 'despaired of Heath's reluctance to spend time reassuring his back-bench colleagues and making them feel their views and feelings were being respected'.[9] In office, he was 'surprisingly short-tempered and impatient, remote and authoritarian'.[10]

As Prime Minister, he carried the '22 in his key policy of applying for UK membership of the European Communities (EC). Opinion in the '22 was divided. Although Ramsden was to claim that there was a strong determination in the '22 to back the policy,[11] a detailed note of the discussion on 6 May 1971 recorded 11 MPs speaking for entry to the EC, 6 against, with 7 expressing doubts or views that 'could not readily be ascertained'.[12] Nonetheless, the decision was taken to back the policy. Despite intense opposition from some Tory MPs, the majority supported the government in the passage of the European Communities Bill.[13] The Bill attracted the most protracted dissent of the Parliament, but other policies – especially those resulting from government U-turns – generated conflict,[14] though opponents used backbench committees rather than the '22 to pursue their opposition. Heath exacerbated the situation by making little effort to garner support in the '22. His relations with the officers and executive of the '22 were, at best, correct and at worst frosty. As Nigel Fisher, a member of the executive, recalled: 'He treated most of his Parliamentary colleagues with ill-concealed contempt, especially the Executive, whose meetings with him appeared to us to be no more than a necessary nuisance as far as he was concerned.'[15]

His failure to engage effectively with the '22 generated problems both in the short and the long term. In the short term, by not listening to backbenchers, he faced public dissent from his own benches. As one long-serving backbencher put it, 'Macmillan always listened, but Heath did not. And if the Prime Minister did not listen to you, then the only alternative was to vote against the Government.'[16] It was a view attested to by other members.[17] If disquiet could not be absorbed within the '22, members went public. The government faced unprecedented levels of dissent in the division lobbies.[18] Heath ploughed ahead with policies, even when warned by Chief Whip Francis Pym that he faced defeat. On six occasions, the government was defeated, three of the defeats taking place on three-line whips.

In the long term, Heath's failure to engage ended his leadership. Backbench dissatisfaction grew and found expression through the election of officers and executive of the '22 as well as officers of backbench committees. The elections were used, as one MP put it, to 'send a signal to Heath'.[19] In 1972, Edward du Cann, a former party chairman who was known to have a difficult relationship with Heath, was approached to stand as chairman of the '22. Those who approached him, he said, were quite clear as to what they wanted: 'someone who would stand up to the Prime Minister … and ensure he was aware of Party opinions. They felt he was ignoring the views of his colleagues in the House.'[20] Du Cann was elected. To ease relationships, in 1973 the new Chief Whip, Humphrey Atkins, organised a dinner for the PM with the officers and executive of the '22. It was described as 'calamitous',[21] with Heath losing his temper. He told one member that he was 'plain ignorant'.[22]

Heath's position worsened after he called an early election in February 1974 and failed to win an overall majority. He sounded out Liberal leader Jeremy Thorpe about a possible coalition. In approaching him, he failed to consult the 1922 and du Cann sent telegrams summoning members to an early meeting.[23] In the event, the Liberals rejected Heath's approach. The party was back in opposition and Heath lacked the levers of power at the disposal of a prime minister. Complaints of Heath's 'presidential style of government' were heard in the 1922 at the end of 1973,[24] but after the election defeat they became louder, and even more so following the loss of the second election of 1974. In the short 1974 Parliament, his handling of opposition was not well received by backbenchers,[25] and at a meeting of the '22 on 9 May, du Cann agreed to convey to Heath the strong sentiments expressed.[26] 'By late May the unhappiness had almost reached breaking point, and the 1922 Executive seriously discussed a planned campaign of revolt', but faced with Heath's intransigence decided to leave the leadership question 'on ice'.[27] The frustration of members was apparent the following month when former minister Paul Bryan demanded that there should be no more 'bogus opposition'.[28] After defeat in the October election, pressure on the leader was very quickly apparent. When the executive met, it was unanimous that there must be a leadership election and du Cann was 'instructed, not invited' to convey this to Heath.[29] At the first meeting of the '22, of 20 speakers, only two spoke in favour of Heath.[30] The officers and executive of the '22 were re-elected *en bloc*, with candidates favoured by Heath failing to be elected.

Pressure built up for Heath to submit himself for re-election as leader, something for which there was no provision. Heath attended a meeting of the '22 on 14 November – 'coldly but politely received', according to MP Airey Neave[31] – at which all the 13 MPs who spoke argued for a reform of the rules.[32] Heath agreed to set up a review of the way the leader was elected. A committee was set up under Alec Douglas-Home, with its recommendations being published on 17 December: they were agreed the following month by the '22 and the party's National Union, and the following week

by peers and the Shadow Cabinet. An election was to take place
three to six months after the start of a new Parliament and annual
ballots thereafter within 28 days of the start of the session. To
win on the first ballot, a candidate needed an absolute majority,
with the majority representing 15 per cent of all eligible voters
and not just of those voting, thus raising the hurdle for a winning
candidate. Responsibility for the conduct of the election remained
vested in the chairman of the '22.

An election was scheduled for February, with the first ballot to
take place on 4 February. Two candidates stood against Heath –
former Education Secretary Margaret Thatcher and longstanding
backbencher Hugh Fraser. Heath expected to win, but his conduct
in office and his failure to maintain contact with backbenchers
counted against him.[33] He came second to Thatcher. She got 130
votes to his 119. Heath withdrew from the race and Thatcher easily won against other candidates in a second ballot. The 1922 had
overseen the election of the party's first woman leader.

Margaret Thatcher was elected more because she was not
Ted Heath than because she was Margaret Thatcher.[34] She was
keen to avoid his style of leadership and spent time with backbenchers.[35] As Butler and Kavanagh recorded, there was a clear
contrast: 'Mrs Thatcher's main strength, unlike Mr Heath's, lay
with the backbenchers.'[36] According to one independent-minded
Tory MP, 'she has more support on the backbenches, which is her
natural constituency, than any other party leader I have known'.[37]
She sought to involve them in the policy process to a greater extent
than Heath.[38] Shadow ministers were encouraged to consult with
the elected officers of backbench committees. However, the performance of the front bench did not always inspire confidence. In
1977, the officers of the 1922 took 'the almost unprecedented step
of expressing dissatisfaction with the shadow cabinet and suggesting a reshuffle'.[39]

Thatcher was assiduous in meeting the officers and executive
of the '22. Unlike under Heath, the meetings 'had the feeling of

real dialogues'.[40] She courted du Cann, seeking his advice, and, as Ramsden noted, 'signalled her recognition of the importance of the 1922 Committee'.[41] Du Cann recalled that if he ever wanted to see her, he was given an immediate appointment.[42] 'Never was I received with anything but courtesy', even when he had advice for which she did not care.[43] She prepared for her appearances before the Committee. Du Cann sent her suggestions as to what to cover. Topics for discussion with the executive were notified in advance. In August 1980, for example, the issues were short- and medium-term economic prospects, House of Lords reform and Northern Ireland;[44] in December 1982, unemployment, tax thresholds and defence.[45] Her PPSs, especially her first, Ian Gow, kept her informed of what transpired at meetings of the '22, not least when addressed by Cabinet colleagues. Once in government, MPs started getting pressure from constituents over policies. At a meeting of the '22 in January 1980, attended by about 100 MPs, party chairman Peter (Lord) Thorneycroft sought to bolster the nerves of backbenchers: 'The important thing was to remain resolute, not to apologise.'[46] Gow recorded that although the speech was delivered 'with all his old fire and style', 'I had the impression, simply from looking at faces during his speech, that some of our younger members did not appreciate the worth and value of the man.'[47]

Some policies were controversial and led to tensions in meetings of the 1922. The 1981 budget attracted particular criticism. At one packed meeting, one Thatcher loyalist attacked another member for criticising Thatcher on the radio. The MP on the receiving end likened it to being put on trial, but some senior figures weighed in to defend the member.[48] Such meetings, though, were exceptional. Under du Cann's chairmanship, the conflicts were addressed not in the full meetings of the '22 – these tended to be short, with no invited speaker – but in the weekly meetings of the executive, where ministers were regular guests.

The executive had a lengthy discussion on the 1981 budget at its meeting on 12 March and agreed to invite the Chancellor to its meeting the following week, 'but to defer a meeting with the Prime Minister until the dust settled'.[49] Sir Geoffrey Howe duly appeared the following week 'and it was thought that his attitude was very robust'.[50] The same year, Environment Secretary Michael Heseltine had a difficult meeting with the executive over provisions of his Local Government Finance Bill; one member wanted him to drop the Bill entirely. It was agreed that the issue would be debated at a special meeting of the backbench finance and environment committees.[51] The criticisms led to dropping the provision for local referendums on proposals to levy a supplementary rate.

On 3 April 1982, following the meeting of the House that morning – a Saturday – to discuss the invasion of the Falkland Islands by Argentinian troops, between 150 and 200 members crammed into a committee room to hear from Foreign Secretary Lord Carrington. Formally, it was a meeting of the backbench Defence Committee, but it was essentially most of the parliamentary party. MPs were highly critical of previous government policy and Carrington was notably defensive. 'He was treated with anger and, by some, with open contempt and undisguised scorn.'[52] He had little experience of the '22 and was stung by the criticism. As he left, he told Defence Secretary John Nott, 'You know, I really think I must go … The Party regard it as all being my fault.'[53] He resigned. The government's position would also have been vulnerable, likely untenable, had it not despatched British forces to retake the islands. While the task force was sailing, the 1922 kept up its pressure on ministers, including Carrington's successor, Francis Pym: 'Tory backbenchers were clearly not in the mood for compromise of any kind.'[54] The successful retaking of the islands bolstered the Prime Minister's reputation. 'The 1922 Committee considered her a heroine and her determination, which had once appeared a dislikeable obstinacy, was now considered resolution.'[55]

By keeping in contact with her backbenchers, Thatcher was able to maintain their support even when government policies were attracting notable opposition. Ian Gow recorded that, after a meeting with the executive in June 1981, 'Edward du Cann, Charles Morrison and Paul Bryan have all said to me that they thought that last week's meeting with the Executive was the best which has been held since you became Leader of our Party.'[56] The minutes recorded that the members 'were very impressed by the knowledge of the Prime Minister and her grasp of affairs at a time when the country was going through a difficult situation economically'.[57] She invited the executive to Downing Street. After one such gathering in 1983, one member of the executive, Nigel Fisher, wrote to thank her, saying 'you created such a happy, friendly and relaxed atmosphere – in striking contrast to the past occasion when your predecessor entertained us, which was a total disaster!'[58]

However, as the decade progressed and Thatcher became more prime ministerial and less a party leader, she came to regard engagement with the '22 and the executive as more of a chore than an opportunity for constructive engagement. As one MP put it, a 'febrile atmosphere' developed in the '22: 'it began with the Westland crisis, was compounded by the poll tax, and Thatcher's oblivious attitude to the change of mood'.[59]

Some tensions appeared in her meetings with the executive. MP Jonathan Aitken noted that, whereas in her first term, she had been respectful, in her second she could be gratuitously offensive.[60] In May 1984, the executive held a post-mortem following a one-hour meeting with her. It was felt that they had focused too much on presentation rather than policy and that the PM was becoming too detached and not talking to people. 'Jill Knight thought that she took the Committee's criticisms of herself including her policies and took these too personally.'[61] Members felt they should hold more regular meetings with the PM. Du Cann committed to raising their discussion with the Chief Whip and also with Thatcher's PPS, Michael Alison, who had come in for criticism at the meeting, one member arguing that he failed to keep Thatcher in touch with the backbenches.

The following month, du Cann reported he had held a meeting with the Prime Minister 'because it was agreed by the Executive that the last meeting with her had not been a satisfactory one'.[62]

Relations did not improve. At her meetings with the executive, one member observed that she tapped her feet with impatience.[63] According to one of her biographers, 'she came to see the 1922 Executive as a bunch of self-important has-beens disappointed at never having won promotion'.[64] Her attitude was noted by Ian Gow in conversation with Thatcher loyalist Alan Clark, who noted in his diary: 'She's storing up trouble.'[65]

At the end of 1985, the '22 chairman, Cranley Onslow – he had replaced du Cann the previous year – asked Thatcher if she would address the '22 on the eve of the Christmas parliamentary recess. When her PPS, Michael Alison, passed on his request, noting that there was no precedent for her to address the '22 more than once a year, she wrote on the memo: 'I think this is a bad precedent. Once a year is better.'[66] Alison recorded that he had pencilled in her diary for the executive to see her on 10 December: she annotated this with 'I seem to remember I addressed them last year which was a mistake.'[67] She appeared to take less care in preparation for her speeches to the '22. In 1987, her notes for her talk comprised a few scribbled words.[68]

The party was badly divided on the issue of European integration, but the issue that proved especially divisive, and essentially sealed Thatcher's fate, was the community charge, or poll tax. It was highly unpopular, generating demonstrations and riots, but the Prime Minister remained unmoveable on the issue. At the start of the 1987 Parliament, she made clear to the 1922 that it was her flagship policy and demanded support for it.[69] As MPs were leaving the meeting, one, Nicholas Budgen, said to another, 'She ain't listening. She ain't listening.'[70] At a meeting with the executive in July 1989, she responded to a range of problems raised by members, not least the poll tax, the conduct of the European Parliament election campaign and the NHS (a 'disaster area' according to Michael Latham).[71]

Reflecting on the exchanges, the members 'all thought that the Executive had put their points more strongly than ever before'.[72]

The meeting of the '22 the same evening was also eventful. The following day, her PPS, Mark Lennox-Boyd, sent a memo: 'I should report to you a small but significant debate which took place at the 1922 Committee last night on the Community Charge', with criticisms levelled by the speakers he listed (Richard Page, Rhodes Boyson, John Wheeler and Charles Morrison).[73] Thatcher's principal private secretary, Andrew Turnbull, annotated the note with 'They are not accepting the basic premise of CC.' Cranley Onslow wrote to the Chief Whip, David Waddington, outlining problems of the community charge that were 'causing colleagues concern'.[74] Onslow also pressed the Treasury to transfer funds from the income tax payer to the community charge payer, but as Kenneth Baker recalled, 'not even the Chairman of the 1922 Committee was listened to'.[75] In December, the executive returned to the issue and decided to seek an urgent meeting with the Environment Secretary, Chris Patten, and the party chairman, Kenneth Baker.[76] Baker reported to the Prime Minister that the executive had been 'very firm and very consistent' and the overall impression was one of 'considerable unease'.[77]

Thatcher's intransigence and detachment generated unease in the parliamentary party. In 1989, she faced a leadership challenge by maverick backbencher Sir Anthony Meyer. His opposition was largely on grounds of Thatcher's stance on European integration. Although Thatcher won easily, by 314 votes to 33, there were 24 spoilt ballots and three absentees, meaning 16 per cent of the parliamentary party had failed to support her. More ominously, up to 60 MPs were reported to have written to her campaign manager saying their support was conditional and, if there was not a change of approach, their support may not be forthcoming in any future contest.[78]

In the event, there was no change of approach – 'she always believed she could face her critics down'[79] – and the political situation was not propitious for the government. When Thatcher had addressed the 1922 in July 1989, one MP, Richard Shepherd, said her reception was more muted than any he had seen in the past ten years. 'The deep uncertainty over the electoral impact of the poll tax hung over the meeting like the shadow of the guillotine.'[80] At a meeting the following March, right-wing MP Tony Marlow said that the Tories could be seen as 'declaring war on the people'.[81]

Thatcher addressed the '22 in July 1990 and wrote afterwards to Cranley Onslow to thank him and the executive 'for all you have done this session especially when things have not been easy ... I thought the spirit of the meeting on Thursday was good and that is the most important thing of all. That is a great tribute to you – my thanks and deep appreciation'.[82] However, the situation deteriorated with the resignation of Deputy Prime Minister Geoffrey Howe on 1 November and with former Defence Secretary Michael Heseltine challenging her for the leadership. Onslow agreed the date of the election with Thatcher – she opted for a timetable when she knew she would be out of the country.[83] She neglected to lobby supporters in the informal spaces of Westminster; Heseltine, in contrast, 'was everywhere'.[84] Thatcher fell short by four votes of the majority required to be declared elected on the first ballot. After seeing members of her Cabinet, she decided to withdraw from the contest. Of candidates in the second ballot (Heseltine, John Major, Douglas Hurd), Major emerged with most votes. Hurd and Heseltine announced their withdrawal from the contest. Onslow said that as chairman of the 1922, he had the discretion 'to override or interpret the rules according to common sense' and that a third ballot was unnecessary and would not therefore be held.[85]

Major's premiership was characterised initially by success, both in terms of handling the Gulf War and in leading the party to an unexpected victory in the 1992 general election. However, thereafter it was downhill, both in terms of standing with electors and with his backbenchers. The government's standing with electors collapsed in the wake of 'Black Wednesday' in September 1992, when the UK withdrew ignominiously from the European exchange rate mechanism: the party's claim to be a competent party of governance was lost.[86] However, the problem within the parliamentary party stemmed principally from Major's stance on European integration. He negotiated successfully over the Maastricht treaty, but perceptions of success were not shared by Eurosceptics in the parliamentary party. A 'no' vote on the treaty in a referendum in the Netherlands gave them the trigger to press for what they termed 'a fresh start with the development of the EEC'. They sought to amend the Bill ('the Maastricht Bill') to give effect in UK law to the treaty. Debate was protracted and was extended after the government was defeated on a Labour amendment. The government agreed that for the measure to take effect, the House had to approve a resolution on the treaty's social chapter. When the motion to comply with this provision was later put to the House, it was lost by 324 votes to 316. The government then tabled a motion expressing confidence in its policy on the social chapter, the Prime Minister making clear that he would resign and request the dissolution of Parliament if it was lost. It was carried by 339 to 299.

Throughout debate on the Bill, the 1922 had been a site of conflict, as much through the election of officers and executive committee members as at its weekly meetings. Cranley Onslow and his successor, Marcus Fox, maintained du Cann's practice of working primarily through the executive.

The executive reflected the wider party in being divided on the issue.[87] In June 1992, 'the general consensus was that we should play it long'.[88] In September, 'there was disagreement as to whether it [the Bill] should be brought back in the foreseeable future without substantial amendment'.[89] At the start of the following year, as the conflict intensified, the executive discussed the question of members of the executive voting against the government on procedural motions on the Bill. 'The Committee divided equally on

**History**

this principle.'[90] Fox did, however, persuade the executive to swing behind Major and in June it issued a statement in full support of the Prime Minister,[91] but such action failed to still an acrimonious debate. In the autumn, supporters of the Prime Minister sought to oust critics from the 1922 executive. They campaigned against five members seeking re-election, though managed only to unseat Sir George Gardiner, the right-wing MP for Reigate. *The Times* claimed that the outcome of the election 'suggests that the parliamentary party wants an end to factional infighting'.[92] If that was the aim, it was never realised. Infighting over Europe dominated the rest of the Parliament. It occurred in 1994 over the European Union (Finance) Bill: eight Tory MPs who failed to support it had the whip withdrawn. Their fate was to feature regularly at meetings of the 1922 executive. Infighting again found reflection in the 1922 elections that year when the chairman, Sir Marcus Fox, seen as loyal to the Prime Minister,[93] was challenged by Eurosceptic Sir Nicholas Bonsor. Fox was re-elected, though reports suggested only by 129 votes to 116.[94]

Major used his appearances before the '22 to rally support. In 1994, after criticisms of his leadership, 'A strong rallying performance before the 1922 Committee on 4 February, which was well received, suggested that a corner may have been turned.'[95] In the event, no corner was turned and critics in the parliamentary party continued to make the running in debate, calling for a referendum on the proposal for a single European currency. They called for the replacement of the Europhile Foreign Secretary Douglas Hurd and by the middle of 1995 were calling for a challenge to Major's leadership. After a meeting with the Fresh Start Group of Eurosceptic MPs, which apparently unsettled the Prime Minister by the level of hostility that was shown, Major decided to force a leadership contest. He had the backing of Fox, who also persuaded the executive unilaterally to declare that it would be the last leadership contest until after the next general election.[96]

64

The divisions over his leadership were apparent in the executive. A statement that the executive fully supported the Prime Minister was agreed when some members were away and at the next meeting, three of them – John Townend, Sir Rhodes Boyson and David Evans – expressed opposition to the statement.[97] The minutes reflect the febrile atmosphere in the executive: 'It was put to them by the rest of the Committee that it would have been better if they had been able to appear personally, rather than be away in Paris or at Lords.' After recording discussion about the leaking of a document considered at a previous meeting, the minutes concluded with 'Differences emerged.'[98] Major was challenged by former Welsh Secretary John Redwood, winning after a bruising contest, by 218 votes to 89. Major was not the only one to face a challenge. Fox was again challenged for the 1922 chairmanship, this time by former minister Bob Dunn, but managed to see off the challenge.

At his appearance before the '22 in July 1996, Major 'decided to let rip … They had to stop fighting each other, he told them, and turn their guns on Labour.'[99] MPs continued to turn the guns on themselves. There was a heated debate in the '22 at the start of December. At its meeting of the executive on 12 December, there was a discussion 'on the previous week's uproar in the main '22 meeting over the single currency. It was agreed that a period of calm was required for a couple of months following which a full appraisal of the negotiations in Europe could take place.'[100]

In the event, there was little the executive could do. As Philip Cowley observed, 'For most of John Major's premiership, the term "Conservative party unity" appeared to be an oxymoron.'[101] There was no respite to the extensive infighting within the party – the Prime Minister was assailed by both Eurosceptic and 'one nation' MPs – which served to exacerbate the scale of the party's defeat in the 1997 general election.[102] The party faced losses on a scale not seen since 1906. Among the casualties was Sir Marcus Fox.

## Hague, Duncan Smith and Howard

In the wake of the election loss and the return of a Labour government, Major resigned. The '22 elected a new chairman, Sir Archie Hamilton. Despite the depleted size of the parliamentary party, and calls from the party's voluntary wing to give party members some voting rights, the '22 executive decided to stick with the existing rules and not extend the franchise for the election of the party leader.[103] To rush into alterations of the existing rules without full consultation with other party bodies, such as the National Union, it believed, 'could prove disastrous'.[104] It accepted the case for a root-and-branch review of the rules and agreed to set up a sub-committee to consult and produce a discussion. However, its adherence to the status quo generated notable tensions with the chairman and executive committee of the National Union.[105]

In the leadership contest, MPs elected 36-year-old former Welsh Secretary William Hague, winning essentially because he was the least divisive candidate. He set about overseeing a restructuring of the party organisation as well as achieving an extension of the franchise for electing the leader, with agreement eventually being reached that the party membership would elect the leader from a choice of two determined by the parliamentary party, following (if more than two candidates were nominated) eliminating ballots. The formula was not only contentious, but, as we shall see, was to prove problematic. Hague submitted himself to a postal ballot of the membership.

Hague led a party that remained divided over the issue of European integration as well as social policy.[106] He had difficulty managing his MPs. Two defected to the Labour Party. He was criticised for how he handled Lord Cranborne, the Tory leader in the House of Lords, after he did a deal behind the backs of the Shadow Cabinet over reform of the Lords. 'Hague's reception at the 1922 Committee held after Cranborne's sacking saw him noisily supported by his backbenchers, but many made it privately clear to journalists that they considered the whole thing an embarrassing mess.'[107] Peter Lilley, the deputy leader, attracted strong criticism, not least at a meeting of the '22, for a speech that was seen as a repudiation of Thatcherism.[108] Hague spoke to the '22, conceding that the presentation had been poor.[109] Various criticisms were raised in the executive and these were conveyed to Hague by Archie Hamilton.

Throughout the Parliament, the parliamentary party suffered from a sense of powerlessness, having difficulty regrouping as a party to face a Labour government with a massive majority and with most Tory MPs having no experience of being in opposition. There was some uncertainty as to how to cope. A good deal of time of the 1922 executive was taken up not only with discussing changes to party organisation, but also the party's financial situation: 'On 19th June [1998] Chairman Archie Hamilton tells the '22 Executive that the Conservative Party is "skint"';[110] Archie Norman, the party's chief executive, 'attends … to brief members on the action that he is taking to balance the books at CCO [Conservative Central Office]'.[111] There were concerns about policy and how decisions were made and the advice the leader was getting. Hague's character, as Nigel Fletcher noted, 'inclined him towards management by clique'.[112] At the one meeting of the executive, 'Eric Forth (Bromley & Chislehurst) is, with good reason, very blunt about the calibre of the people William has around him.'[113]

The party lacked any clear sense of direction – there was no clear vision,[114] and for most of the Parliament it trailed Labour in the opinion polls, with little likelihood of winning the next election. The 2001 election was effectively lost, like the 1997 election, as a consequence of 'Black Wednesday' in 1992. The party duly lost the election – only 166 Tory MPs were elected, a net gain of one – and Hague resigned as leader. Archie Hamilton also stepped down as chairman of the '22. He was succeeded by Michael Spicer. The party acquired a new leader, after the party membership opted for Iain Duncan Smith, who had served in the Shadow Cabinet, over former Chancellor and long-serving MP Kenneth Clarke, the final two candidates selected by MPs.[115] Spicer, as chairman of the '22, oversaw the procedure.

An inherent problem of the new rules was demonstrated in the fact that Duncan Smith made it to the final two with the support of only one-third of Tory MPs (see Chapter 13). He was elected primarily because he wasn't Ken Clarke, who was thought to be too divisive on the issue of Europe. However, as leader, he never managed to stamp his authority on the party. He was beset by what Hayton and Heppell neatly summarised as 'internal divisions and ineffective leadership'.[116] He was, as they noted, 'an incredibly poor political communicator'.[117] That applied both to his public performances and to his appearances before the '22 Committee.

His attempts to take the initiative in focusing on public services and social justice were derailed by his attempts to maintain unity on other issues. Instead of treating it as a conscience issue subject to a free vote, he imposed a three-line whip to oppose allowing gay and unmarried couples to adopt children. The negative reaction by some Tory MPs led him to declare that the whip would remain in place but not be enforced. More than 40 MPs ignored the whip (8 voted for the measure, 35 abstained) and one frontbencher (John Bercow) resigned.[118] Duncan Smith then called a press conference. Over the past few weeks, he said, 'a small group of my parliamentary colleagues have decided consciously to undermine my leadership'. The vote on adoption had been an attempt to challenge his mandate to lead the party. 'We cannot go on in this fashion', he declared. His message, he said, was 'unite or die'.[119] His reaction suggested someone prone to panic, if not paranoia. He also clashed with Tory peers and some of his MPs after he decided unilaterally to support a largely elected second chamber and dismayed some MPs by his unequivocal support for Tony Blair's decision to back the United States in invading Iraq. More Tory MPs voted against than voted for the leader's position on Lords' reform in a series of votes in 2003 and 16 voted for an anti-war amendment over Iraq.[120] He made further enemies on his own benches when in 2002 he removed David Davis as party chairman. He also clashed with the Party Board after he sacked the party's chief executive and replaced him with a former MP who had been a Maastricht rebel under the Major premiership; in so doing, he was acting *ultra vires*, as the decision was one for the Board.

His appearances before the '22 were often problematic,[121] sometimes heard in silence; on one occasion he was virtually inaudible because of a faulty sound amplification system.[122] As Michael Spicer recorded of one meeting: 'Sullen meeting of '22 with IDS. Virtually no questions. He made same speech as at 1992 [sic] dinner two weeks before. Storm clouds could be gathering. The feeling is growing that he is making no impact.'[123] Concerns were expressed at meetings of the executive – 'need identity to which everyone can relate'[124] – and relayed by Spicer to the leader.[125] There was a perception among some MPs that he simply was not up to the job. As one of them, Gary Streeter, put it, 'Iain was not electable as Prime Minister. It was just about his personal leadership … he just wasn't up to it.'[126]

In January 2003, the executive had two lengthy discussions on the state of the party,[127] and the following month had a notably bad-tempered meeting with Duncan Smith, the secretary not pulling any punches in writing the minutes. The leader sought to justify his actions in reorganising Central Office and claimed newspaper reports were untrue. Disagreement with the Party Board had solely been about the leader's ability to sack and fire people as he wished. His defence appeared to elicit no support from the executive. One member said that this was not the first crisis to engulf the leader because he was receiving bad advice. 'The Party is in a shambles and there is no way that it can win the next General Election.' Duncan Smith responded by saying 'that he doesn't take lectures from anyone'. Others attacked his changes at Central Office: it was a serious mistake, according to one member, to appoint someone to run Central Office 'who is self-righteous and opinionated and that he [Duncan Smith] should not be surprised at the outrage which followed'. One 'conveyed the view from the grassroots, he said they were becoming desperate because the Party Leader was not winning the hearts and minds of the people'. The minutes concluded with 'Anthony Steen commented that the leader was floundering.'[128]

Spicer believes that the beginning of the end for Duncan Smith came with the leader's speech – 'muddled, without substance and ill prepared' – at the dinner the following month (March 2003) to commemorate the 80th anniversary of the 1922 Committee.[129] Even before then, some MPs had begun to make clear their lack of confidence – one (Crispin Blunt) had called for Duncan Smith to go – and speculation had begun as to a possible successor. After a poor performance by the leader at the party conference, MPs began announcing that they had put in letters to Spicer calling for a confidence vote. In October, the executive divided 10 to 7 in favour of writing to demand a vote of confidence.[130] The Chief Whip, conscious of support ebbing away, told Duncan Smith he should consider his position.[131] Duncan Smith made clear that he would not go voluntarily.[132] On the morning of 28 October, Spicer announced that the threshold had been reached and that there would be a vote the following day. The executive met at 3.00 p.m. and agreed that the statement on the ballot paper would be 'I have confidence in IDS as Leader of the Conservative Party' with a box for 'yes' and 'no'. (It also agreed the procedure in the event of a 'no' vote winning.) At 2.30 p.m. the following day, Duncan Smith appeared at a packed meeting of the '22 in Committee Room 14 and made possibly the best speech of his career in defence of his leadership.[133] Speaking for about 20 minutes, he conceded that he had made mistakes, had learned from them and was proud of what he has achieved. He believed he had got the measure of the Prime Minister. He finished to a banging of desks. I turned to one senior MP and asked his opinion: 'Too late' was the laconic response. The ballot opened at 3.30 p.m. and closed at 6.30 p.m.

Duncan Smith was voted out by 90 votes to 75. As Peter Snowdon observed, he became the first party leader in opposition since Austen Chamberlain to be removed before having a chance to fight a general election.[134]

Duncan Smith may have been deposed sooner had it not been for the rules for electing the leader. The prospect of more than one candidate standing, leading to a divisive and lengthy contest, acted as a deterrent. Once he was voted out, former Home Secretary Michael Howard was nominated to succeed him and other potential candidates, such as David Davis, decided against standing. At a meeting of the '22 on 6 November, Spicer was able to declare that there was only one nominee and that therefore Howard had been elected.[135]

Howard was leader for two years, during which, as David Cameron claimed, 'there was a sense that the grown-ups and the professionals were back in charge'.[136] However, there were tensions over policy proposals as well as decisions by the leader that generated dissent in the '22. There were clashes over Europe, Lords reform (Howard for an elected House, the '22 executive against) and identity cards. In 2004, Howard's decision to support the government's policy of introducing identity cards proved especially controversial,[137] splitting the Shadow Cabinet and the parliamentary party. He defended his policy at the '22, arguing that he did not want Labour to be able to say that the party opposed them. As Michael Spicer recorded: 'Usual appeal for loyalty – re identity card issue. MH makes the – in my view unconvincing – argument that when he was Home Secretary the police wanted them … Douglas Hogg pleads that he take account of "liberal" view in the party.'[138] The following year, Howard withdrew support for the government's planned legislation on the subject. His decision just before the 2005 general election to prevent Tory MP Howard Flight, the party's deputy chairman, from standing as a candidate following a controversial speech, was seen by many MPs as a massive over-reaction. There was also a wider unease in the parliamentary party about a lack of direction. In July 2003, Spicer more than once warned Howard that the parliamentary party was becoming restive,[139] and in December there was a 'Very outspoken '22 meeting. Nick Winterton, Howarth, Heathcoat-Amory and Leigh all speak for greater sharpness in policy, especially re low taxes. Letwin defends the view that it is "too early to give hostages to fortune". This does not go down well as we are some 8 points behind Labour in the polls. Bizarrely, MH [Michael Howard] sits at the back of the room listening.'[140]

Although Howard had regular contact with Michael Spicer as chairman of the '22 – they were friends and got on well together[141] – there were problems in ensuring a regular dialogue with the party leadership. The whips proved especially problematic. Spicer echoed Gervais Rentoul's concerns that the whips viewed the '22 as a problem and sought to work around it. 'David Wilshire (ex-whip) comes up to say that he has written evidence that the whips want to cut down '22 to size. The eternal tension between whips and '22 goes on!'[142] The withdrawal of the whip from Howard Flight added to the tension. There was also an attempt by Howard in 2005 to call a meeting of MPs to discuss constitutional changes in the party rather than hold it under the aegis of the '22. Spicer persuaded him to change his mind.

The meeting to discuss constitutional changes took place after the party had lost the 2005 general election. Howard announced his intention to resign as leader after some party reorganisation had been achieved. A package of reform proposals, covering rules for electing the leader as well as wider party organisation (including a central membership and head office control of party candidatures), were put to a packed meeting of about 180 MPs and peers in the Grand Committee Room off Westminster Hall on 24 May. When the meeting was told it was a take-it-or-leave-it package, there was a notably hostile reaction. Douglas Hogg was cheered when he argued it should not be taken as a package and that there should have been consultation with the 1922. MPs crowded into

Committee Room 14 the next night for the regular meeting of the '22, as they did in the two subsequent weeks, to discuss the proposals, which proved largely friendless. On 20 July, Michael Spicer announced that MPs had voted by the requisite two-thirds majority (127 votes to 50) for the election of the leader to revert to MPs. The party's constitutional college failed to mobilise the two-thirds majority required for the change.

Howard's handling of the affair generated opposition in the '22 and some members started putting in letters of no confidence,[143] though the frontrunner to succeed him, David Davis, proved reluctant to encourage his supporters to do so.[144] In the event, Howard resigned in October and the extant leadership rules, other than for some minor drafting changes, were employed to elect his successor. The two candidates placed before party members were former party chairman David Davis and Shadow Cabinet member, albeit an MP for only four years, David Cameron. Cameron had started with few declared supporters, but he developed a momentum that carried him to victory, winning 134,448 votes to 64,398 for Davis.[145] His victory was attributed to the party wanting a clear break with the past.

Cameron was to lead the party into a new era of party governance, delivering not only electoral success, but also under his premiership a referendum outcome that was to generate a period of political turmoil and a role for the 1922 Committee as a major political player. The Committee was to be led by the longest-serving chairman in its history and one whose name was to regularly adorn the news headlines. The Committee had come of age.

## Chapter 5

# The maker and slayer of leaders: from Cameron to Sunak

David Cameron was elected party leader in 2005, with party members looking to him to deliver electoral success. There was no expectation that the 1922 would not continue as it had in recent years, ready if necessary to remove a leader who was deemed a likely electoral liability, but otherwise ready to sustain, though not necessarily uncritically, the person they had elected to lead them. In the event, Cameron was to deliver electoral success, but also preside over a referendum outcome that was to generate political turmoil and catapult the 1922 Committee into a role as a major, and very prominent, player in British politics – and to make its chairman virtually a household name.

### Cameron and May

As party leader, Cameron set about stressing what the Conservative Party was for rather than what it was against, adopting a value-driven approach and emphasising the 'big society' rather than big government.[1] He set up policy groups to advise on policy, their recommendations being considered by the Shadow Cabinet, with input from the 1922 Committee, before being adopted as policy. He effectively resuscitated the party as a party of governance.[2] However, though respected, he did not have a close relationship with his backbenchers. He encountered criticism when he stood by his Shadow Education Secretary, David Willetts, after he made a speech that was interpreted as an attack on grammar schools. Willetts had a bruising meeting of the '22, with only two MPs prepared to speak in his defence.[3] 'Dangerously, his critics came from all wings of the party. Sitting in the front row and looking sulphurous was Michael Howard, who loudly banged the desk in support as the blows rained down.'[4] Cameron exacerbated the situation by challenging the critics. The Shadow Europe Minister, Graham Brady, resigned in protest. The impression was given of a divided party.

Cameron also attracted criticism from backbenchers for his handling of the 2009 scandal surrounding MPs' expenses. Although the parliamentary party generally accepted the need for action on the issue,[5] the scheme devised to address it generated dissent. Cameron set up a scrutiny panel which was accused of meting out summary justice, some MPs being forced to stand down as candidates at the next election. 'What really caused resentment among a number of backbenchers was the charge of favouritism.'[6] He was viewed as detached and reliant on a core group of trusted advisers and this reliance, and a sense of self-confidence, meant that the parliamentary party did not warm to him. This created problems when he failed to translate an opinion poll lead into a clear victory in the 2010 general election.[7]

The failure to win an overall majority led Cameron to offer to negotiate with the Liberal Democrats to form a government. As negotiations got under way, he called a meeting of Conservative MPs to report on progress. It was a body summoned by the party leader, not a meeting of the 1922 Committee. The purpose was not to endorse a deal, but rather to acquiesce in a proposal for a referendum on the alternative vote (AV) for parliamentary elections. The alternative, according to Cameron, was a Lib–Lab coalition that may introduce AV anyway.[8] Not all Tory MPs were persuaded of the case for a coalition – favouring instead a minority Conservative government – or of the commitment to a referendum. However, they were left feeling that they had no choice.[9] The Coalition Agreement also stored up problems for relations with the parliamentary party, given that on constitutional issues the two parties adopted diametrically opposed positions and the agreement conceded more to the Liberal Democrats than to the Conservatives.[10] Cameron also generated tensions with back-benchers by calling a meeting of MPs to get them to agree to ministers serving as voting members of the 1922 Committee. It was viewed as an attempt to prevent the independent-minded Graham Brady being elected to succeed Michael Spicer as chairman. As we shall see (in Chapter 6), the attempt ultimately failed.

Cameron's continued use of trusted advisers, and a failure to generate, as Harris put it, 'a directing idea',[11] left him vulnerable to criticism within the party. He had to try to balance maintaining the support of the Liberal Democrats in the House while keeping his own backbenchers on side. Various measures, such as the Fixed-term Parliaments Bill, attracted dissent from Tory MPs, though not on a scale to threaten the government.[12] Dissent, however, became marked over the 2011 referendum campaign on whether to replace the existing first-past-the-post voting system for the House of Commons with the alternative vote. Cameron's aim was not to play a prominent role in the campaign. However, when the AV campaign looked as if it may succeed, pressure from the 1922 made him change his mind. Party chairman Baroness Warsi had a difficult meeting with the '22, facing criticism over the party's failure to commit resources to the campaign. Graham Brady and the executive committee saw Cameron and told him that he could have the distinction of being the last Conservative Prime Minister.[13] He thereafter threw his weight behind the 'No' campaign, much to the annoyance of his Deputy Prime Minister, Liberal Democrat leader Nick Clegg. Relations with Clegg were further soured when Cameron was not able to deliver on House of Lords reform, the Bill to provide for a largely elected House having to be abandoned after 91 Conservative MPs voted against it, and a further 19 abstained, on Second Reading.[14] Cameron had a stand-up row immediately after the vote with backbencher Jesse Norman, who had led the campaign against the Bill.

Cameron also took up the cause of same-sex marriage, initiating a government Bill that was disliked by a large portion of the parliamentary party. Some took issue with the fact that it was not included in the party's manifesto. The issue was raised by Graham Brady in one of his regular meetings with the PM. 'The letters are pouring in, he tells David. He needs forty-six letters from the MPs to trigger a leadership contest … Only Brady himself knows exactly how near that trigger we really are.'[15] In the event, there was no challenge and the Bill made it to the statute book, despite more Conservative MPs voting against than for it.

However, the issue that caused most friction between Cameron and his backbenchers was that of European integration. When Tory MP David Nuttall achieved a debate on a motion to hold a referendum on the UK's continued membership of the European Union, Cameron imposed a three-line whip to oppose it. Despite a heavy whipping operation, 81 Tory MPs voted for the motion. The outcome cheered Cameron's critics in the parliamentary party. 'The coalition had picked a fight with the Conservative Party and had been given a bloody nose.'[16] Some members were reported to have submitted letters of no confidence to Graham Brady.[17] Cameron realised he needed to secure his base in the parliamentary party. He said he would negotiate reform of the UK's membership and put the renegotiated terms to the people in a referendum. Some MPs pressed him to go further and commit to a referendum in the next Parliament. In May 2013, two backbenchers moved an amendment to the motion on the Queen's Speech regretting the absence of any mention of a Referendum Bill. No fewer than 114 Conservatives voted for it. The PM's response was to produce a draft Bill providing for a referendum before 31 December 2017. It was introduced as a Private Member's Bill – the Liberal Democrats blocked it being a government measure – and

Cameron lobbied for it. The Bill failed to make it through the House of Lords.

Despite the change of heart, Cameron's relationship with the 1922 remained somewhat detached. He developed a working relationship with Graham Brady and his speeches when he addressed the '22 were generally well received, and delivered without notes, but were the sort of speeches one could imagine him giving to any Conservative gathering.[18] He appeared aloof and tended to take decisions without reference to the '22. As one MP put it, 'There's lots of contact, not much listening.'[19] His deputy chief of staff noted how few MPs the PM could count as true loyalists.[20] The party also suffered from advances made by the UK Independence Party and by the defection of two MPs to join it: they resigned to fight by-elections and both won. Cameron committed the party in its 2015 manifesto to holding an in/out referendum on the UK's membership of the EU before the end of 2017 and to honouring the outcome, whatever the result. It was a means of holding the party together, but it was also to seal his fate.

Cameron led the party to victory in the 2015 general election, achieving an overall majority. He achieved passage of a Bill providing for a referendum. He did not achieve changes to the terms of the UK's membership to the extent he sought, but he pursued the referendum campaign to remain in the EU, believing it would triumph. On 23 April 2016, by 52 per cent to 48 per cent, electors voted to leave the EU. The following morning, Cameron announced his resignation. Five candidates stood to succeed him. The two who topped the final poll of MPs were Home Secretary Theresa May and Environment Secretary Andrea Leadsom. In the event, Leadsom withdrew after an interview in which she commented on May not having children, but she had already contemplated withdrawing because she recognised that she lacked support in the parliamentary party.[21] May had received an absolute majority of votes in the final ballot of MPs and, rather than re-running the election, Graham Brady announced that May was elected.

## The maker and slayer of leaders

By her own admission, Theresa May was not prone to spend time socialising in the tea room or corridors of the Palace of Westminster. She relied on a close body of advisers and tended to keep her views to herself.[22] Her principal challenge was to deliver on the referendum vote for the UK to leave the European Union. Members of the parliamentary party were divided over membership, some opposed to withdrawal, some favouring a 'soft' and others a 'hard' Brexit. May was also conscious of the party's small overall majority of 12. To bolster her position – having previously denied any intention to hold an early election – she sought, and achieved, a general election under the terms of the Fixed-term Parliaments Act. The campaign proved disastrous, a large lead in the opinion polls evaporating and, in the June 2017 election, the party losing its overall majority. To maintain a majority, negotiations were undertaken with the Democratic Unionist Party.

May appointed one of the party's defeated MPs, Gavin Barwell, as her chief of staff, asking him 'to focus on improving relations between No. 10 and the parliamentary party'.[23] His first task was briefing her for an appearance before the 1922, which took place on Monday 12 June.[24] Committee Room 14 was packed. It was not clear when she went into the meeting that she would survive as Prime Minister. She made a powerful speech, essentially one of contrition. Having appeared wooden in performance during the election campaign, she now came across as human. She acknowledged the need for a broader consensus on Brexit and said she had got the message about being more open and receptive. She accepted responsibility for what had happened and said she had got the party 'into this mess', adding 'I'm the one who will get us out of it.' She would serve the party as long as it wanted her to. Help, she declared, would be provided to those who had lost their seats, an announcement that went down well with the assembled MPs. She not only got an ovation, but a standing ovation. She then spent an hour answering questions from about 20 to 30 MPs, mostly tackling issues to be addressed rather than critical of her leadership.

According to Seldon, the 'aim of the game that evening was not her political survival – that was not in doubt – but giving MPs the grounds on which they could forgive her and reset a new relationship'.[25] When she entered the room, her political survival was in doubt. The speech in effect saved her premiership, at least for the time being. It deterred potential leadership challengers. She had the space to craft a withdrawal agreement.

During the first half of 2018, Brexit did not figure significantly at meetings of the '22. They were given over mostly to hearing from Cabinet ministers speaking to their departmental responsibilities, typically to an audience of 20 to 30 MPs. The Prime Minister spoke on 28 March, to a packed room of 150–200 MPs, receiving a standing ovation. In a short 10-minute speech, she sounded upbeat, stressing successes, such as an improving economy. Of the few questions that were asked, none was critical.

Divisions within the party increased as the year progressed, with ministers, beginning with Brexit Secretary David Davis, resigning following the Prime Minister revealing her 'soft Brexit' plans at Chequers at the start of July. However, she received a loud ovation when she addressed the '22 on 18 July. She stressed what had been achieved outside of Brexit and how well the party had done in the local elections. One MP said he had put in a letter of no confidence, but he had withdrawn it as the Prime Minister needed the freedom to negotiate. Several called for a united front to avoid a Corbyn premiership – a recurring theme at meetings of the '22.

However, the division within the party's ranks became more pronounced as May struggled to win the party round to her strategy. The outcome of the election and the composition of the parliamentary party meant that she lacked a parliamentary majority to deliver on whatever agreement was negotiated. She faced a European Research Group (ERG) that favoured a hard Brexit and MPs who favoured remaining in the EU. There was particular concern over the position of Northern Ireland and the need to avoid a 'hard' border with the Republic of Ireland. At a '22 meeting on

5 September, addressed by the new Brexit Secretary Dominic Raab, Brexiteers such as John Redwood and Bernard Jenkin argued that it was not the problem it was being made out to be. As the Prime Minister began to lose ministers who were not prepared to back her policy, MPs started submitting letters of no confidence to Graham Brady. May appeared before the 1922 on 24 October, which she handled more effectively than critics had expected.[26] It was another meeting with standing room only. She received sustained applause and stressed what she wanted to achieve, primarily to get Brexit done by the next election. It proved a temporary reprieve.

The withdrawal agreement was published in November, but instead of being put to a vote in the House in December, when it looked as if it would be defeated, it was announced that it would be delayed, an announcement that proved the final trigger for some members, who submitted letters of no confidence. On 11 December, Graham Brady announced that the requisite 48 letters had been received. He agreed with May that the vote would take place the next day, a Wednesday. At the 1922 meeting the following evening, 251 MPs gathered to hear the Prime Minister say that she would not lead the party into the next election. Four hours later, Brady announced that she had won the vote by 200 votes to 117. Although she was the victor, a large proportion of the party had not supported her. As the *Daily Telegraph* observed, she had 'emerged deeply wounded by a result that puts her own future and Brexit itself in doubt'.[27] The following Wednesday, May returned to the '22 and spoke briefly to say that it was the party's 'solemn duty' to stop Jeremy Corbyn getting into Downing Street.

Although May won the confidence vote, she was not so fortunate with the withdrawal agreement. When put to the House in January 2019, it went down to the largest recorded government defeat (by 432 votes to 202) in modern political history. For many Tory MPs, what had been negotiated on Northern Ireland proved unpalatable. When the agreement was again twice put to the House in March, it was defeated, albeit by smaller majorities. The House, by

# History

312 votes to 311, also agreed a motion moved by Tory MP Oliver Letwin, to take control of the parliamentary timetable in order to enact legislation that tied the government's hands in negotiations.[28] May was in the classic case of being in office but not in power.

As the situation worsened, there were again calls from some Tory MPs for the PM to resign. In March, May appeared before two meetings of the '22, the first on Monday 11 March, when 225 MPs crowded into the Attlee Suite in Portcullis House to hear her, and the second on 27 March, when, to try to ease passage of the withdrawal agreement on the 29th, she said, her voice wavering at times, that she recognised that there were those who believed there needed to be fresh leadership once Brexit was achieved. 'I am prepared', she declared, 'to leave this job earlier than I intended in order to do what is right for our country and our party.' However, no date was given for her departure, much to the annoyance of members of the ERG who believed they had agreed with her that she would announce her departure date at the meeting.[29]

After the agreement was voted down for a third time, criticism of May intensified. The 1922 executive came under pressure from some members to change the rules on confidence votes to allow one before the 12 months elapsed after the last vote, Brady's two predecessors having stated publicly that it was open to the executive to change the rules. As Theresa May was later ruefully to observe, 'The mood music on this was not helped by members of the '22 committee being willing to give their views to the media!'[30]

The executive was itself divided on the issue of Brexit, with members drawn from both sides of the divide. With strong remainers like Antoinette Sandbach and arch-Brexiteers such as Steve Baker and Bernard Jenkin in its ranks, there was little likelihood of it taking a united stand on the principle. There was occasional shouting and storming out.[31] It focused on process, primarily the rules for electing the leader.

At a meeting of the '22 on 3 April, some members asked Graham Brady if they could write to him calling for a leadership election and if he would announce if more than half the parliamentary party wrote to him. Brady said they could write to him, but that the rules were clear. On 24 April, he made a statement on behalf of the executive. It had resolved that there would not be any rule change; that any member could write to the chairman; and that the Prime Minister had been asked to indicate a schedule for her departure from office. In response to a question, he confirmed legal advice had been taken and that it was open to the executive to change the rules.

The decision not to change the rules had apparently been agreed by a narrow majority. The executive returned to the issue the following month. The executive voted in a secret ballot, with Brady keeping the voting slips in an envelope, to be opened only if May did not announce that she was leaving office by 12 June. Brady informed May, who received the news badly. On 16 May, the executive saw her in her office at the Commons to discuss the date of her departure as leader. On 21 May, she sought to bolster support for the agreement by offering a vote on whether to hold a second referendum, a decision that prompted another Cabinet resignation and in the minds of some Brexiteers the belief that her position was untenable. Early on Friday 24 May, Brady went to see May to tell her time was up, but she had already made the decision. She went outside No. 10 to announce her resignation. She would quit as party leader on 7 June, but she would remain as Prime Minister until a successor was elected.

During May's premiership, the 1922 Committee, and especially the executive, had been kept busy. At one point, Brady was almost in daily contact with the Prime Minister.[32] She acknowledged the importance of seeing him to 'get his take on the mood of the backbenches'.[33] Brexit was the principal issue consuming members' interests. Other than meetings addressed by the Prime Minister – the number and large attendances resembling the days of the Suez Crisis – there were sharp exchanges at some of the regular meetings, some MPs, notably Brexiteers, complaining about ministers being allowed to dissent and not being disciplined. When the party chief executive, Sir Mick Davies, attended a '22 meeting and observed that most significant party donors tended to support remaining in the EU, he received some barracking. When one MP, a leading Brexiteer, argued that the vast majority of the party was of one view, implying a minority were disloyal, another shouted dissent and stormed out, almost knocking his chair over.

There were other issues exercising backbenchers. Complaints were raised about the conduct of the Speaker, John Bercow, not only over Brexit, but also over his tendency to let questioning of the Prime Minister run on, notably so in April 2018 over the decision to agree air strikes in Syria in conjunction with France and the United States. Graham Brady said the issue had been discussed by the executive.

Once May had announced her resignation, the process for electing a new leader began, this time overseen by the two vice-chairmen of the 1922, Charles Walker and Cheryl Gillan, Graham Brady having recused himself as he may be a candidate. In the event, he was not, with the final two candidates placed before the party membership being former Foreign Secretary Boris Johnson, who had been a leader of the campaign to leave the EU, and Foreign Secretary Jeremy Hunt, who had voted for remaining. Johnson was elected by a two-thirds majority.

## Johnson, Truss and Sunak

Johnson was not someone with a notable body of parliamentary supporters – he had pursued other interests while a backbencher – but was acknowledged to be an effective campaigner. He sought to impose some discipline, in September withdrawing the whip from 21 MPs who failed to support the government over Brexit. He addressed the '22 on 16 October, attracting laughter, not least with jokes about the Brexit Party and the Liberal Democrats. He said members must come together as a party. He said nothing about Brexit negotiations and did not take questions. He left to applause, but not a standing ovation. He achieved a renegotiation of the withdrawal terms with the EU and mobilised a majority to give a Second Reading to the Bill to give effect to it. It was passed by 329 votes to 299. However, he failed to get a majority for the Bill's timetable motion. An attempt to call an early general election under the Fixed-term Parliaments Act was thwarted three times before he achieved enactment of a free-standing bill to hold a general election on 12 December. The Conservatives were returned with an 80-seat majority. A modified version of the withdrawal Bill was then passed, enabling the UK to leave the EU on 31 January 2020.

The start of 2020 was the high point of the Johnson premiership. The government shortly thereafter faced the COVID-19 pandemic, MPs having largely to disperse, Parliament having first given major emergency powers to government. Johnson himself was hospitalised with COVID-19, but he survived. The government's handling of the period of lockdown, especially attempts to get sufficient personal protection equipment (PPE) and pursue a 'test and trace' policy attracted widespread criticism. Lockdown restrictions began to come under attack from MPs. In September, over 40 MPs added their names to an amendment tabled by Graham Brady requiring a vote 'as soon as reasonably practicable' on any future lockdown restrictions.[34] 'His intervention is a sign of the scale of disquiet among Boris Johnson's backbenchers about the way he is handling the pandemic.'[35] Critics formed a Covid Recovery Group (CRG) and continued to challenge Johnson's cautious approach. The number of dissenters grew over the course of 2021 and at the end of the year 98 Conservatives voted against further, albeit less stringent, restrictions, the government only winning the vote because of opposition support.

However, what undermined Johnson's position was revelations that he had attended farewell parties in No. 10 during the period of lockdown, subsequently being issued with a fine after investigation by the Metropolitan Police. After initially telling MPs that all rules had been complied with, he then conceded parties had taken place.

Some MPs began to submit letters of no confidence. Johnson was further undermined by attempts to soften the punishment recommended for Tory MP Owen Paterson for breaching lobbying rules, leading to a backlash in the media and among some backbenchers. There was no co-ordinated effort by any group within the party to oust Johnson, but rather a string of individual MPs deciding, and in some cases making public, that they thought he should resign.[36] By the end of May 2022, 27 MPs had made public their opposition. They included former Cabinet ministers Mark Harper and David Davis, and the former chair of the ERG, Steve Baker. By June, it was rumoured that the number of letters submitted to Graham Brady was close to the requisite number (now 54) needed to trigger a vote. On 6 June, Brady announced that the figure had been reached and that the vote would take place that evening. Appearing before the '22, Johnson stressed what had been achieved and 'whatever else they may say about me, do you really think that anyone else would have done it?'[37] It was an up-beat performance, with no contrition. Johnson won by 211 votes to 148.

The size of the dissenting vote – 41 per cent of the parliamentary party – indicated that his tenure in No. 10 was limited. 'Far from moving on', declared *The Economist*, 'the result is paralysing.'[38] In the event, his position was soon rendered untenable, not by the actions of the 1922 Committee, but by his own ministers. Having faced various scandals, he was brought down by his failure to admit, after initially denying it, that he had been informed of complaints of sexual assault against the MP he had appointed as Deputy Chief Whip. Cabinet ministers, led by Health Secretary Sajid Javid and Chancellor of the Exchequer Rishi Sunak, resigned, followed by other ministers. Following a record number of resignations, Graham Brady saw him to discuss his position.

Brady told him that the executive had agreed to bring forward the annual election of officers and members of the executive to the following week so that it would have a fresh mandate before discussing any changes to the rules governing leadership elections. He told Johnson that in his view 'given the mood of the parliamentary party, it is inconceivable that the new executive would be more averse to changing the rules'. It was almost inevitable that a vote of confidence would take place the following week. 'It is fairly obvious you would lose it.'[39]

Johnson was adamant that he was going to stay, but the following morning called Brady to say that he had reflected on their conversation and that he had concluded that it was in the interests of both the country and the party that he should go. A lectern was erected in Downing Street and Johnson delivered a defiant resignation statement. It was later reported that had Johnson sought to stay in office by requesting an early general election (something war-gamed as one of several scenarios by Johnson's close allies), a 'golden triangle' of Graham Brady, the Cabinet Secretary and the Queen's private secretary would have ensured it did not happen, with the Queen being 'unavailable' to speak to Johnson.[40]

Johnson's resignation triggered another leadership contest, several candidates being whittled down to former Chancellor Rishi Sunak and Foreign Secretary Liz Truss, the latter fighting the election on a tax-cutting platform and winning with just under 60 per cent of the votes of the party membership. In the event, Truss' tenure as Prime Minister proved to be the shortest in history. A mini-budget delivered by Chancellor Kwasi Kwarteng on 23 September 2022 proved disastrous, generating a loss of confidence in the markets and among electors. At the party conference, Kwarteng announced a U-turn on a proposed scrapping of the upper tax rate of 45p in the £: 'It was', *The Times* reported, 'the inevitable conclusion of a day of crisis meetings and phone calls in which senior Tories including Sir Graham Brady, the chairman of the 1922 Committee of Conservative backbenchers, made it clear to the chancellor and prime minister that the policy had to go.'[41] Brady had seen the PM and told her that 'she did not have the numbers to ram a tax cut for the richest 10 per cent through Parliament, and that trying to do so would likely bring her down'.[42]

Truss dismissed Kwarteng and replaced him with Jeremy Hunt, who proceeded to scrap the principal provisions in the mini-budget. MPs were reported to be submitting letters of no confidence, even though under the rules a newly elected leader could not face a vote of no confidence for 12 months. Some publicly called for her to go. As many as 100 MPs were reported to have written to Brady. On 12 October, Truss addressed the 1922 Committee. There was a banging of desks as she arrived. She said there would be a major policy announcement the next day and that those present would be invited to a briefing at No. 10 by the new chief of staff. She said the whips were being moved back into 12 Downing Street (from No. 9) and that there would be no election until 2024, a statement that elicited some cheering. However, her speech failed to rouse the audience and some questions were barbed. One MP, Robert Halfon, pointedly told her that she had 'trashed the last 10 years of workers' Conservatism'. Another told waiting journalists that the PM had 'done absolutely nothing to reassure colleagues whatsoever'; another said the situation was impossible.[43] The following week, there was confusion during a debate on fracking as to whether the government had made the vote one of confidence; there were altercations outside the division lobbies and rumours that the Chief Whip had resigned, the PM being reported to have run after her to persuade her to stay. 'Confusion reigned supreme in Parliament as drama turned to farce, with MPs baffled as to whether they could rebel or not.'[44] The chaotic situation suggested a government in disarray.

The following morning (20 October), Graham Brady met Truss, at her invitation, at Downing Street, slipping in through a back door. She had already decided that it was not possible to continue. Brady confirmed that she had lost the support of the parliamentary party. He had received 'too many letters' for her to stay in office.[45] She said she had reached the same conclusion. She followed her two predecessors in making a statement in Downing Street announcing that she was stepping down.

The executive of the '22 decided that a long leadership contest was undesirable. In her resignation statement, Truss said that she and Brady had agreed that there was to be a leadership election 'to be completed in the next week'. There was a clear feeling that it would be ideal for there to be only one candidate. To deter too many candidates coming forward, the executive agreed that the number of signatures needed for a nomination to be valid would be 100. Supporters of Boris Johnson, Rishi Sunak and Penny Mordaunt started collecting signatures. By the time of the nomination deadline, Sunak had achieved the requisite number. Penny Mordaunt just fell short. It was later confirmed by Brady that Johnson had met the 100-signature threshold. However, he decided against running, recognising that he would not lead a united party. As a result, Sunak was declared elected and on 25 October accepted the invitation of the new King, Charles III, to be Prime Minister, becoming the youngest Prime Minister for over 200 years and the nation's first British Asian holder of the office. At the last meeting of the '22 that year, on 14 December, he thanked Graham Brady and the members of the executive for all that they had done 'in what has been an unusually busy year'.

## A century on...

In February 2023, Sir Graham Brady presided over a dinner to mark the 1922's centenary year. The '22 had come a long way since Gervais Rentoul and a few fellow MPs gathered in April 1923 to set up a group to assist new members. At the time, the '22 was little noticed. A century later, the 'influential' and 'powerful' 1922

Committee had become a staple of newspaper reports, its chairman being better known to television viewers than probably most ministers. In good Conservative fashion, it had evolved. From being a self-help group for new MPs, it had become a significant political body with notable consequences for the British political system. Those consequences are the focus of Part III.

# Part II

# Organisation and leadership

## Chapter 6

# Who and when: membership and meetings

The 1922 Committee comprises Conservative MPs and meets weekly when the House of Commons is sitting. That statement is correct, but it does not fully reflect who attends meetings – or rather who is eligible to attend – nor the activity of the Committee. *Membership* does not include all Conservative MPs. *Attendance* at meetings can and does extend beyond members of the Committee. Many of the functions of the 1922 – discussed in Part III – are carried out by smaller bodies that meet at other times. The executive of the 1922 is, as we shall see in Chapter 8, the workhorse of the Committee. Until the end of the twentieth century, Conservative MPs were more engaged in the work of party backbench committees (see Chapter 7) than they were in the weekly meeting of the 1922 Committee. The weekly meeting is the formal gathering of the 1922 Committee, but the Committee is much more than the meeting.

## Membership

There is a difference between being a member of the 1922 and being entitled to attend meetings. As we shall see, at different points, parliamentarians other than Tory private members have been invited to attend, with the 1922 ending the first century of its existence being close to constituting, in terms of attendance though not voting rights, the Parliamentary Conservative Party.

93

## Extending the membership

The 1922 was open initially only to those Tory MPs first elected in 1922, but shortly after it was formed the executive received a letter from the MP for Hereford, Mr S. Roberts, asking if membership was available for all members of the party. After discussion, 'it was decided that the names of any "older" members of the Conservative Party (viz those not elected for the first time to this present Parliament) who may express a desire to join the Committee should be considered by the Executive, and a recommendation be made to the next meeting of the full Committee'.[1] On 7 May, Roberts was elected as the first 'older' member. Others followed.

At the start of 1924, it was agreed to invite all Conservative MPs newly elected in the December 1923 election to become active members. Reflecting the changed composition, the minutes throughout 1924 refer to the '1922/23 Committee'. Former members of the Committee (that is, those defeated in the election) were also invited to attend the meeting to discuss the outcome of the election. In March 1924, there was a discussion as to whether to change the name of the Committee and to widen the membership, but it was decided to maintain the current position.[2] After the 1924 election, which saw a notable increase in new Tory MPs, new members were invited to join and by the end of the first session, the Committee had 185 members.

However, the most important decision regarding membership occurred in December 1925. At a meeting of the executive on 21 December, Rentoul reported that he had discussed with the Chief Whip inviting all private members to join the Committee and dropping '1922' from the Committee's title. The executive decided to retain the name, but approved inviting all private members on the Conservative benches to join. Rather than being a body for a minority – one that over time would diminish and eventually wither away – it was now a body open on a continuing basis to all Tory MPs, other than the leader and ministers. By the end of 1928, it had almost 300 members.

The membership was open to any Conservative private member, but not to any other parliamentarian. Reports apparently circulated in 1934 that it had a wider membership. The *Yorkshire Post and Leeds Intelligencer* reported that 'Contrary to reports which have recently appeared, the Committee is open only to Conservative MPs. There is no truth in the assertion that it has ever thrown open any of its meetings to other Government parties.'[3]

In 1947, the Liberal National Party and the Conservative Party merged at the constituency level. (The Liberal Nationals also changed their name to National Liberals at this stage.) Although the National Liberals were to retain a separate identity in the House of Commons, including having their own whip, up to the 1960s, they became an integral part of the Conservative ranks in the House. As a result, the National Liberal MPs became members of the '22.

For almost the whole of the first 50 years of the 1922's existence, Ulster Unionist MPs were part of the parliamentary party. They attended '22 meetings and one, Sir Hugh O'Neill, a former Speaker of the Northern Ireland parliament, became chairman in 1935. Another, Knox Cunningham, served as the Prime Minister's eyes and ears at meetings when he was Macmillan's PPS from 1959 to 1963. An Ulster Unionist was also on occasion elected to the 1922 executive – Sir David Campbell in the 1950s, Lord Robert Grosvenor in the 1960s, followed by Stratton Mills. The Ulster Unionists remained part of the '22 until they split from the Conservative Party in 1972, following the introduction of direct rule of the province from Whitehall.[4] Stratton Mills, the MP for Belfast North, may have been the last Ulster Unionist to address the '22, speaking at a specially convened meeting on 27 March 1972 to discuss direct rule in the province.[5]

## Peers, MEPs and members of other elected bodies

Private members in receipt of the Conservative whip remain the only members of the '22, though the Committee may invite others to attend. In February 1969, the '22 Chairman, Sir Arthur Vere Harvey, 'advised the Committee that in order to strengthen the links with Conservative peers, that in future two Members would be invited to attend the 1922 Committee meetings'.[6] It was later agreed to open meetings to any peers who wished to attend. In 2002, Michael Spicer confirmed that peers were 'encouraged to attend and speak at the 1922 Committee meetings if they so wished'.[7]

Important meetings, as when addressed by the party leader, may be swelled by the attendance of several peers and some may attend, and speak, when a meeting engages their interests. The number is usually in single figures. Other than this writer, there are few peers who are regular attenders. On rare occasions, when a significant meeting looks as if it may be standing room only, peers may be asked not to attend or at least discouraged from adding to the pressure on space. Meetings of the '22 are nonetheless more inclusive than meetings summoned by the party leader, which tend usually to be confined to MPs. When David Cameron summoned the meeting of Tory MPs in May 2010 to report on coalition negotiations with the Liberal Democrats, it was made clear that peers were excluded.

The executive also addressed relations with Conservative members of the European Parliament. On occasion, the leader of the Conservative group in the Parliament was invited to speak, either to the '22 or the executive: in June 1999, the leader, Edward McMillan-Scott, and other MEPs attended the '22 to discuss whether the party should affiliate to the European People's Party (EPP) – a meeting that was lengthy and contentious[8] – and in 2014 Syed Kamall MEP, the new leader of the group, addressed the executive on the strategy for European elections and their effect on domestic politics.[9] The executive also discussed opening meetings to MEPs. In July 1989, it agreed to invite MEPs to attend the meeting on 20 July being addressed by the Prime Minister.[10] (It is not clear whether any did so.) In 2001, it discussed and agreed that representatives of the Conservative group in the Parliament could attend meetings of the executive at the chairman's invitation. None appears to have done so and it was another 12 years before the executive returned to the subject. In 2013, it was agreed that MEPs be invited regularly to meet the Committee.

One MEP, who did attend the occasional meeting of the 1922, recalled that the Committee never really seemed that keen on their involvement, which was attributed to the fact that executive committee members were somewhat sceptical of the European Union.[11] When David Cameron became party leader, the leader of Conservative group in the European Parliament was occasionally invited to Shadow Cabinet meetings, but no similar relationship was established with the 1922.

In June 2003, the executive agreed that Conservative members of the Welsh Assembly and Scottish Parliament should be allowed to attend '22 meetings on request to the chairman.[12] There is no record of members of devolved legislatures attending meetings, other than as speakers. Allowing Conservative members of other legislative bodies to attend did not extend to members of the Greater London Authority (GLA). The executive in July 2003 agreed that GLA members should not have access to 1922 meetings.[13]

## Ministers

In 1943, as we have seen in Chapter 1, membership was opened to ministers. The change was one of several proposed by a senior member, Oliver Stanley. The 1922 appointed a six-member delegation to discuss the proposal with the Prime Minister and other ministers. Churchill welcomed the idea and at meetings held on 24 February and 10 March, the '22 agreed that all Conservative MPs in receipt of the whip would be eligible for membership.[14] Churchill expressed the view that it would be undesirable for ministers to stand for office or vote in elections for officers and members of the executive, and this was agreed. There was also the practical point noted by *The Times* that it was doubtful whether very many of them would be able to attend.[15] However, the key point, given later developments, is that the decision to admit ministers was one taken by the 1922. Although the proposal came from outside, it was recognised that it was a matter for the '22. To reflect the inclusion of ministers, the name was changed to the Conservative and Unionist Members' Committee but reverted to its former membership, and name, in 1945.[16] Ministers were not eligible to attend when the party returned to power in 1951.

In 1952, as already noted (see Chapter 1), whips were invited to attend as observers on a sessional basis. In writing to extend the invitation, the chairman, Derek Walker-Smith, reminded Chief Whip Patrick Buchan-Hepburn that attendance conveyed no voting rights. 'I look forward', he wrote, 'to seeing members of the Whips Office at our weekly meetings and to a pleasant co-operation with them at all times.'[17] Whips became regular attenders, though the number attending now varies. Chief Whips until recently expected all whips to attend, unless they had chamber duties. As Chief Whip from 2001 to 2005, David Maclean used to attend regularly.

The whips feed back to the Chief Whip and party leaders any problems that arise. A similar role is fulfilled by the party leader's Parliamentary Private Secretary (PPS) who is eligible to attend as a member of the '22. As we have seen (in Chapters 3–5), some PPSs, ranging from George Harvie-Watt under Winston Churchill in wartime through to Ian Gow under Margaret Thatcher, have been especially assiduous in keeping the leader informed. Others have not necessarily been so assiduous, with some – such as Peter Morrison under Margaret Thatcher – being rather patrician and not mixing well with members of the '22.

On rare occasions, junior ministers were invited to attend a '22 meeting, notably one on the Suez Crisis in 1956,[18] one addressed by the Prime Minister, Sir Alec Douglas-Home, in July 1964,[19] and one addressed by Prime Minister Margaret Thatcher in July 1982, her PPS, Ian Gow, erroneously informing her that 'As you know, for the first time, Ministers not in the Cabinet have been invited to attend the Committee.'[20] Such invitations were issued by the executive. A proposal was made in 1971 to allow junior ministers to attend as a matter of course, but in view of divided opinion on the issue, it was decided not to proceed with the suggestion.[21] The issue was raised again in 1975, when one former junior minister, William van Straubenzee, wrote to the chairman suggesting that in future periods of Tory government meetings should be opened up to ministers.[22] Edward du Cann recognised that the issue was worth considering, but no action was taken.

No further action was taken on opening up meetings to ministers until 35 years later when it was agreed before the 2010 general election that when in office, ministers should be permitted to attend. However, the party leader, David Cameron, once returned to Downing Street had more ambitious intentions.

## Cameron thwarted

Even before he became Prime Minister, David Cameron had a reputation for not having a benign view of the 1922. At a meeting of the executive in March 2007, it was confirmed 'that there was no truth in the rumour the Leader wanted to rid himself of the 1922 Committee'.[23] However, concerns about his view of the '22 as then constituted appeared to be borne out following the 2010 general election.

Decisions as to eligibility for membership of the 1922 Committee are taken by the 1922 itself. However, there was an attempt by Cameron following his appointment as Prime Minister to expand membership to include ministers. According to one Conservative MP, Cameron 'seemingly became obsessed with the risk that the Conservative 1922 Committee would do for him as it had done with some of his illustrious predecessors'.[24] He quoted another member as saying 'Cameron is launching a takeover bid to limit the power and influence of the 1922 executive. He wants to put his people in to make sure he is not given any problems by the committee.'[25] Cameron sought to justify his actions by claiming that he wanted to foster greater unity across the party: 'nowhere was the "one team" spirit more important than in our parliamentary party'.[26]

He summoned at short notice a meeting of all Conservative MPs on 20 May 2010 and about 20 minutes prior to the meeting saw the two prospective candidates for the chairmanship, Graham Brady and Richard Ottaway, and informed them of his plan. In the 25-minute meeting, he argued the case for the change on the grounds of unity. The proposal was agreed, with 168 voting for the motion 'The 1922 Committee should change to encompass the whole of the Parliamentary Party,' against 118 supporting 'The 1922 should retain its existing structure.' However, as Elliott and Hanning recorded, 'the victory proved to be pyrrhic'.[27] Not only was there a large dissenting vote, but Cameron was confronted by Tory MP and solicitor Bill Cash, who challenged the legality of the exercise. He argued at the meeting that it was not lawful and subsequently sought advice from a leading QC, who confirmed his opinion. A meeting of MPs summoned by the leader had no standing in determining the rules of the 1922 Committee: 'not only was it unlawful under the Conservative Party's Constitution, but there was no power at all through an ad hoc meeting of the parliamentary party to override the entrenched functions of the 1922 Committee as set out under the Conservative Party constitution itself'.[28] Under threat of legal action, Cameron conceded defeat.

The result, as Robin Harris observed, was that the attempt to prevent 'the awkward squad' getting elected to the 1922 executive did not succeed. 'It had the opposite effect: they now dominate it.'[29] Cameron was believed to want Ottaway as chairman rather than Brady, who had resigned from his front bench team and was seen as the more independent of the two. Brady was elected. It also had three other consequences. One was that it alienated newly elected MPs who, as Elliott and Hanning noted, 'arrived quite willing to be loyal'.[30] Another was to reduce the size of the electorate in '22 elections. Although it was claimed that the Prime Minister had achieved a compromise in that ministers were to be able to attend, but not vote at, meetings of the '22, it was no such thing. The '22 in the previous Parliament had agreed that in the new Parliament, ministers could attend meetings, but not vote. Michael Spicer had reminded members of this decision at a '22 meeting in March 2010. The '22 was simply implementing a decision previously taken. The whips interpreted the change as meaning no members of the government's 'payroll vote' could take part in elections.[31] This included parliamentary private secretaries, although this had little effect in the elections following the 2010 election, as by that point few PPSs had been appointed. The third effect was noted by the new chairman, Graham Brady, when the '22 met in June: it made it unlikely, he said, that there would be much need in the future for extraordinary meetings of the parliamentary party. His observation was met with murmurs of approval and was followed by Bill Cash presenting him with a copy of Goodhart's history of the 1922 Committee.

The episode essentially created unnecessary problems for the new government with its own supporters. As one senior MP told Elliott and Hanning, 'We didn't need to have all that agitation at the beginning.'[32] Cameron himself conceded, 'I had intended to hit the ground running on party management, but was left limping away, frustrated.'[33]

## Meetings

The Committee has generally met weekly in one of the committee rooms of the Palace of Westminster. Before the Second World War, it was normally, though not always, Committee Room 10 and since then Committee Room 14. On rare occasions, the Committee has met outside the Palace of Westminster. The special meeting in February 1924 to discuss the outcome of the general election was held outside Parliament, at 1 Hans Place, SW1. During the war, the Committee variously met in the 'Annexe' (Church House, Westminster) when Parliament relocated there. Meetings held with parliamentary candidates have also been held at venues outside the Palace of Westminster, such as at the Central Hall, Westminster.

Meeting days have changed. It was initially Monday at 6.00 p.m., but moved in wartime to Wednesday, at 5.00 p.m., and in 1945 to Thursday at 6.00 p.m. On occasion, special meetings have been held, as, for example, in February 1924 to discuss the Committee's response to the loss of the 1923 general election, in April 1928 to discuss election expenses under the Franchise Bill, in 1956 during the Suez Crisis, in 2005 to discuss Michael Howard's plans for party reform, and in 2019 during the discussions on the government's EU withdrawal agreement. During the General Strike in 1926, it was announced by Gervais Rentoul that the Committee would meet daily from Monday to Thursday inclusive.

The Thursday 6.00 p.m. slot was a fixture until the 1990s. In November 1950, a suggestion by Cyril Osborne, the MP for Louth, that the Committee should meet in the morning was not agreed.[34] However, attendance came under pressure in the 1990s as parliamentary activity, and demands on MPs' time, changed. Members were often keen to get back to their constituencies on Thursday evenings. It was decided in 1995 to bring the meeting time forward to 5.00 p.m. The following year, there was a proposal to move the meeting day to a Wednesday. Members were split initially: in March, 49 voted to retain Thursday as the meeting day and 45 voted for Wednesday. In November, the executive decided unanimously to move the meetings to a Wednesday.[35] At the start of the new year 1997 it moved to Wednesdays at 6.30 p.m. The time was changed, briefly, to 6.15 and then reverted to 6.30. It was later brought forward to 5.30 p.m. and, under Graham Brady's chairmanship, to 5.00 p.m.

## Format

The format has generally followed the same pattern since the 1920s. After the minutes are read by one of the joint secretaries, the whip on duty announces forthcoming business. (In the early years, this was not always taken after the minutes, but it became the normal practice.) According to one Chief Whip, Andrew Mitchell, 'Some care was taken in preparing for this each week, since, in a moment of potential terror for the whip on duty, he could be asked questions, not necessarily out of desire to elicit information but to show up the whip's lack of knowledge.'[36] The script is rehearsed with fellow whips in advance.[37] In practice, there are occasionally queries to the whip, though according to Gyles Brandreth, the more daunting aspect of being the whip on duty is that one's fellow whips are at the back of the room sitting in judgement.[38]

The whip's announcement of business is generally short and straightforward, with no significant questioning. There were two occasions, both in the 1980s, when answers to questions notably rose above a simple explanation. One relatively new whip in 1984 was questioned by a senior member as to why a particular vote was made a three-line whip, allegedly receiving the response that it should be 'bloody obvious even to the most stupid member', a reply that is deemed to have doomed his career as a whip. In 1989, when the whip Greg Knight was asked whether he could confirm that the Chancellor of the Exchequer, Nigel Lawson, had resigned, he stood up to confirm that he had. (Just before going into the meeting, Knight had been authorised by the Deputy Chief Whip to do so.) This was the first occasion, in an era before social media, that the news was known to MPs.

Since 2007, the minutes and business statement have been followed by a report from the chairman, or a member of the executive committee, of the Association of Conservative Peers (ACP). In May 2005, the executive decided that the ACP should attend on a regular basis,[39] and in April 2007 Michael Spicer announced that the ACP would henceforth provide a brief report at the beginning of every meeting of the '22.[40] This in effect was to establish a reciprocal relationship, as a member of the 1922 Committee executive reported each week to the meeting of the ACP. The ACP chairman – unlike chairmen of the '22 (see Chapter 8), usually a former Cabinet minister and sometimes a woman – reports on what has been happening in the Lords and often who has addressed the ACP. Given the increasing brevity of the minutes of the 1922 Committee meetings, coverage of the ACP report often takes up more space than coverage of the principal business.

Up until the 1997 Parliament, any reports from backbench committees were also taken. The committees, as we shall discuss in Chapter 7, were core to backbench activity for most of the years from 1924 to the 1990s. Though not formally committees of the '22, they necessarily comprised members of the '22 and over time the '22 effectively oversaw their activity and, as noted in earlier chapters, occasionally had to address disputes that arose in them.

Any issues that members wish to raise precede the main item, which is the address by the invited speaker. The practice of inviting speakers has varied, with some chairmen being sparing in inviting a minister or frontbencher to speak. As we have seen, after the 1930s, it became usual to hear from ministers rather than outside speakers. On occasion, an outside guest may be invited; this may be a leading party officer (talking about the party's election preparations) or parliamentary official (talking for example on security or fees), or a public figure. Among those in the last category have been Bank of England Governor Eddie George in 1999 and Microsoft founder Bill Gates (who suffered the double indignity of having to wait until a division finished and then using a PowerPoint screen that malfunctioned) in 2011. Occasionally, the speaker has been closer to home. On 22 November 2000, 'Lord

Norton of Louth spoke to his paper "Strengthening Parliament" and answered questions.'[41]

Without a speaker, meetings can be short, ending within 10 or 15 minutes. This was notably the case in the 1970s under the chairmanships of Harry Legge-Bourke and Edward du Cann. Short meetings, though, do not necessarily equate to unimportant meetings. Members may raise points of pressing concern that may resonate with other members, be it issues of public policy, as with the poll tax in 1989, or more direct concern, such as actions of the party organisation or constituency associations. Attempts to de-select an MP can cause particular concern. With no speaker or other scheduled business, it is the issues raised from the floor by members that gain the attention of the chairman and officers as well as the whips. Anodyne minutes may mask or certainly not always convey the strength of feeling expressed on such occasions.

Certain topics have regularly been raised. Some essentially House of Commons matters have engaged members, not least members' pay, parliamentary accommodation, the broadcasting of proceedings (first discussed in March 1926 – 'unanimously resolved that the proposal was most undesirable'),[42] problems of getting called in debate, election law, and reform of the House of Lords, an issue that has engaged the '22 on occasion from 1932 (when members heard Lord Salisbury on the subject) through to 2012 and the Coalition Government's House of Lords Reform Bill. At times of crisis for the party, the need for unity will be stressed by some members, including the party leader. As we have seen in Chapter 5, in the 2017–19 Parliament, the need to avoid a government led by Labour leader Jeremy Corbyn was regularly deployed to engender a united stance. The calls for unity have usually fallen on deaf ears.

The minutes may also demonstrate nuanced changes over time. When Margaret Thatcher was Leader of the Opposition from 1975 to 1979, the minutes generally refer to her as receiving 'a warm welcome'.[43] When she was Prime Minister, the reaction appears more mixed. When she addressed the '22 in April 1983 she 'received a standing ovation'.[44] When she addressed it again three months later, the minutes as originally typed read: 'The Prime Minister, Mrs Margaret Thatcher, addressed the meeting and received a standing ovation'. The entry was changed to read: 'The Prime Minister addressed the meeting and was warmly received.'[45]

One change has been the move from holding votes on issues – as we have seen in Chapter 2, in pre-war years members on occasion moved motions – to the chairman summing up. This results in the chairman exercising significant influence in discerning the mood of the meeting. Other than for the election of officers and members of the executive, and on procedural matters, the last recorded vote took place in 1942.

The weekly meeting is preceded by a meeting of the executive committee. On rare occasions, as when it met to discuss the issue of the party leadership following the October 1974 general election loss (see Chapter 4), the executive has become the focus of media coverage, but generally it operates away from the media spotlight. Whereas meetings of the '22 are formally private, but with the proceedings subject to frequent leaking, meetings of the executive generally do manage to maintain their confidentiality.

## Attendance

Attendance at meetings of the 1922 has fluctuated, depending on the business and political events. At times of tension, the meeting room has been packed. The most dramatic meetings, as during the Suez Crisis and over Brexit, attracted more than 200 members. The minutes, depending on who the secretary is, have often expressed attendance in round figures which may at times be essentially impressionistic, but one can see from the numbers recorded how much attendance has varied, with standing room only some weeks and with swathes of empty seats in others. On one occasion, for reasons that are unclear, the precise attendance figure became a matter of discussion at the executive. On 26 July 1984, it discussed attendance at the previous week's '22 meeting addressed by the Prime Minister and 'it was agreed to alter the figure from 175 to 200, although both Secretaries were convinced that their original figure was the correct one'.[46]

The fluctuating attendance is an important form of political intelligence, enabling the officers as well as the whips to gauge the mood of backbenchers. It has tended to be more issue-sensitive than the backbench party committees. It can adapt quickly to a developing situation and summon a minister to attend. The attendance inside the committee room may also be reflected in the number of journalists hovering outside the room, hoping to catch a fleeting snippet of what is being said and waiting to waylay members as they leave. The banging of desks when the leader attends, or a minister who has some major achievement under their belt, is taken as an indication of the strength of feeling among members.

Without a speaker, the attendance at meetings has tended to be low. (On one occasion, attendance was so low that I got a cheer when I entered the room.) A notable feature of recent years has been low turnouts when there has been a speaker. Even a senior Cabinet minister may not draw a large attendance if there are no contentious issues relating to the minister's department. Fewer than 30 MPs turned up in February 2023 to hear the Foreign Secretary, James Cleverly, and fewer than 20 the following month to listen to the Education Secretary, Gillian Keegan.

The issue of low turnouts has been raised on various occasions in recent decades, both in the full '22 and in executive meetings (see Chapter 7), but the problem has been most marked in the twenty-first century. One long-serving member attributed it to a decline in a communal spirit among MPs, given that the House no longer sat late, and with a parliamentary week of basically two-and-a-half days and with MPs working in their individual offices when in Westminster.[47] There was also less incentive to attend to hear the business for the next week, given that business was now covered for two weeks in advance. The pandemic of 2020 was also seen as militating against new MPs getting involved.

## The 'blue light' 1922

For much of the time, meetings of the 1922 are routine. Julian Critchley opined that the 'run-of-the-mill weekly meeting is to be avoided', before noting that 'when the party's dander is up, the '22 can be every bit as Gothic as its High Victorian surroundings'.[48] It can offer an element of drama, he argued, which the Commons' chamber seemed reluctant to provide.

As we shall see in Part III, meetings of the '22 have significant consequences, though in many respects its political impact derives from what it can do as much as what it does do. One long-serving MP, Sir Peter Bottomley, who became Father of the House in 2019, likened it to a 'blue light service'.[49] When there is a crisis, it comes into its own. Tory MPs cram into Committee Room 14 in a way that would induce apoplexy in a health and safety inspector. At other times – when, to follow the Bottomley analogy, there is no need to put the emergency lights on – the activity has consequences that do not attract the headlines, but which matter, not only for the Conservative Party in the House of Commons, but for the wider political system.

## Chapter 7

# Engaging members' interests: backbench committees

For three-quarters of the first century of its existence, the principal activity that absorbed the energies of members of the 1922 Committee was not the weekly meeting of the '22, but backbench subject committees that were not even formally part of the 1922.[1]

When the 1922 Committee was formed, it created a series of sub-committees, but as we have seen in Chapter 2, these were superseded by backbench subject committees established by the party leadership in 1924, apparently on the initiative of the Chief Whip, Eyres-Monsell.[2] They built on some unofficial committees that previously existed, especially the Unionist Agricultural Committee.[3] Some of the newly created committees had a short existence due to a lack of interest, but others, covering agriculture, finance, foreign affairs, imperial affairs and trade and industry, became well established and developed a pattern of activity that was to become the norm for party committees. They met regularly, elected a chairman and secretary, and heard from speakers, including ministers. That covering agriculture – known formally as the Agricultural Committee – was especially active. Chaired by Sir George Courthorpe, the MP for Rye, it appointed sub-committees, sent delegations to meet ministers and ranged widely in the subjects it discussed. Any Tory MP could attend a committee meeting and meetings of the Agricultural Committee regularly attracted a good attendance. A meeting to consider the Minister of

Health's poor law reforms drew an audience of 150.[4] It maintained close links with agricultural bodies outside the House and in 1937, alarmed at the state of the poultry industry, persuaded Baldwin to meet a delegation to discuss the serious situation in the industry,[5] as well as, unusually, promoting a Bill, through the chairman of its Poultry Sub-Committee, Robin Turton, under the ten-minute rule procedure, to amend the Agricultural Marketing Act 1933.[6]

The committees flourished during the 1920s and 1930s. In the 1930s, the India Committee notably engaged members' interests, on occasion attracting over 200 members to meetings,[7] as did the Foreign Affairs Committee.[8] 'You see these unofficial committees are always crowded', Churchill observed in 1931, 'the House empty and the unofficial committees full.'[9] They were seen as carrying weight within the party. Their popularity was such that in the 1930s, the whips had to step in to regulate the timing of meetings, committees having chosen the most popular (and hence competing) times in the week to meet.[10]

The committees tended to engage members in a way that the 1922 Committee did not. Indeed, the '22 appeared to gain some traction from organising meetings jointly with the backbench committees. A joint meeting with the Public Health Committee was organised in 1928 to discuss the Local Government Bill: it was attended by both Neville Chamberlain, the Health Minister, and Sir Kingsley Wood, the Parliamentary Secretary for Health. *The Times* anticipated a large attendance.[11] There was a joint meeting with the India Committee in 1933: it attracted about 200 members and lasted two hours.[12] In 1937, Air Minister Lord Swinton spoke at a well-attended joint meeting with the Air Committee;[13] his successor, Kingsley Wood, also did so the following year, addressing the problems of the Air Ministry. He impressed 'a large and representative meeting of backbenchers'.[14] The same year the chairman of the Agricultural Committee, Sir Edward Ruggles-Brise, and the chairman of the '22, Sir Hugh O'Neill, met the Prime Minister to press for the withdrawal of the Milk Industry Bill.[15] The activity of the Agricultural Committee appears more significant than that of the '22. A meeting to discuss the issue attracted about 100 MPs and the committee was claimed to be instrumental in ensuring that the Milk Bill did not proceed to a Second Reading.[16]

The committees continued to meet throughout the Second World War and were reorganised in the 1945 Parliament. In the 1950–1 Parliament, Churchill appointed the committee chairmen, usually selecting the frontbench member covering the subject. In so doing, he was formalising the practice that had been adopted in practice in previous periods of opposition. The committees elected the other officers. In government, the committees elected all the officers. The committees grew in number, the subject committees being complemented by some regional committees. As we shall see, they remained active until the 1990s, influencing policy and fulfilling a range of functions. They suffered, as in the 1930s, from their success, the 1922 executive having to intervene in an attempt to regulate elections and meeting times, before falling foul of a range of other activities that came to occupy backbenchers' time.

## Consequences

The committees in their permanent form 'fulfilled a number of valuable roles. Unlike previous unofficial groups, there was no suggestion of conspiracy about them and no imputation of disloyalty when MPs expressed frank views at their meetings'.[17] They were a means of backbenchers engaging with ministers and, in opposition, directly and consistently with the relevant frontbencher. 'The committees were both a safety valve and an information forum, and the latter role was reinforced by the habit of having the responsible Cabinet or junior minister attend meetings from time to time, especially to explain forthcoming legislation.'[18] Any significant problems would also be noted by the whip in attendance. As one MP expressed it, 'if a committee really blows off steam, it's in Cabinet the next day'.[19]

The strength of feeling on an issue could be expressed not only by voice, but also by presence. A large attendance could reflect the extent of interest on the part of members and at times the extent of concern. As we have seen, some meetings in the inter-war years, not least on the subject of India, attracted large audiences. The ability for any member to attend

> made them a key arena on important and divisive issues, as happened particularly with the India Committee in January–March 1931, the Foreign Affairs Committee in 1935–9, and the Fuel and Power Committee over the coal industry in the Second World War … It was more effective to transmit expressions of concern directly to the Leader; when more emphasis or speed was needed than was possible by leaving it to the whip to report back, the most effective tactic was to appoint a deputation to seek an interview.[20]

The importance of backbench committees as a means of expressing dissatisfaction was well illustrated by the experience of Austen Chamberlain. As he wrote to his sister in May 1935, reporting on when he had spoken the previous week to the Foreign Affairs Committee: 'When I first joined it on leaving office only a dozen or 15 people attended. This time there must have been over a hundred (well over, I should think) all anxious & on the verge of revolt against [Foreign Secretary, Sir John] Simon by name. I expressed their dissatisfaction with policy while avoiding any mention of Simon's name.'[21]

When Chamberlain again appeared before the committee in December 1935, arguing that the Hoare–Laval pact was the least bad option available, the opposition to it was such as to induce Chamberlain in summing up to argue against it as a betrayal of the League of Nations.[22] 'Reports from the whips about the mood at this meeting was a crucial factor in the Cabinet decision to sacrifice the Foreign Secretary in order to save the Government.'[23] Indeed, the Foreign Affairs Committee provided a key forum for Tory MPs in the 1930s. It was important both in expressing its dissatisfaction with government policy, but could also be a notable ally of the leadership. Churchill in 1936 failed to persuade it to his view on the role of the League of Nations: the committee was deemed by Leo Amery to be 'practically solid' against his position.[24] A meeting attended by about 200 MPs in January 1938, following Anthony Eden's resignation as Foreign Secretary, 'was clear in its swing towards Chamberlain's position'.[25]

In an era before departmental select committees were established in the House of Commons, they also provided a means through which backbench MPs could specialise in a particular policy sector. In the early 1950s, Earl Winterton, MP for Horsham, claimed that the chamber contained only a handful of members because young MPs thought that they 'could best serve the interests of the party and advance the prospects of their own careers by becoming immersed in the affairs of the numerous committees and sub-committees of the party'.[26] One detailed analysis of backbench committees found that nearly 90 per cent of backbenchers claimed to attend subject committees on a regular basis, with attendance overwhelmingly a consequence of a member's prior interest in the subject.[27] 'Active businessmen, for instance, were particularly prominent in the Trade and Industry Committee, while teachers took much interest in the Education Committee, and farmers and rural landowners in the Agriculture Committee.'[28] A study of the Industry Committee in the 1980s found that the emphasis in discussions derived more from expertise than ideology: 'detailed understanding of, and attention to, the daily concerns of industry outstripped general ideological debate as the main preoccupation of regular committee members'.[29]

Being elected as an officer enabled new MPs to get involved and make a mark in the House. Malcolm Rifkind, elected to the House in 1974, noted that in the late 1970s, when he had the opportunity to develop his interests, not least in foreign policy, 'I became Joint Secretary of the influential Conservative backbench Foreign Affairs Committee.'[30] In the 1979–80 session, 40 of the 53 committee secretaries were newly elected MPs.[31]

Committee chairmanship came to give an MP some standing, including in being called in debate. Iain Macleod's position as chairman of the Health Committee enabled him to be called early in the Second Reading debate on the National Health Service Bill in 1952: he followed Aneurin Bevan and launched a savage attack on him, essentially establishing his parliamentary reputation.[32] After the weekly meeting of a committee, recalled one MP, 'the chairman could request (in effect, demand) an immediate meeting with the relevant minister to warn him of anxieties about emerging policies'.[33] Brand noted that there appeared to be a consensus among members and the media that the Conservative chairmen carried more weight than their Labour counterparts. 'This may be associated with the sorts of people who become officers: on the Tory side there is a much higher proportion of ex-ministers – who therefore have experience – and of young MPs who are thought to be on the way up.'[34] During the period of opposition in the 1966–70 Parliament, Heath developed the practice of using committee officers to speak on a temporary basis from the front bench.[35] Each committee was chaired by the relevant shadow minister, and the vice-chairman (in effect, the senior elected backbencher) would speak in support. In the 1987 Parliament, several chairmen were used to advise on the party manifesto and some formed parts of the groups drawing it up.

Recognition that chairing a backbench committee carried some weight was not confined to the Palace of Westminster. Peter Rawlinson recalled when he was elected to chair the backbench Broadcasting Committee, at a time when both the BBC and ITV wanted a second channel that was becoming available:

> For several months I experienced the envy not of artists, but that of television tycoons. I was lunched by Sir Ian Fraser of the Independent Broadcasting Authority and dined by Sir Hugh Carleton Green, Director General of the BBC. The former was lofty and gave the impression that lunching me was personally distasteful but somebody had told him that he should. The other smiled and smiled, with

the eyes narrowing behind the gleaming spectacles while more and more invitations arrived to appear on 'Any Questions'.[36]

## Voice and influence

The committees were useful private fora in which views could be expressed and relayed to the party leadership through the whip who attended: 'indeed, much of the point was for it to be a channel of aid and effective communication to those in authority'.[37] The interest and concerns raised by a particular issue could be reflected through the committees in three ways. One, as we have already seen, is through attendance. Once members were in attendance, they could ensure their views found an outlet through election of the committee officers and through giving voice to their concerns.

Election of committee officers was in the early decades normally unopposed. 'In only a few cases, where the committee was already something of a battleground, did it become contested or the whips seek to influence the choice.'[38] This changed in the latter half of the century, when the election of committee officers attracted slates from particular wings of the party. In the 1950s, the One Nation group of MPs, in order to influence party thinking, 'decided in advance which candidates to support for election as officers of party committees, including the '22 Committee, and voted accordingly when the elections took place'.[39] In 1967, opponents of the liberal policy of the Shadow Education Secretary, Sir Edward Boyle, crowded a meeting of the backbench Education Committee to elect a vice-chairman (Boyle was automatically the committee chairman) who was opposed to Boyle's policies. They succeeded in electing one of their number, Ronald Bell, to replace the moderate incumbent.[40] During the period of the Heath government, neo-liberal critics of the government's 1972 U-turns on the economy and industrial policy managed to get one of their number, Nicholas Ridley, elected as chairman, and two others as vice-chairmen, of the Finance Committee,[41] and another, John

Biffen, as chairman of the Industry Committee.[42] The following year, government loyalists crowded the annual meeting of the Finance Committee to vote Ridley out of the chair.

Critics of government policy found them a valuable outlet for their views. As one MP in the 1990s observed, 'if you disagree with a government policy, it is a good position from which to bowl a few googlies at the wicket – and be noticed by the media, who always relish an internal battle'.[43] The dissidents were generally more committed than other members to turning up at meetings and giving voice to their concerns. During the period of the Heath government, backbench opponents of government policy, especially on the economy, tended to congregate in the backbench committees;[44] the Finance Committee became 'a rallying place for critics of Government policy'.[45] Although a small minority of the parliamentary party, they were able to dominate in the confines of a committee attended by about 20–30 members. Electing critics to chair the committees also enhanced their position, given the status accorded to committee chairmen in chamber debates.

The committees variously constituted part of policy networks – forming, according to one committee officer, a vital 'machinery of linkage' between industry and ministers[46] – and put pressure on government ministers to at least justify or, more substantively, change a policy. 'There can be little doubt', wrote Peter Richards, 'that backbench pressure can be exerted effectively through this network.'[47] Several committees 'took a conspicuous part in the discussions which resulted in the withdrawal of the original proposals made in 1937 for a National Defence Contribution'.[48] In essence, as Henry Fairlie noted, they essentially fulfilled the role that parliamentary reformers wanted committees of the House to fulfil.[49]

There were notable instances of committee influence in the period of Conservative government after 1951. 'The government', recorded Brand, 'withdrew its threat to reduce subsidies [to farmers] after a visit by the Chairman of the Conservative Agriculture Committee: Sir Anthony Hurd.'[50] Hurd was especially influential, not least given that he had declined junior ministerial office in order to chair the committee. He had close links with the farming community and for many years had been the agricultural correspondent of *The Times*. In 1953, the Fuel and Power Committee called for an inquiry into the functioning of the National Coal Board, and the demand was discussed at a meeting of the 1922: the Minister of Fuel and Power, Geoffrey Lloyd, who had pressed to attend rather than wait to be summoned,[51] justified the government's position. The Committee accepted his position, though some MPs, led by the chairman of the Fuel and Power Committee, Victor Raikes, persisted, and in the event the National Coal Board itself requested such an inquiry.[52] The Fuel and Power Committee had a further impact in 1957 in getting changes made to the Electricity Bill.[53]

In the debate over the government's negotiations for Britain to withdraw from the Suez Canal Zone in 1953, there was

> considerable Cabinet discussion over the best way to defuse the incipient rebellion. On [Chief Whip] Buchan-Hepburn's recommendation, it was agreed that [Defence Minister] Alexander should address the Foreign Affairs Committee, rather than the smaller Defence Committee, on military strategy and economic facts of the case to detach a large number of restive backbenchers and isolate the hard core.[54]

The following year, 'First Selwyn Lloyd, Nutting and Dodds-Parker faced the Foreign Affairs Committee on 12 July 1954 … The following day Churchill, Butler and Head addressed the Army subcommittee convened specifically to discuss the Suez question further before the forthcoming Commons debate.'[55]

The Foreign Affairs Committee remained a key body when the Suez operation got under way in 1956. Charles Mott-Radclyffe, MP for Windsor, chaired the committee. As such, 'I was the buffer between my fellow back-benchers, including of course "the rebels", on the one hand and Anthony Eden and Selwyn

Lloyd on the other ... This was a period when the Foreign Affairs Committee seemed to be almost permanently in session, meetings being convened, interrupted and re-convened at all hours of the day and night.'[56] Mott-Radclyffe also recorded that ministers outside the Cabinet knew little of what was being decided and asked if they could attend the meeting of the committee being addressed by the Prime Minister 'in the hope that they might discover what was afoot'.[57]

The Commonwealth Affairs Committee also proved an important forum in 1961 for discussion of the government's policy in central Africa. The minister, Iain Macleod, appeared three times before it to explain and defend the policy. There was a group of about 40 MPs implacably opposed to the government's approach, but when Macleod spoke to the committee in February, with about 180 MPs present, they were in a minority and he appeared to be winning over some critics.[58] However, when the Prime Minister of the Federation of Rhodesia and Nyasaland, Sir Roy Welensky, addressed a packed meeting of the committee – there were about 200 MPs present – he attracted support for his policy. (Macmillan, having received a report from his PPS, Knox Cunningham, noted that he 'made a bitter attack on Macleod [Colonial Secretary] and by implication on me'.)[59] Both Knox Cunningham and the committee chairman, Major Patrick Wall, advised Macmillan that he had carried most of those at the meeting.[60] In pressing for the British government to accept his proposals, Welensky let it be known that he was prepared to return to the UK to put his case not only to the government, but also to Parliament and public opinion.[61] In the event, Macleod managed to negotiate an agreement that obviated the need for Welensky to return.

The Trade and Industry Committee was notably engaged in the debate over abolishing resale price maintenance (RPM) in 1964. President of the Board of Trade Edward Heath spoke to a packed meeting of the committee – about 100 MPs attended – and 'was listened to in almost total silence'.[62] Members objected principally to the timing of the measure, which members thought would be electorally disastrous for the party. Heath returned to address the committee after the Bill was published. A steering committee was established, with three officers of the committee and seven other members, both for and against the Bill: it met daily, acting as a body to reach a compromise on amendments. However, in the face of Heath's determination to enact the measure, only minor changes were achieved. The key point was how central the Trade and Industry Committee was to the debate over the Bill. It was the principal arena in which the minister faced his critics. He did so in the full 1922 Committee, but the Trade and Industry Committee was able to address the issue on a more intensive basis and act as an intermediary between the Department of Trade and interested bodies lobbying on the issue.

The committees were also notably active during the period of Heath government from 1970 to 1974. In 1972, the Home Secretary appeared before the Home Affairs Committee to defend the immigration rules. He annoyed members by his refusal to make concessions, with the result that MPs took their opposition as far as voting against the rules in the division lobbies, leading to a government defeat.[63] The following year, following criticism of the Maplin Development Bill at a meeting of the Aviation Committee, the government delayed the Second Reading of the Bill until it could be sure of a majority.[64] The committees, as already noted, proved an arena for critics of government policy to meet and challenge what ministers were doing.

Under Margaret Thatcher, the practice developed whereby each year the chairman of a particular policy group would report to the relevant backbench committee on progress within the group and seek comments from the committee. Thatcher also encouraged shadow ministers to consult backbench committees before pursuing an initiative.[65] The elected officers of the committees also served in the Business Committee which met weekly, drawing them together with shadow ministers. Whips would attend meetings and report back any problems to the Chief Whip. In government, Thatcher's PPS, Ian Gow, also attended some committee meetings and reported back. He prepared a lengthy note of a meeting of the Constitutional Committee on 23 January 1980 at which the Lord Chancellor, Lord Hailsham, argued the case for Lords reform, devolution and a bill of rights. Gow noted some support for Lords reform, but added: 'However, there is also considerable opposition to such reform and I think that even among reformers, there is no unanimity as to what reforms are desirable.'[66] Ministers variously discussed issues with committees. Home Secretary William Whitelaw met weekly with the officers of the Home Affairs Committee.[67] Chancellor Nigel Lawson had pre-budget meetings with the Finance Committee, taking with him his entire Treasury team.[68] In Lawson's clash with the Prime Minister's economic adviser Alan Walters, the committee gave the Chancellor 'a resounding vote of confidence'.[69]

The committees thus absorbed the interests and commitment of members of the parliamentary party, usually more so than the weekly meeting of the '22. Their activity variously figures in Jack Brand's study of the policy influence of British parliamentary parties. The 1922 Committee receives virtually no mention, other than to claim that 'there is no weekly meeting specially dedicated to the discussion of policy or tactics as in the Parliamentary Labour Party, and the 1922 is not normally well attended'.[70]

Despite his comment on the importance of the committees, Brand nonetheless cautioned against over-estimating their importance.

> One should not exaggerate the importance of back-bench committees on either side. With one or two exceptions, the turnout rarely exceeds a dozen, and the well-attended meetings are those where a minister or a well-known outsider is to speak. Within these constrains, however, the committees do constitute a 'public' for the minister.[71]

Influence may have been sporadic, but that reflected the occasions when policy generated disquiet on the backbenches.

When not engaging with frontbenchers, the committees met to hear outside speakers. On those occasions, only a handful of committed members would attend. This assessment was borne out by the study of backbench information by Barker and Rush, published in 1970. As they found, attendance tended to be lowest when an outside expert spoke on a topic not related to current policy concerns. Even the heads of major companies could find themselves speaking to a fluctuating audience of four to six MPs.[72] As we shall see, the low attendances were ultimately a contributory factor to the committees' demise.

## The committees and the 1922

During the period from 1924 through to their demise at the start of the twenty-first century, the backbench committees were not formally committees of the 1922 Committee, although as we have seen in Part I, they could and did present reports to it. However, the distinction between being autonomous formal party entities and committees of the '22 is a narrow one. The members were necessarily members of the '22 and the executive of the '22 took an increasingly proprietorial approach, especially in the post-war years, occasionally recommending – acknowledging that it could do no more than recommend – when committees should meet and organise elections, before being more assertive and essentially overseeing how they were organised. The discussions were prompted by pressures on committees, not least, as we shall see, competing demands that undermined the attendance and engagement of members.

The problems associated with committee meeting times, the election of officers and increasingly members' attendance became a regular topic of discussion in the '22 executive and on occasion at the meetings of the '22. The issue came up as early as 1961, when it was reported that the executive had considered the procedure for the election of committee officers. 'The '22 had no power to tell Party Committees how their affairs should be conducted but the Executive recommended that the conduct of their elections should follow the pattern set in the 1922 Committee itself.'[73] Twenty years later, the executive took a somewhat firmer view of its capacity to intervene.

The method of electing the committees was raised again in 1982 and it was decided that the executive would look at the matter.[74] Two years later, at meetings in April and July, it discussed what could be done to address the problems, not least declining attendances.[75] Although the value of the committees was acknowledged by some members of the executive, others focused on the reasons for poor attendance, including the creation of select committees and some MPs now having offices in the Norman Shaw Buildings. Cranley Onslow made the point that MPs would do what they wanted, and if they did not want to support party committees, nothing was going to make them do that.

In November, Edward du Cann invited suggestions from members of the '22 as to how committee elections could be improved and said that, with the agreement of the executive, he would be writing to committee chairmen inviting them to let him know what plans they had to improve the effectiveness of their committees in the coming years.[76] The following year, he reported that the executive had considered possible changes to the procedure for elections, but had concluded that they should remain unchanged. 'It was recommended, however, that the Secretaries of these Committees should co-ordinate the timing of meetings through the Whips, particularly those concerned with the election of officers.'[77]

However, by the 1990s, the committees were having difficulty attracting enough members to attend to make meetings, especially those with outside speakers, worthwhile. The executive on more than one occasion appointed a sub-committee to review the operation of the committees. It decided in November 1991 to appoint one to consider the process of electing officers; the following March it approved new rules for the elections.[78] In May 1992, in response to a letter from an MP, who said there were too many committees, it set up another sub-committee.[79] Two weeks later, the chairman announced that the conduct of committee elections would be held under the responsibility of the '22 executive and that a working party would make recommendations in due course for the better functioning of the committees.[80]

Three years later, in February 1995, Robert Dunn returned to the issue, raising the question of lack of activity in the committees.[81] The following week, it was agreed that parliamentary private secretaries (PPSs) should be able to hold committee positions. However, attempts to halt the decline in attendance failed to bear fruit. Onslow's observation that MPs would do what they wanted was borne out; the committees were in clear difficulty.

## Demise and resurrection

During the 1980s and 1990s, the committees had to compete with other demands on MPs' time, including departmental and other investigative select committees, a greater volume of public business, burgeoning constituency correspondence, a growing number of all-party groups and a need for members to engage in profile-raising activities.[82] Attendance declined throughout the 1980s and by the 1990s, as a regular attender at the Agriculture Committee observed, it was 'good if six MPs attend'.[83] The Foreign Affairs Committee was reluctant to invite an ambassador to speak for fear of an embarrassingly small audience. A member of the Trade and Industry Committee said that there were too many competing interests to attract a high attendance. 'Occasionally there is an embarrassingly low turn-out'.[84]

A consequence was more irregular meetings of committees, with some effectively becoming moribund. Another was that ministers, or at least some ministers, no longer took them as seriously as before. 'It cuts no ice with the department' was how one minister described the committee covering his department.[85] In 1992, one senior Cabinet minister, when told it was the usual practice to meet committee officers each week, replied exasperatedly 'Must I?' and kept the meetings short.[86] Serving as a committee officer also ceased to be seen by many new MPs as a route for promotion to ministerial office, preferring instead to serve as PPSs. (Of junior ministers serving in 1989, almost three-quarters had served as PPSs.)[87] The combined effect of these developments was to threaten the future of the committees. They were, in the words of one MP, 'withering on the vine'.[88] A fundamental blow came in the outcome of the 1997 general election. The parliamentary party was halved in number, from 336 to 165. Sustaining committees in the way that had been possible before now became virtually impossible. The party was in opposition and essentially demoralised.

At a meeting of the executive at the start of 2000, Archie Hamilton introduced a paper on the structure of the backbench committees and it was agreed (a) that there was no support for a radical amalgamation of the committees – 'they should be left as they are but encouragement should be given to joint Committee meetings' – and (b) Shadow Secretaries of State should be expected to seek additional MPs beyond the support groups to participate in meetings.[89]

Six policy groups were also established, headed by shadow ministers, but at a meeting of the executive on 20 March 2002 – despite the chairman having said at its meeting on 6 March that the groups were going well – it was reported that the groups were running into problems and that discussion was needed with the Shadow Cabinet about the groups' leadership and direction.[90] At a meeting of the executive in May, 'disappointment was expressed that some were not performing well and their attendance was low'.[91] At the end of 2003, the executive took the view they should be closed down: they were viewed as having little influence and had never been party to the deliberations on the party manifesto.[92] The groups appear to have continued, albeit – as the chairman reported in 2004 – with mixed results.[93]

Since then, there have been attempts to create successor bodies to the backbench committees, though this time as agents of the 1922 Committee, in effect a reversion to what happened when the '22 was first created in 1923. In practice, it primarily made formal what was previously the reality; the 1922 had effectively made the committees its own. The attempts to get the new bodies up and running have not always borne notable fruit, coming up against essentially the same pressures that undermined them in the 1980s and 1990s.

Some groups were established towards the end of the 2005–10 Parliament under Michael Spicer's chairmanship, but moves to embed them were especially marked under the chairmanship of Graham Brady. In the 2010 Parliament, he sought to institutionalise them, with five being created, with each having an elected chairman. They met fortnightly, sometimes more frequently, and in at least one instance the chairman used the position as the basis for making public pronouncements and not simply for internal party deliberations. Attendance varied. Some meetings attracted few members, whereas a meeting with Caroline Spelman on the sale of forests attracted an audience of over 100.[94] Conservative Secretaries of State met their respective committees to get feedback and met with the chairs on an ad hoc basis. Reports from the committees were occasionally given at meetings of the '22. The primary roles of the committees were to serve as sounding boards for Conservative ministers and to feed in to deliberations of policy commissions established by David Cameron. They also had a role in monitoring the fulfilment of Conservative parts of the Coalition Agreement.

The committees were reestablished in the 2015 Parliament, one novel feature being that they were utilised to establish links with, and draw on the expertise of, the Association of Conservative

Peers. One of the vice-chairmen of each committee was a peer. Not being subject to the same pressures as MPs, peers appeared more committed to meetings than those MPs who served as officers. Although the parliamentary party was a larger body than in the 1997 Parliament, there was not the time or commitment, not least on the part of new MPs, to engage with them and use them as fora for information sharing and influencing ministers. They made little mark within the party. After the 2017 general election, one member of the executive commented that they had been ignored, as evidenced by the 'appalling' party election manifesto.[95]

Another set of committees was established following the 2019 general election and on this occasion some became active, much depending on the commitment of the chairman. The Defence and Treasury Committees were among the more active.[96] The Foreign Affairs Committee, under Giles Watling, the MP for Clacton, also held regular meetings – during 2022, it heard from a range of speakers, including the chief executives of the TaxPayers' Alliance and the British Red Cross. Others hardly appeared on members' radar.

However, they were not the force they once were. They did not report to meetings of the '22. After 1997, the focus shifted, more or less exclusively, to meetings of the '22. For members first elected at that and subsequent elections there was no institutional memory of the pre-1997 backbench committees and the weight they carried, nor of how much they had engaged the energies of backbenchers. The means of backbench influence were no longer dispersed, but instead concentrated.

## Chapter 8

# Transforming or presiding? Leadership in the '22

Leadership of the 1922 is provided by the officers and members of the executive committee. The chairman is the most prominent figure. By 1989, Tory MP Julian Critchley was able to describe the chairman as being 'as politically important as the chief whip'.[1] By the end of the first century of the Committee's existence, he was also at times a prominent public figure. The chairman is supported by the executive committee, an oft-neglected body in the study of British politics, which serves as the workhorse of the 1922, meeting prior to the weekly meeting of the 1922 and typically having a full agenda.

When Gervais Rentoul and other new MPs met for their second meeting on 23 April 1923, they proceeded to elect officers and members of an executive committee. Rentoul was elected to the chair, four others as officers (deputy chairman, treasurer, joint secretaries) and eight as members of the executive. Those elected are listed in Table 8.1. Since then, the number of officers has increased by one, with the appointment of a second deputy chairman, and the members of the executive increased from eight to twelve.

### The chairman

The key position in the 1922 is that of the chairman. Eighteen men have held the position, while another served briefly as acting

**Table 8.1** The first 1922 executive

---

Meeting of the 1922 on 23 April 1923.

The Committee proceeded to the election of officers as follows:

Chairman: Mr G. Rentoul

Deputy Chairman: Captain Erskine-Bolst

Treasurer: Sir John Hewett

Joint Secretaries: K. Vaughan-Morgan and R. Clarry

The following were then elected to serve on the executive committee in addition to the chairman, deputy chairman, treasurer and secretaries who were appointed *ex officio* members: Mr Mitchell Banks, Major Edmondson, Admiral Sir Guy Gaunt, Major Ruggles-Brise, Mr A. A. Somerville, Lord Titchfield, Mr Luke Thompson, Colonel Woodcock.

---

chairman (see Table 8.2). They have varied in background as well as how they have led the Committee. Some have led, while others have presided. Those who have demonstrated leadership have been Gervais Rentoul, Alec Erskine Hill, John Morrison, Edward du Cann, Michael Spicer and Graham Brady.

Some have had short tenures, leaving prematurely because of election loss, promotion to ministerial office or in one case ill-health, while others have served long terms, with five serving for nine years or more. There has been a notable inversion in terms of length of service between the chairman of the 1922 and the party leader. Between 1922 and 2001, the average tenure of a party leader was just under eight years, whereas that of a chairman of

**Table 8.2** Chairmen of the 1922

| | |
|---|---|
| January 1923 – December 1932 | Gervais Rentoul (Lowestoft) |
| December 1932 – December 1935 | William S. Morrison MC (Cirencester and Tewkesbury) |
| December 1935 – July 1939 | Sir Hugh O'Neill Bt (Antrim) |
| September 1939 – November 1939 | Sir Annesley Somerville *(acting)* (Windsor) |
| December 1939 – December 1940 | William Patrick Spens KC OBE (Ashford) |
| December 1940 – December 1944 | Alexander (Alec) Erskine Hill KC (Edinburgh North) |
| December 1944 – June 1945 | John (Jock) McEwen (Berwick and Haddington) |
| August 1945 – November 1951 | Sir Arnold Gridley KBE (Stockport South) |
| November 1951 – November 1955 | Derek Walker-Smith (Hertford) |
| November 1955 – November 1964 | John Morrison (Salisbury) |
| November 1964 – March 1966 | The Rt Hon. Sir William Anstruther-Gray Bt MC (Berwickshire and East Lothian) |
| May 1966 – July 1970 | Sir Arthur Vere Harvey CBE (Macclesfield) |
| July 1970 – November 1972 | Sir Harry Legge-Bourke KBE (Isle of Ely) |
| November 1972 – November 1984 | The Rt Hon. Edward du Cann (Taunton) |
| November 1984 – April 1992 | Cranley Onslow (Woking) |
| April 1992 – May 1997 | Sir Marcus Fox MBE (Shipley) |

(Continued)

**Table 8.2** (Continued)

| | |
|---|---|
| May 1997 – June 2001 | The Rt Hon. Sir Archibald (Archie) Hamilton (Epsom and Ewell) |
| June 2001 – May 2010 | Sir Michael Spicer (Worcestershire South) |
| May 2010 – | Graham Brady (Altrincham and Sale West) |

the 1922 was just over three. Most leaders experienced more than one chairman of the 1922: Churchill during his leadership had four. The situation changed after 2001, the party having seven leaders up to 2023 (an average of just over three years in office), but only two chairmen of the '22 (an average of 11 years in office). Michael Spicer was '22 chairman under three leaders and Brady under five: exceptionally, three of the five relinquished office following a meeting with Brady.

Those elected to chair the Committee have generally been educated at independent schools and Oxbridge, not unusual for Conservative MPs of the period. This only changed with the election of Marcus Fox, who was educated at a state grammar school, followed later by Brady, educated at Altrincham Grammar School. All bar three (Harvey, Fox and Hamilton) have gone to university (or, in the case of Legge-Bourke, Sandhurst). Of those university educated, seven went to Oxford and five to Cambridge. W. S. Morrison studied at Edinburgh University, Gridley at Bristol and Brady at Durham.

They have tended to come from professional and landowning backgrounds, especially for the first seven decades of the Committee's existence. Lawyers dominated for most of the period up to 1955: Rentoul, W. S. Morrison, Spens, Erskine Hill and Walker-Smith were barristers; the elderly Annesley Somerville, who was acting chairman in 1939, had been a long-serving teacher, McEwen served as a diplomat, and Gridley was a consulting engineer. Of the four chairmen from 1955 to 1972, three – John Morrison, Anstruther-Gray and Legge-Bourke – were land-owners. Harvey was the first to be drawn from a career military background – he was an Air Commodore – though most prior to du Cann had seen wartime service: two had been awarded the Military Cross, W. S. Morrison in the First World War and Anstruther-Gray in the Second. (Anstruther-Gray had also served as a member of the Shanghai Defence Force and Harvey as an adviser to the Southern Chinese Air Forces.) Du Cann was the first to come from a business background (though his continuing business connections were ultimately to taint his political career), Onslow served in MI6 as an intelligence officer, and Fox was the first to come from a modest background: after military service, he worked as a bank clerk and sales manager, before becoming a com-pany director. His successor Archie Hamilton was a more arche-typal Tory (son of a baron, Eton, Coldstream Guards). Spicer was primarily a financial journalist, while Brady worked in public rela-tions before his election to Parliament.

Before 1945, most chairmen had Scottish or Irish links. O'Neill and Somerville were Irish and Rentoul was part-educated in Ireland, while W. S. Morrison, Erskine Hill and McEwen were Scots. Since 1945, eleven – that is, all bar William Anstruther-Gray, a Scot sitting for Berwickshire and East Lothian – have been Englishmen sitting for English seats (though Morrison also owned land in Scotland and Legge-Bourke in Ireland), seven of them sit-ting for seats in the southern half of England and four (Gridley, Harvey, Fox and Brady) sitting for northern seats.

Of the 18 chairmen, eight have not held, nor gone on to hold, ministerial posts. Three went on to hold office after serving as chairman. W. S. Morrison, who clearly had political ambitions, held several ministerial posts before becoming Speaker of the House of Commons. His successor, Hugh O'Neill, went from chairing the 1922 to hold junior ministerial office. Walker-Smith served as a junior minister in the Treasury and Board of Trade, before becoming Minister of Health. Seven had held ministerial office prior to their election, four – du Cann, Onslow, Hamilton and Spicer – reaching minister of state rank. Anstruther-Gray served briefly as Assistant Postmaster-General and both McEwen and Fox served as whips and junior ministers.

Three were already privy councillors at the time of becoming chairman, Anstruther-Gray because of his service to the House (he was Deputy Speaker and Chairman of Ways and Means until 1964) and du Cann and Hamilton because of their ministerial service. All at some stage received knighthoods (or baronetcies) or peerages, or both. Though titles were variously bestowed, Erskine-Hill was the only one to undergo a name change while chairman, changing his name from Hill to Erskine-Hill.

So far, the 1922 has never elected a woman nor a former Cabinet minister as chairman, though it has occasionally had the opportunity to do so. Hamilton was elected in 1997 in preference to former Education and Transport Secretary John MacGregor, Spicer in 2001 in preference to former Education Secretary Gillian Shephard, and Brady was re-elected in 2021 after a challenge from former junior minister Heather Wheeler.

## Leading or presiding

'Of all the influential positions in the Conservative Party', wrote Alan Clark, the chairmanship of the 1922 Committee 'is the one most dependent on the personality and force of character of the incumbent.'[2] The role itself is a multi-faceted one, serving to hold backbenchers together, ensure the views of backbenchers are heard by party leaders (and nowadays the Party Board), that frontbenchers engage with the '22 and that the processes of communication are maintained and, since 1965, that the rules for electing the party leader are applied effectively. The chairman needs a good ear to discern the mood of the parliamentary party – gleaned not only through the weekly '22 meeting, but by being around the tea room and corridors (and nowadays through WhatsApp groups)[3] – and through being willing to convey that mood to leaders. The chairman is in the distinctive position of being the leader's only adviser who has not been chosen by the leader.[4] Some have been more active than others in carrying out the tasks.

Rentoul was arguably the most important chairman of the 1922. The fact that he was a successful barrister prior to being elected as an MP is relevant in that his focus was the law and not politics. The son of a judge, he graduated with a first in jurisprudence and was called to the Bar. Insofar as he had an interest other than the law, it was drama. He came to public prominence as a result of a successful defence in a celebrated murder case. He would likely have continued his career at the Bar had not his wife read to him an advertisement placed by the Lowestoft Conservative Association seeking a candidate for the 1922 election. (They wanted someone of independent mind who could pay his own election expenses.) He applied and was duly selected and elected. The salient point is that he entered the House of Commons not having had any prior engagement with parliamentary activity. The House of Commons was thus novel territory to him, hence his sense of bewilderment and a desire to do something about it.

The 1922 Committee was his brainchild and he helped steer it through the first decade of its existence. He was energetic and a good speaker as well as apparently popular with other members. He appeared keen for the 1922 to have some influence in the party, as evidenced by the response to the loss of the 1923 general election. He did not enjoy unchallenged dominance. In 1929, there was a contest for the chairmanship, but Rentoul was re-elected. 'There was a contest for the position, but Sir Gervais is very popular … He has a fine presence, which is enhanced by a quick sense of humour, and a natural courtesy that is not always met with among MPs.'[5] As we have seen in Chapter 2, his chairmanship was to end in controversy, following the decision to create an Economy Committee and publish its report without the prior agreement of the '22. It was an unfortunate end to his parliamentary career, though he went on to distinguish himself in judicial office.

Rentoul's three successors presided, but do not appear to have made much of a difference to the work of the Committee, if anything contributing to Stuart Ball's view of its limited role and impact. Morrison, 'extremely popular with all and sundry',[6] was not lacking in ambition – he once casually told Churchill's wartime PPS, George Harvie-Watt, he might be a future Tory leader[7] – but he was not 'an energetic innovator'.[8] He appeared focused on climbing the ministerial ladder. He combined his chairmanship of the '22 with being PPS to the Attorney-General and went from the chairmanship to being Financial Secretary to the Treasury. The 81-year-old Somerville simply stood in as acting chairman in 1939, after O'Neill had become a minister, and Spens, 'a short, plump, amiable lawyer with agricultural interests',[9] was regarded by some members to be 'too amiable a man to lead the fight for influence and position which clearly lay before the 1922 Committee'.[10] His tenure was so short and unremarkable that his entry in the *Oxford Dictionary of National Biography* makes no mention of it. His main claim to fame is that in 1943 he was (unexpectedly) appointed Chief Justice of India.

Spens was succeeded by someone who was prepared to fight for influence and position. Alec Erskine Hill was a Scottish lawyer who proved an energetic chairman, possibly too energetic, or possibly too thrusting, for the likes of some ministers. Some senior figures clearly took against him. Butler in 1943 deemed him to be 'too stupid to do anything but intrigue'.[11] However, his intrigue was to bear fruit in terms of advancing the position of the '22. He exploited the situation created by the wartime coalition to elevate the status of the Committee. He had, as Goodhart noted, 'a well-developed taste for political combat on and off the main stage'.[12] According to Channon, writing in his diary in 1941, he 'is a huge man of 47 and looks 60 or more. As chairman of the 1922 Committee he holds a certain position in the party and yields [sic] some influence'.[13]

As we have seen in Chapter 3, Erskine Hill saw off an early attempt by Churchill to prevent ministers addressing the '22. In so doing, he 'had won his spurs'.[14] His influence thereafter derived from his energetic efforts to keep MPs on side at a time of war. As one MP recorded, 'he did fine work in these years of stress and strain by his part in ensuring that differences of opinion among Conservatives in regard to the conduct of the war should not degenerate into personal feuds or cause bitterness'.[15] He drew members together, frequently around a dinner table. Churchill's PPS, George Harvie-Watt, observed that 'One of the busy bees was a Scottish QC, Erskine-Hill. He was a most ambitious man, Chairman of the Conservative Backbench Committee … He gave many little working dinner parties throughout the war and did admirable work for the Conservative Party.'[16] David Maxwell-Fyfe was among the members who acknowledged the value of his activity:

> This is always a delicate job, but it was particularly so in wartime when so many Members had criticism on matters which it would have been unpatriotic to broach in the Chamber. Alec dealt with the situation in two ways. In the first place, he determinedly saw Ministers. 'Having a word with Alec' became one of the best-known phrases in Ministerial circles … Alec's second method was to give them dinner. He would collect about fifteen colleagues, including, of course, the real expert, and ask the relevant Minister to dine with us in a private room at the Dorchester – with, of course, fair warning of the trouble.[17]

Cuthbert Headlam recorded in his diary for 22 January 1942:

> At the House this morning I had a talk with Erskine Hill, chairman of the '1922 Committee'. He is reputed to be a coming man but I find him a bit heavy in hand and I doubt somehow whether he is really the man to get a move on among the Tories – however, he

professes to be trying to do so and I have agreed to work with him. There is no doubt today a feeling of great unrest in the Party, and in the House generally, against the Government.[18]

He on occasion had to assuage Churchill's anger. When things were going badly in the Far East, and the government was being criticised by MPs, the PM summoned Erskine Hill: 'He was rather a stout man and readily sweated with the least expenditure of energy and had continuously to wipe his brow with a coloured handkerchief.'[19] On one occasion in 1943, Erskine-Hill sought a meeting with Churchill. 'He always wanted interviews on major issues. The P.M. agreed most reluctantly because he couldn't stand Erskine-Hill.'[20] Erskine-Hill arrived late, Churchill was fuming. 'Poor Alex had to battle his way alone. I'm bound to say he did quite well considering, although there was no need for him to have seen the P.M. at all. He was merely being important.'[21] He conveyed the feelings of the 1922 about a possible return to government by Beaverbrook, but – as Harvie-Watt and Chief Whip James Stuart had kept Churchill informed of opinion – he wasn't adding anything to Churchill's knowledge.

Erskine-Hill, in short, did not always endear himself to others by his self-important manner, but nonetheless had a notable effect, essentially ensuring that the '22 was seen as a key medium for expressing backbench opinion. The fact that Churchill was not only prepared to see him, but also on occasion summon him, demonstrated the status that the Committee had acquired. Erskine-Hill worked hard to facilitate that recognition.

Subsequent chairmen developed the role of the '22 and were prepared to press the case of the '22 as well as hold regular meetings with the leader. 'Thus it was that Churchill, under polite but firm pressure from the Chairman of the 1922 Committee, Sir Arnold Gridley, ended up promising his MPs (at a testy meeting held just after the Party's failure to take Hammersmith South) that he would indeed respond to their demands that he draw up a statement of party policy.'[22] Under Gridley's successor, Derek Walker-Smith, the chairman and executive began to hold regular meetings with the Prime Minister.

Walker-Smith's successor, John Morrison, was a particularly influential figure. He was very much in the mould of traditional Tory patrician. One MP, who served under eight chairmen, recalled that he was 'the most fatherly and benevolent' chairman he had ever encountered.[23] He was highly regarded and someone who wielded influence away from the public gaze. He acquired the nickname of 'Major Shrewd'.[24] He appears to have been on close personal terms with Macmillan, whom he invited to holiday at his island retreat in Scotland.[25] Macmillan described him as 'a very loyal friend'.[26] During his nine years in post, he saw Macmillan to express, at times strongly, concerns expressed at meetings of the '22,[27] and, as we have seen, was a pivotal figure in determining who should succeed Macmillan. He manipulated the process without being publicly visible in so doing, the responsibility for the choice of the Earl of Home being largely visited on others.

Morrison's three successors did not replicate his impact, in part because one (Anstruther-Gray) served only 16 months, his parliamentary tenure cut short by losing his seat, and another (Legge-Bourke) retired after two years in the chair because of ill-health.

The election of Edward du Cann in 1972 to succeed the ailing Legge-Bourke marked a new era for the Committee. As we have seen in Chapter 4, he was elected in order to ensure the voice of backbenchers was heard by the Prime Minister. He was, in the words of Alan Clark, 'witty, sympathetic and authoritative'.[28] He knew the party in the country – he had been party chairman – as well as in the House. He worked hard at keeping backbenchers on side. As one MP, David Waddington, recalled: 'It was said of Edward du Cann when a young member asked him the time he put an affectionate arm round his shoulder and said: "What time would you like it to be, dear boy?"'[29] Hugo Young characterised him as an intriguer, 'at once furtive and oleaginous, smiling and ruthless, publicly smooth and privately rough'.[30] He represented the '22 under two determined, and very different, leaders, clashing with Heath over the role he played in Heath's loss of the leadership: Heath clearly saw him as a manipulator, seeking to remove him from office, whereas du Cann saw his role as one of a facilitator, ensuring the views of backbenchers were heard. Under Margaret Thatcher, he worked hard, and largely successfully, to ensure good relations with the PM. As we have seen, he liaised with her office to ensure she was briefed on topics for discussion with the executive.

Although du Cann provided long service, he was not universally popular. While the party was still in opposition, some MPs tried to persuade Francis Pym to stand against him: one told du Cann he would vote for anyone who stood against him.[31] In the event, du Cann survived until being ousted by Onslow in 1984.

The deterioration in relations between Thatcher and the '22 detailed in Chapter 4 can be ascribed to a combination of the Prime Minister becoming more detached from Parliament, a series of parliamentary crises and du Cann being replaced by Cranley Onslow. Controversy over du Cann's business dealings and a feeling it was time for a change appear to have sealed his fate. Although the description of Onslow as a 'a bluff character in the tradition of fishing-and-shooting Tories down the ages' belies his work in military intelligence,[32] he appeared the wrong person for the role under a strong-headed Prime Minister. He was able at times to convey unpalatable information, including effectively telling Trade and Industry Secretary Leon Brittan that it was time to go, but was not notably influential in the face of the PM's intransigence over controversial issues, especially the poll tax. Though reportedly not afraid of her,[33] he appeared not naturally inclined to challenge her. As one journalist recorded, Onslow 'unlike his predecessor Sir Edward du Cann at the time of Edward Heath's downfall, saw it as part of his job to protect the leader of the party'.[34] This was not surprising given that he was, according to Chief Whip Tim Renton, felt to be 'firmly on her side'.[35] Even at the end of her premiership, when she consulted leading figures after the result of the first ballot in the 1990 leadership contest, he failed to give a clear line. 'The challenge of reconciling the opposing views of his fellow officers proved beyond Onslow's stolid Toryism.'[36] He also appeared initially not to understand the election rules he was overseeing.[37] Onslow also mishandled the announcement of the results of the 1990 leadership contest,[38] a fact that some MPs held against him and was believed to have been influential some two years later in voting him out of office and replacing him with a very different figure in Sir Marcus Fox.

Whereas Onslow was keen to stay out of the limelight and rarely ventured into a television studio, Fox was notable for his willingness to give interviews. He was an activist chairman, letting ministers know when policies were causing concern or when they had lost the trust of the parliamentary party, but was criticised for using his public appearances to defend the government against backbench critics, and in 1995 for being a vocal supporter of John Major's candidature at a time when he was the returning officer for the election. As we have seen in Chapter 4, he persuaded the executive to swing behind Major in his battle with critics in the parliamentary party. He was twice challenged for the chairmanship, but survived both challenges, albeit apparently by a narrow margin on the first occasion. His loss of the chairmanship was determined not by backbench MPs, but by the electors. He was one of the many Tory MPs who were swept away in the Labour landslide of 1997, a defeat that he apparently took badly.

In opposition, the depleted parliamentary party acquired a chairman who was markedly different to Fox: Archie Hamilton, as we have noted, came from a more traditional Tory background and was a physically commanding presence, in contrast to the diminutive Fox. Hamilton's first challenge was in ensuring the prerogatives of the '22 were maintained in the election of the leader, with the party's MPs remaining the exclusive electorate. Hamilton's twin role was in maintaining the morale of a parliamentary party that was not used to being in opposition, certainly not in such reduced numbers, and adapting to the practical challenges of such reduced numbers. One effect was somewhat paradoxical. The small size of the parliamentary party served to remove the capacity to maintain backbench party committees (see Chapter 7), effectively giving greater weight and focus to meetings of the '22. There were no competing fora in which MPs could make their views known privately to fellow Tory MPs and the party's leadership. The whips could focus exclusively on the meeting of the '22. Party leader William Hague's PPS (Desmond Swayne) was a regular attender.

Hamilton played a central role in determining how a leader could be removed from office. In January 1998, he chaired a meeting of the executive at which he put forward a package of recommendations to cover a no confidence vote in a leader, primarily that 15 per cent of the parliamentary party would be required to trigger such a vote (with no minimum or maximum number required), that a simple majority would suffice for an incumbent to survive, a defeated incumbent would not be eligible to seek re-election, and a leader should be permitted to precipitate a vote of confidence. 'It was stressed that the rules and conduct of leadership elections will remain under the authority of the 1922 Committee.'[39] The recommendations were approved unanimously by the executive.

As we have seen, the new rules have been employed since, three party leaders having been subject to confidence votes. We shall consider later some of the implications (see Chapter 13). One consequence for the chairman of the 1922 was to provide a greater public profile whenever a leader came under attack and backbenchers started to submit letters of no confidence: the recipient of the letters became the focus of media attention.

Hamilton chaired the Committee for one Parliament, stepping down in 2001. He was succeeded by two long-serving chairmen, Michael Spicer and Graham Brady. The quietly spoken and fairly cerebral Spicer was elected in a three-way contest (Spicer received 79 votes to 66 for Gillian Shephard and 11 for John Butterfill) and remained in post until he retired in 2010. He was described as 'a charming, amiable and clever man with an entirely human fallibility of liking to be liked'.[40] Although elected with the support of a particular faction, he worked to be above faction and held the parliamentary party together. Some colleagues felt he lacked a killer instinct, but he presided effectively over two Parliaments, with no challenge to his position. He oversaw the no confidence vote in Iain Duncan Smith and the fraught meetings to discuss Michael Howard's proposals for reforming the party constitution. As we have noted (see Chapter 4), Spicer dissuaded Howard from calling a meeting of Tory MPs to discuss the proposal, ensuring proceedings instead remained under the auspices of the '22. One executive committee member observed that when David Cameron was elected leader, Spicer, coming from the right of the party, was able to act as something of a safety shield, with those from the same wing of the parliamentary party being prepared to trust Spicer's lead. He was also good at knowing when to fudge an issue and bring a discussion to a close.[41]

When Spicer stepped down, David Cameron sought to enlarge the membership of the '22 to include ministers, a move believed to be designed to favour Cameron's preferred candidate for the chairmanship, Richard Ottaway, a vice-chairman of the Committee and former shadow minister, against Graham Brady, known to favour a minority Conservative government in preference to a coalition and seen as a more independent figure. As we have seen, the move ultimately failed and Brady was elected.

As chairman, Brady had to convey backbench sentiment to successive leaders, imparting on occasion unwelcome views. Despite the relationships at times being fraught – at one point, Johnson was seen carrying a note penned by his political secretary, Ben Gascoigne, saying that he should not see Brady without the Chief Whip being present – he managed to develop working relationships with each. Behind the closed doors of Committee Room 14, he was seen as an effective chairman of the executive and of '22 meetings, taking up points raised by members, and in public as an inscrutable figure, notable for being tight-lipped about the number of letters of no confidence received. The only knowledge of letters submitted came from MPs announcing (whether truthfully or otherwise) they had submitted letters. The challenges Brady faced were severe from the moment he was elected, encompassing tensions caused by being in coalition, by the issue of Brexit and consequences of the 2016 referendum, and divisions over the party leadership as well as individual policies, including the response to the COVID-19 pandemic.

During the period of the three premierships of May, Johnson and Truss, Brady was a key figure, in each case seeing them to confirm that it was no longer viable to continue as leader. In the case of May and Truss, they had come to the same conclusion. Johnson, as we have seen in Chapter 5, after initially indicating his intention to continue, came the next day to realise that he had to go.

Brady was a pivotal figure, variously praised by MPs for the way he presided – one long-serving MP with experience of several chairmen described him as 'exceptionally good in the chair'[42] – and in handling difficult situations. At a '22 meeting in October 2019, one retiring MP said he had been an outstanding chairman. However, at times he came in for criticism. Some MPs thought him too sympathetic to May after the 2017 election.[43] In 2020, he faced a challenge for the chairmanship from Bill Wiggin, though the reasons for the challenge were not clear; one suggestion was that some MPs were critical of his decision to recuse himself during the 2019 leadership contest. He was re-elected. He was challenged again the following year. Some MPs were critical of his role as one of the sceptics over the COVID-19 lockdown. Two potential challengers emerged, Robert Goodwill and Heather Wheeler, but Goodwill stood aside to let Wheeler have a clear run. Goodwill had said the 1922 'should not be allowed to become some sort of opposition party within a party'.[44] Wheeler accused Sir Graham of leveraging his position to promote his own views.[45] The challenge had the not-so-tacit support of No. 10. Goodwill did not deny that he had government support. In the event, Brady saw off the challenge and was re-elected, enabling him to become the longest-serving chairman in the history of the 1922.

## The executive

The executive is the workhorse of the parliamentary party. 'Whatever the formal minutes of the Committee's proceedings may say', wrote Edward du Cann, 'it is generally agreed that the largely unrecorded work of Executive members has been the foundation of the Committee's success.'[46]

The executive meets for up to an hour before the weekly meeting of the '22 and has usually an agenda covering a range of items. It summons ministers or frontbenchers to discuss policies, especially if contentious, and will address issues that are concerning members. The officers also meet the Chief Whip after each week's meeting of the '22. It has also acquired significance because of its role in determining the rules for electing the party leader.

## Membership

Initially, membership appeared to be of worthy backbenchers and was not seen as a particularly important position to hold within the party. Among the more noteworthy members of the first executive to be formed was Admiral Sir Guy Gaunt, an Australian who was UK naval attaché in Washington at the outbreak of the First World War, and seen as a key figure in facilitating the US's entry into the war, who was elected as MP for Buckrose in East Yorkshire in 1922. (He left the Commons in 1926 after a divorce scandal.) Membership of the executive became more sought after once the '22 started to acquire a more influential role in the party.

Membership started to include more senior figures in the parliamentary party. 'By 1945, election to the executive … afforded a position not previously considered desirable in Conservative politics, of a group outside the leadership accredited with the duty of vocalizing the feelings of rank-and-file MPs.'[47]

Members are elected by ballot, though the method of election was modified in 1955 after 'Mr John Vaughan-Morgan, having acted as a scrutineer at the ballot for the office of Vice-Chairman, reported that Members seemed to be having difficulty in putting the crosses in the right place. The chairman agreed that in any future election the system of crossing out names should be established in order to avoid mistakes.'[48] This practice was maintained until more recently reverting to the original format.

Nominations for membership usually exceed the number of places available, not least because the elections, like elections to party committees (see Chapter 7), have been used to promote particular interests in the party, sometimes a particular cohort of MPs returned at the same election or more frequently groups representing a particular strand within Conservative thought. The practice of running slates of candidates is well established. Some of the unofficial groups in the party – the number having grown in recent years – have put forward candidates or caucused to decide which candidates to support.[49] In the 1950s, the One Nation Group decided which candidates to support for the executive as well as the party backbench committees.[50] Later groups to run slates included the 92 Group on the right of the party and the Lollards on the left.[51] Following the elections to the '22 in 1979, the Prime Minister's PPS, Ian Gow, sent a memo to the PM: 'As usual, the list of unsuccessful candidates is most revealing. The new Members (not always on the Left) have been well organised and have done well. Generally, the Left has done rather well.'[52] In more recent decades, there has been notable electioneering by groups on the right, such as the 92, the Cornerstone and No Turning Back groups, and the European Research Group (ERG) supporting Brexit. In 2001, Michael Spicer gained the backing of the 92 Group in his bid to become chairman of the 1922,[53] and mounted a campaign that, according to one of his challengers, was conducted 'with military precision'.[54]

The groups putting forward or endorsing candidates have not been confined to ideology. In some Parliaments, newly elected MPs have got together to influence the outcome. In 1980, MPs of the 1979 intake organised a slate of candidates and were notably effective.[55] A similar situation arose in 2012. The 301 Group – comprising MPs of the 2010 intake generally supportive of the Prime Minister – produced and published a list of candidates. As Tim Bale noted, 'The willingness and capacity of various right-wing clubs … to run "slates" of candidates for such contests was testimony to their initial vigour, although it was noticeable that Cameron loyalists in the so-called "301 Group" of mainly younger MPs managed to put together their own slate in 2012 to deny the right complete control of the '22.'[56] Indeed, eight of its candidates were elected. As *The Guardian* reported, 'The 12 members of the executive represent a mix of the 301 Group and those who were not supported by the group.'[57] The results reflected the shift of balance in the party, given the results of the 2010 election, and ensured that the executive could not be characterised as a body of unrepresentative malcontents.

Having members drawn from different wings of the party has been seen as important in ensuring that the executive can fairly represent the views of the parliamentary party. One member, writing in 1977, noted that 'It has not always been so, but in the previous few years the Executive has covered the entire spectrum of political opinion in the Parliamentary Party.'[58] At times, one element may dominate, limiting its claim to speak for backbenchers as a whole, but, as we have seen in Part I, attempts to remove members generally had limited success. When there has been a clean sweep, as with the re-election *en bloc* of members in 1974, against a slate committed to Ted Heath, it has sent a message to the party leadership.

For the first 17 years of the executive, the membership was wholly male. In 1940, one of the new secretaries, Allan Chapman, suggested that a woman be co-opted to the executive, and Lady Davidson (wife of Sir John Davidson – she had succeeded him as MP for Hemel Hempstead in 1937) agreed to serve. In 1951, she was elected in her own right. She was followed by Edith Pitt, the MP for Birmingham Edgbaston (who had hardly begun her term when she was made a minister), Lady Tweedsmuir, the MP for South Aberdeenshire (and also later to be a minister) and Betty Harvie Anderson, MP for Renfrewshire East (and later to be the first woman to serve as a Deputy Speaker). Since then, other women have been elected, including as officers. Jill Knight in 1983 became the first female joint secretary, and others later held office as vice-chairman (Marion Roe, Cheryl Gillan and Nusrat Ghani). It has also proved more diverse in having non-white members, such as Priti Patel, from a Ugandan-Indian background, and Kashmir-born Muslim Nusrat Ghani.

## Activity

The executive has a more diverse and usually fuller agenda than that of the full '22. It has the advantage that, unlike meetings of the '22, proceedings are not usually leaked to the media. The occasions when it has attracted notable media attention are rare. It gained notable coverage in 1974 when meetings held at Edward du Cann's home and then his business headquarters to discuss Heath's leadership were covered by reporters. The latter meeting, in Milk Street, led to the description of the 'Milk Street mafia'.[59] (Du Cann issued a libel writ to stop the term being repeated.)[60] Discussions in 2003 following a clash with the Party Board over constituency autonomy were reported in the *Mail on Sunday*.[61] Mostly, though, there is little leakage from meetings of what has transpired.

## Transforming or presiding?

The executive has shared with the chairman the role of a sounding board. As one leading Tory MP recalled, 'Leading members of the 1922 Committee … are also frequently used as conveyors of opinion between backbenchers and their leaders'.[62] In the immediate post-war years, in the preparation of the Industrial Charter, 'Oliver Poole was responsible for ensuring that the whole thing would fly with the parliamentary party, a task he accomplished by maintaining a running commentary with the Executive of the 1922 Committee'.[63] In 1958, when backbenchers were largely opposed to a proposal to integrate Malta with the UK, the Chief Whip reported to the relevant minister, Alan Lennox-Boyd, that the executive foresaw 'very great trouble in the Party if the proposals for integration are proceeded with'.[64]

The executive can be especially alert to issues directly affecting members, not least relations with the national party organisation and constituency associations as well as how members are treated by the leadership. After the withdrawal of the whip from eight Tory MPs in 1994, members of the executive became exercised by the failure to restore the whip. Although initially divided over whether it should be restored,[65] in March 1995, it was agreed 'to pass on the view of the Executive that those who had the whip withdrawn should now be offered the opportunity to have it restored',[66] the executive returning to the issue in subsequent meetings that month. Michael Howard's withdrawal of the whip from MP Howard Flight (see Chapter 4) also caused some tension with the leader. Since 1997, there has been one issue that has regularly put the executive at variance with the leadership and that has been House of Lords reform, which to some extent impinges on the role of MPs given that many members believe an elected second chamber would threaten the primacy of the House of Commons.

The executive meets with the party leader as well as with other ministers. As Chancellor, Nigel Lawson had pre-budget meetings with the executive.[67] The meetings with the leader used to vary in their frequency, but in 2006 Michael Spicer reported to the executive that it had been agreed with David Cameron that the executive should meet him three times a year,[68] a practice since maintained. Meetings with the leader tend to be substantial, enabling members to express views on the topics being discussed. On 11 November 1975, Margaret Thatcher met the executive, along with her deputy, William Whitelaw, and the Chief Whip, to discuss devolution. Each of the 13 members present expressed a view before there was a general discussion and the chairman, du Cann, proposed that a party committee on constitutional matters, chaired by Whitelaw, be established.[69] Advance notice has usually been given of points to be raised. In November 1980, du Cann asked that Thatcher address the short- and medium-term economic prospects with particular reference to unemployment, House of Lords reform and Northern Ireland. She was also advised that 'Bill van Straubenzee will raise the question of public sector pay' and 'Peter Hordern will argue that the privatisation of BNOC [British National Oil Corporation] should be achieved by the sale of shares, and not by the sale of bonds.' The note prepared by Ian Gow concluded: 'If there is time, the Executive would like to have a discussion about the legislative programme for the new Session.'[70]

Meetings with the leader can be amicable. Macmillan recalled of one meeting in March 1961: 'I also have seen the executive ctee of the 1922 Ctee – this was a most useful meeting.'[71] At other times, they can be difficult, members raising concerns with a leader who may take issue with them. As we have seen in Chapter 4, meetings with Margaret Thatcher became somewhat tense at times in the latter half of her premiership, with the executive holding a post-mortem following one meeting to discuss why it had been so problematic. The usefulness of the meetings with her 'was reduced by her tendency to hector rather than listen'.[72] John Major had a difficult lunch with the executive in October 1992 over the issue of pit closures, the day after Environment Secretary Michael Heseltine had made concessions following backbench pressure.

The executive sought to convey how badly the issue had been handled: 'the PM turned on them, admonishing them for not giving him the public backing he needs'.[73] At times, the effectiveness of the leadership has been an issue and whether the leader is conveying a sense of direction. 'Further disquiet at '22 Executive. Touchy-feeling phase has run its course…'[74]

At times, concern may extend to ministers collectively and individually. The executive gave voice to its disapproval of Cabinet infighting over the issue of Europe under John Major's premiership. 'So serious … did the leaks from and in-fighting in the Cabinet become that in February 1995 the Executive of the 1922 Committee … actually warned their leader that he had to warn his colleagues to stop.'[75] Two days later, Major told the Cabinet that he had met the executive, 'where dismay and anger at reports of Cabinet differences over Europe had been put to him "in the bluntest terms".'[76]

Iain Duncan Smith also encountered tense meetings. Spicer confined to his diary: 'Acrimonious meeting between '22 Executive and IDS. Issues raised appointment of Legg, "lies" about Stephen Gilbert's "sacking"/"unsacking", briefing against members of the party.'[77] During the early days of David Cameron's leadership, 'a meeting with the Executive … during which Cameron tried to persuade them that groups such as Cornerstone … needed reining in did not go well.'[78] Occasionally, they have been disastrous, as witnessed by the meeting between Heath and the executive, engineered by the Chief Whip to 'be a grand rapprochement. It proved to be calamitous.'[79]

Difficult meetings have also occurred with ministers, invited to meet the executive when they are pursuing policies generating concern within the party. Under Thatcher's premiership, for instance, as already recorded (see Chapter 4), Chancellor Geoffrey Howe was summoned to discuss his 1981 budget and, in the same year, Environment Secretary Michael Heseltine to address concerns about his Local Government Finance Bill. Opposition was such that a joint meeting of the backbench Finance and Environment Committees was arranged to discuss the measure. Energy Secretary Nigel Lawson was summoned to discuss gas prices a week ahead of a Commons' debate on the subject. 'I had been warned to expect trouble,' he recalled.[80] As Chancellor, he was also told 'privately but forcibly' by the executive that the party could not cope with an attack on the taxation of pensioners.[81] Nor have those invited to meetings been confined to the leader and front-benchers. In 2002, for example, the programme included meetings with Jacqueline Foster, chair of the members of the European Parliament, and Sam Younger [though the minutes refer to him as Miss Sam Younger], chair of the Electoral Commission.[82]

However, discussions with ministers and others is but one part of the executive's work. Like the chairman, its role is multi-functional, encompassing, as we have seen, essentially domestic concerns relating to party matters as well as policies being pursued by government. Among the former is the issue most often discussed, that of MPs' pay and pensions. In opposition, issues of pay and rations have tended to be more frequently considered than issues of policy. Even in government, it can be to the fore. It occupied time in the executive in the 1979–80 session, with du Cann devoting considerable time to the Boyle report on MPs' pay. There was a special meeting of the executive and du Cann and two vice-chairmen saw the Speaker to discuss it. The Leader of the House, Norman St John-Stevas, also attended the executive to consider the recommendations. After 2010, the executive and the '22 were regularly exercised by the work of the Independent Parliamentary Standards Authority (IPSA), with complaints regularly being expressed and with the 1922 vice-chairman pursuing members' complaints with the House of Commons Commission.

The executive also serves an important role in determining the leadership rules. Following Sir Antony Meyer's challenge to Margaret Thatcher for the party leadership in 1989, it set up a sub-committee to examine the leadership election rules.[83] It did so again in 1995 following the leadership election triggered by PM John Major. It was particularly concerned to address the longer-term method of holding elections 'with a view to removing the annual threat to a sitting Prime Minister'.[84] In 2001, it considered proposals from one senior MP, Andrew Tyrie, that party members should be given a wider choice than two candidates and that peers and MEPs should be involved in the parliamentary stage of voting and that the Party Board should be involved when the voting went out to the party leadership.[85] The last of these was immediately rejected and at the following week's meeting, a majority were against the other proposals, though accepting they needed further discussion. The executive has essentially been protective of the 1922's role as the body for determining the rules for the election of the party leader.

The work of the executive is thus varied. The minutes of its meeting on 14 December 1989, when it had a relatively short agenda, convey the range and importance of its work:

> Cranley Onslow in the chair.
>
> It was agreed that a review body consisting of the Chairman, 2 Vice Chairmen, Sir Charles Morrison and Sir Paul Bryan should look into possible changes in the Leadership procedures.
>
> A Sub-Committee of Ian Gow, James Pawsey and Donald Thompson was appointed to review the Backbench Committee Elections procedures. They were asked to report back in February, 1990.
>
> A discussion took place on the Hong Kong passports problem.
>
> The Community Charge was discussed and it was decided to arrange an urgent meeting with the Environment Secretary and the Chairman of the Party.[86]

The demands on the executive became if anything more severe after 2015 and the outcome of the Brexit referendum and 2017 general election and the pressures on successive leaders. Nusrat Ghani, a vice-chairman from 2020 to 2022, observed that the work was all consuming and was not confined to leadership contests. Colleagues came with issues like 'dealing with security, or people coming forward with whether they were happy or not impressed by government policy'. It was, she said, 'incredibly difficult, sensitive and time consuming'.[87] The work was largely unrecognised outside, and possibly not always that much within, the parliamentary party.

Over post-war decades, the '22 chairman became the public face of the Committee, especially after the provision for a vote of no confidence in the leader was introduced – and the announcement of election results began to be televised (Spicer in 2003 was the first chairman to announce in front of the cameras who was to be the new leader) – but the executive became the powerhouse of the '22. It came to exercise what amounts to hidden-hand leadership.

# Part III

# The impact of the 1922

# Chapter 9

# What's going on?
# Bedding in and being heard

Institutions and processes are not neutral in their effect. The creation and activity of the 1922 Committee have had consequences for Conservative MPs individually and collectively, as well as for the Conservative Party and the political system. In this chapter, we address the consequences for members individually. In subsequent chapters, we address the consequences for Tory MPs collectively (Chapter 10), for the party (Chapter 11) and for the political system (Chapters 12–13).

When MPs at a crowded meeting of the 1922 Committee give vent to dissatisfaction with a policy, or the leadership, of the party, it makes headlines. Journalists, sensing controversy, assemble outside the room and wait to ask MPs 'what happened?' Other weeks, either a lone or no journalist is present. When MPs leave a meeting that has been sparsely attended and has lasted only a few minutes, journalists do not rush to enquire 'why are you here?' 'A few Tory MPs attend weekly party meeting' is not going to make a riveting headline. Regular but unspectacular activity nonetheless has consequences. The relevance of that is sometimes most apparent when the behaviour ceases. The outbreak of the COVID-19 pandemic in 2020, forcing MPs to decant Westminster and operate largely as discrete entities, highlighted the problems of not being able to meet collectively. Although it proved possible to arrange hybrid meetings, they were no substitute for members coming together in person to interact.

Before the 1922 came into being, there was no structured means for gaining a knowledge of the procedures and norms of Parliament. MPs were left to fend for themselves, exploring and imbibing the ways of Westminster, and to rely on written communication from the whips as to forthcoming business. The existence of the 1922 has served to remove both the isolation and the exclusive reliance on the party leadership. It has provided a means of socialisation into the party in Parliament and into the House of Commons. It has served as a means of information exchange, a platform and a safety valve.

## Bedding in

## Socialisation

Until the 1990s, new MPs were left to acclimatise themselves to the ways of Westminster, learning by observation how to behave in the House and utilise the resources available. Until relatively recently, the House authorities provided no formal induction for newly elected members and what was provided was not always absorbed or even utilised by all new arrivals. What guidance was provided came principally from the whips, but that was, until the start of the twenty-first century, essentially on an individual basis.[1]

The *raison d'être* for the formation of the 1922 Committee was, as we have recorded (see Chapter 2), to provide a means of assisting in dealing with parliamentary questions and 'in order to enable new members to take a more active interest and part in Parliamentary life'. For this purpose, it provided talks by senior figures and at the start of a new Parliament arranged briefings for the new Tory MPs. It facilitated the new members learning the practices and norms of Westminster. As we have noted, this is likely to be especially valuable for those members with no prior experience of the institution.

As Rentoul recounted, 'the new M.P.s soon began to realize, as many had done before, the complete insignificance of an inexperienced rank-and-file member lost in the maze of parliamentary procedure'.[2] The 1922 was designed to help them understand the maze and have some input into the proceedings. Its value in this respect was reflected not only in the number of newly elected members who joined, but also in the number of longer-serving MPs who were keen to be involved in its activities.

At times, the '22 has not only assisted new members to understand what happens in Westminster, but it has on occasion engaged in a form of prior socialisation by arranging meetings with party candidates. This has most often and understandably been prior to a general election, but it has also occurred at other times. In July 2003, for example, the executive agreed to organise a function at that year's party conference for prospective parliamentary candidates.[3] In 2007, Charles Walker produced a paper about involving candidates, proposing a reception for them and also recommending that the chairman write to them, with the letter including information about the work and role of the 1922 Committee.[4]

Newly elected MPs have also been able to participate in social events occasionally organised by the '22 for all its members. Other than an annual reception, and a dinner addressed by the leader, there have been occasional dinners. Early in the twenty-first century, one member of the executive, Sir Patrick Cormack, each year organised two get-together social events for members. The executive in January 2004 agreed that in the run-up to the general election, prospective parliamentary candidates should be invited to attend.[5] Later that year, it discussed how the 1922 Committee and Association of Conservative Peers (ACP) could work more closely together. 'Patrick Cormack suggested that we would gain more if we saw more of each other and in his inimitable way, and not unexpectedly, suggested we should have a summer supper and a Christmas dinner.'[6] Although such joint gatherings did not make it to the regular schedule of events, their proposal illustrates a recognition of the value of drawing members together, essentially as a bonding exercise.

In the next Parliament, the chairman, Michael Spicer, gave a brief report to the executive, at the start of 2006, on a meeting with new MPs and a discussion took place as to why a greater number of members was not turning up for '22 meetings. It was noted that 67 per cent of the Conservative Parliamentary Party had been elected since 1997. It was agreed that the executive should organise a social event with new members as soon as possible.[7] The following month, the chairman was able to report that the reception for members of the 2005 intake was considered a success.[8] Prior to the 2015 general election, the executive agreed the importance of the first full meeting of the '22 after the election 'being one of a meeting of the entire Parliamentary Party to reinforce the message, particularly to new Members, that the 1922 Committee *is* the Parliamentary Party'.[9]

The significance of the '22 in helping new MPs acclimatise to Westminster is found not only in bespoke activities to assist new MPs in learning about the House, but also in the very fact of holding regular scheduled meetings, enabling members not only to hear, and ask questions about, forthcoming business, but also to meet fellow members, hear the concerns they raise, and to hear from the leader and frontbenchers. The leader's appearance before the '22 offers a relatively rare opportunity for a backbencher to put a question, one that they may not wish to pose publicly, and to gauge not only the leader's response, but also that of fellow MPs. By being a regular feature in a member's diary, meetings of the '22 provide a sense of belonging, knowing one is with allies (usually) and being able to use the gathering not only to hear the formal proceedings, but also to engage informally with other members. When meetings are well attended, the chairman may need to call for order, sometimes more than once, to commence the meeting.

Not all new members necessarily imbue the value of '22 meetings.[10] In 2011, the executive 'expressed concern' that one new MP, Louise Mensch, had told Channel 4 News that the 1922 Committee 'was a waste of space'.[11] This may explain why attendance at times has dipped and been an issue discussed by the executive, but for other new MPs even short meetings serve a purpose. On these occasions, the issues raised acquire greater prominence. As one MP, Robert Hayward, first elected in 1983, expressed it, it was an opportunity to get a feel for the matters that were concerning members. The fact that there were no speakers made members feel freer to air issues. For new members like him, listening to what was being raised was a valuable means of getting an understanding of issues and parliamentary processes in a way that was not possible through other avenues.[12] As we have seen, even a short discussion on the community charge in July 1989 was sufficient to prompt the Prime Minister's PPS to send her a note alerting her to the criticisms levelled.

The importance of meeting physically each week was highlighted when it was not possible to do so. In 2020, three months after new MPs had taken their seats, the COVID-19 pandemic denied many of them the opportunity to take part in the weekly meetings in the Palace of Westminster, leaving a sense of detachment or disorientation; it took time for some members of the 2019 intake to appreciate the role of the '22 once full meetings were resumed.

The value of the '22 in enabling members to fit in and feel comfortable with their existence in the House extends to all its members. The fact that membership of the '22 is exclusive and entails meeting privately may reinforce that sense. The chairman and other members of the executive also fulfil a pastoral role, serving, as one put it, as an 'agony aunt'.[13] One member of the executive noted in 2023 that it was a role that had expanded in recent years, meetings with members taking place late at night and at weekends, assisting 'colleagues going through tough times, either through the media, their own actions, or other causes. It is different support to that "offered" by Whips or the Party (if they offer anything at all)'.[14] Indeed, the problem on occasion may be a member's relationship with a whip or the whips. The 1922 executive, as we have already noted, was much exercised in 1994 by the position of the eight MPs who had the whip withdrawn.

## Information exchange

The '22 has always served as a conduit for the exchange of information.[15] Members get to hear not only from the whip on duty what business is scheduled, but also from a speaker (if there is one) and from other members if they have points to raise. For ministers, it is an opportunity to inform and persuade. Education Minister Edward Boyle in the 1960s came in for criticism because of his policies, but said that 'I felt with the 1922 Committee that I was winning over a bit more support, or neutralizing a bit more opposition, each time I spoke to them.'[16] Members have the opportunity to listen and to question. Not only are they able to raise points, but also to comment on those raised as well as put questions to the whip on duty, the chairman (or representative) of the Association of Conservative Peers (ACP), and the speaker. Most questions will go the speaker, though on occasion a point raised by a member may generate discussion; the chairman of the ACP may also be pressed about developments in the House of Lords or the issue of Lords reform.

Questions to speakers vary both in number and range. Some ministers speaking to their departmental briefs may encounter relatively few, though those leading large ministries with a range of responsibilities may have to field a wide range that go on for some time. Whereas a typical meeting with a speaker may last no more than half an hour, some will go on, exceptionally, for an hour or even more. When Health Secretary Steve Barclay addressed the '22 in January 2023, he spent an hour fielding questions from most of the MPs who were present.

The value to members of '22 meetings is that they provide an opportunity for exchanging information and doing so in a party environment, away from the public gaze. Although details of meetings may leak when there is controversy, and a minister – especially the Prime Minister – is under pressure, most meetings are not prone to generating headlines.

The value to the leadership is that it is a means of keeping in touch with backbench opinion. 'In particular, it [the 1922] tries to surmount the problem which bedevils so many leaders, namely loss of contact with their own supporters.'[17] Although not formed for the purpose, it has served to avoid the lack of contact that characterised the relationship between leaders and the led in the early twentieth century.

## Being heard

### Platform

Meetings of the '22 serve not only to share information, but also as a platform for members to pursue particular issues or ostensibly raise issues as a means of promoting themselves. The value is not confined to backbenchers. Ministers may use it as a means of mobilising support.

Members have used the weekly meeting as a way of ensuring contentious issues are addressed or for seeking support for particular action, the initiative coming from the floor rather than the officers or frontbenchers. In November 1962, for example, Dame Irene Ward opened a discussion on the Vassal case and the resignation of the minister Tam Galbraith.[18] In 1981, when Sir Geoffrey Howe's budget proved controversial, one member, John Loveridge, asked for support for a motion backing the Chancellor 'and Sir Anthony Kershaw and other Honourable Members appealed to the Party to keep its nerve'.[19] In 1983, Sir Anthony Meyer took to the floor to highlight the impact of boundary changes on his constituency and the choice of candidates 'and a number of views, mainly expressing concern were put to the Committee'.[20] The issue was discussed again at the following week's meeting, one MP, Michael Mates, voicing concerns that there may be further examples.

Members may also use it as a means of challenging the stance taken by party leaders or at least raising issues that are contested. In 1976, Peter Blaker opened a discussion on the Shadow Cabinet's decision to have a three-line whip for the vote on the Second Reading of the Devolution Bill. Nineteen members spoke.[21] In 1990, Anthony Marlow raised the matter of the community charge (poll tax).[22] In July 1992, Ray Whitney used the opportunity to raise the question of the Maastricht Bill,[23] as did another member, Nicholas Budgen, in the October meeting;[24] whereas the June meeting lasted only 11 minutes, this one went on for almost 50 minutes.

Some members use the '22 as a platform for advancing not only their own views, but on occasion their political ambitions. As we have seen, Macmillan used it to promote his bid for the premiership in 1957. One Cabinet minister during the May premiership, having engineered an invitation to speak, ostensibly on his departmental brief, used the occasion to establish himself as a potential leadership candidate.[25] However, whereas Macmillan was speaking to a packed room, the Cabinet minister was addressing about 30 MPs.

Some members have used meetings of the 1922 more than they use the chamber to raise issues. Their reputation may thus be established more in Committee Room 14 than on the floor of the House. Some intervene with erudite comments. Sir Peter Tapsell, an MP from 1959–64 and 1966–2015 and an assiduous attender of meetings of the '22, had the same reputation in the 1922 as he achieved in the chamber, that of a grandee who would offer informed observations drawn from his knowledge of finance and international affairs. Some members can be brief, whereas others, usually a small number, go on at length. As one member of the '22 executive noted in 2023, 'some MPs fancy themselves as wordsmiths and meetings can be subjected to ranty soliloquys not even thinly disguised as questions'.[26] Some are regular contributors. In recent decades, among the more frequent contributors have been former ministers Douglas Hogg (an MP 1979–2010) and John Redwood (an MP since 1987) and erstwhile backbenchers Sir Patrick Cormack (1970–2010), Sir Bill Cash (an MP since 1984) and Michael Fabricant (an MP since 1992).

The existence of the '22 as a platform has also been of value to party leaders, over and above using it for personal advancement. It is a means of rallying support. As David Dilks, a noted historian covering the period of the 1930s, wrote of the 1922, 'On the whole this committee has been a source of strength to the established leadership of the Conservative Party, not least because it has given loyal members of Parliament a platform previously available only to the rebellious.'[27] As we have seen in Chapter 7, dissident backbenchers tended to congregate in the backbench party committees rather than the weekly '22 meeting. Some leaders have attended the '22 to mobilise support. Neville Chamberlain had a notably supportive '22. Few leaders have been able to arouse support since to the same extent, though the '22 has provided a valuable means of appealing to members. The '22 rallied around Margaret Thatcher for much of her premiership. That support was not guaranteed – the parliamentary party was never wholly Thatcherite in the way that the party was Chamberlain-supporting in the 1930s[28] – but it supported her for much of her premiership, until in the late 1980s the party faithful swung against her.[29] She was generally better in her relations with her backbenchers than she was with her ministers.

John Major, as we saw in Chapter 4, sought to use the '22 to rally support for his policy on Europe. Some leaders have used it to prepare members for election campaigns. As with Major's attempts to rally support, meetings have not always gone according to plan. When David Cameron and George Osborne addressed a special meeting of the '22 in January 2010, ready for the general election, they proved difficult to hear above a loud air-conditioning system and employed PowerPoint presentations with print that was too small to be read by everyone. The half-hearted applause at the end suggested the troops had not been enthused. (Cameron made a better, more well-received speech the following month.) The key point, though, is not the effectiveness or otherwise of the meetings, but rather the existence of the platform, a ready-made platform, afforded by the '22.

## Safety valve

The 1922 Committee, opined *The Scotsman* in 1945, had proved to be 'an efficient – perhaps too efficient – safety valve'.[30] Meetings can enable those unhappy with government policy to blow off steam without necessarily going public and voting against the government.[31] 'Senior ministers', declared one long-serving MP, 'don't always realise how frustrated backbenchers can be.'[32] The 1922's function as a safety valve was well expressed by Chris Patten: 'Looking back a year later on the 1973 meetings that Central Office had organized with the 1922 Committee, Patten recalled that "it turned out MPs mostly wanted to grumble about policy".'[33] It was a sentiment reiterated by a later government Chief Whip who recalled that whenever the officers came to see him after the weekly meeting of the '22, the members generally wanted to complain.[34] It was also a view to be taken by Margaret Thatcher later in her premiership. After a meeting with the 1922, she said she was fed up with the party: they 'do nothing but complain'.[35] The '22 has throughout its existence formed an arena in which members can vent their frustrations, be it with specific policies, the actions of ministers or general direction being taken by the party, though this has been most pronounced in the years since 1940.

Meetings can serve to absorb some level of dissent, members feeling it is sufficient to have been heard at the '22, especially if a minister or frontbencher is present to respond, and not taking it further. Much will depend on how a minister deals with the pent-up feeling. On some occasions, there is an opportunity for members to vent disagreement, indicating that they will take it beyond the confines of the committee room. Expressions of dissatisfaction may also induce attendance by frontbenchers to justify their position.

In June 1951, for instance, a discussion took place on the party's actions in not voting on the increases in income tax. 'Sir Herbert Williams criticised the action taken and other members took part in the discussion. Captain Crookshank agreed to pass on to Captain Lyttleton the gist of the views expressed, the majority view being that the Party should have voted on that occasion.'[36] In 1955, the Cabinet's decision to keep the Road Services network in public ownership was raised. 'The 1922 Committee was furious…'.[37] John Boyd-Carpenter, the Minister of Transport, attended a meeting along with the Lord Chancellor, Lord Kilmuir (David Maxwell-Fyfe), to justify the government's position. 'Between us while we did not mollify some of the less sophisticated Members we reduced the situation to a manageable one. David spoke with great authority. His manner was exactly what the situation required.'[38]

The tactics of the party have been the subject of some exasperation. As we have seen in Chapter 3, the tactics employed in opposition were raised under Churchill's post-war leadership. Unpopularity when the party is in government can also generate tensions. The Orpington by-election of 1962, in which a supposedly safe Tory seat fell to the Liberals, generated shock among Tory MPs. The party chairman, Iain Macleod, appeared before the '22, facing 'a barrage of complaints from anguished MPs, many of whom suddenly felt that their seats were not as safe as they had imagined'.[39] Similar meetings have occurred when the party is in trouble, ministers and party officials attending to explain their approach to presentation or tactics and steps being taken to improve the situation.

# The impact of the 1922

In October 1974, at a packed meeting attended by about 220 members, Kenneth Lewis raised the question of the party in opposition, initiating, according to the minutes, 'a full discussion' – the word 'constructive' was crossed out – to which 21 members contributed.[40] In 2001, concerns were raised that opposition tactics were not being correctly targeted. 'The Chairman undertook to report this to the Chief Whip.'[41] The floor of the '22 was also used to express concern when the leadership endorsed policies of a Labour government, as over the stance taken by the leader, Michael Howard, to endorse the introduction of identity cards (see Chapter 4). The '22, as we have seen, has also been a site for the outlet of conflicting views on the issue of European integration, though notably failing to confine those views to the privacy of the '22 meetings. In this case, it was not so much a safety valve as a split pipe, the views of members being spewed out publicly. Nonetheless, the '22 served a valuable role in enabling different views to be heard and for party leaders to respond to them within a party setting.

The '22 executive has also served to take up members' concerns with party leaders, not least over presentation and the effectiveness of frontbenchers. As recorded in Chapter 4, the officers in 1977 made clear their dissatisfaction with the Shadow Cabinet and recommended a reshuffle. Following some poor performances by ministers in 1980, Margaret Thatcher recalled: 'Not surprisingly, when I met the executive of the '22 Committee … I found that they had a low view of ministers' efforts at presentation.'[42] The executive also conveyed members' concerns over the leadership's failure to get involved more centrally in the 2011 referendum campaign on AV, members' frustrations having been vented in a meeting with the party chairman, Baroness Warsi. The '22 was also an outlet for MPs' frustrations about how the party leader was reacting to the expenses' scandal of 2009. It was a matter that exercised the executive, not least the threat by David Cameron to deny re-selection to any MP who failed to pay what Sir Thomas

Legg, who was carrying out a review of expenses, said they should repay. It was agreed that the chairman should see Cameron and that points to be raised should include the need for an appeals system, the issue of process which should be interactive and iterative and that Legg should not be allowed to change the rules retrospectively. 'The rule of law, arbitrariness, estoppel and the need for appeals were reiterated.'[43] As we shall see, the '22 has also been used by members to express their disquiet over both policy and the actions of ministers, including the Prime Minister, at times to such an extent as to induce change.

The impact of the '22, as detailed in Part I, became significant in the years after 1940 and acquired a new, and powerful, dimension when the method of electing the leader passed from one of 'emergence' to election by the party's MPs and later still the parliamentary party acquired the formal power to de-select a leader. From 1965 onwards, every member of the '22 ceased to be a bystander and instead became important as a voter. After 1998, each member also became of interest to the media when the party leader was under pressure: 'Have you submitted a letter of no confidence?'

# Chapter 10

# Collective action: a trade union for backbenchers

The 1922, wrote an MP who became one of its joint secretaries, 'is to all intents and purposes the trade union of Conservative backbench MPs'.[1] David Cameron described it 'as a trade union-style meeting comprising, of all people, Tory MPs'.[2] Both Archie Hamilton and Graham Brady described their position as chairman as akin to that of a 'shop steward'.[3] As Edward du Cann put it, the 1922 'represents the backbenchers; it's there to put their point of view'.[4]

The 1922 speaks for the interests of backbenchers not only to party leaders, but also to other bodies, including the House authorities, not least on issues such as pay and standards. It will on occasion make common cause with the Parliamentary Labour Party (PLP) and other parties in defence of members' interests. In 1978, for example, the 1922 and the PLP made a joint submission regarding improvements to the parliamentary pensions scheme. Indeed, there is on occasion appreciation of the work of the other party body. In 1944, one member of the 1922 suggested anyone who cared should subscribe to a leaving present for the secretary of the PLP.

We can distinguish between those issues that are essentially party matters, to do with party organisation and MPs' relationship to other party bodies, and House matters, those affecting, and decided by, all MPs. The issues under the former include the, at times fraught, relationship of members with the professional and voluntary wings of the party, as well as local constituency parties.

## Collective action

The issues coming under the latter include the subject that has attracted the most debate in the 1922, that of MPs' pay, as well as related issues and the administration of the House.

## Party matters

The 1922 speaks for backbenchers to the rest of the Conservative Party, as well as to other bodies. On party matters, it has weighed in on party organisation, not least where actions or proposed changes impinge on members' interests. Though an unofficial body until 1998, it enjoyed close links with the official national party organisation. As we have seen in Chapter 2, as early as February 1925, it was reported that arrangements had been made for Mr J. Green of the Central Unionist Office to act as secretary to the Committee.[5]

## Status within the party

Links became more formalised after the war. The 1948 Maxwell-Fyfe report on party organisation resulted in the creation the following year of an Advisory Committee on Policy to advise the party leader on policy.[6] It comprised members drawn from different sections of the party, including five appointed by the 1922 Committee. Meeting once a month when Parliament was sitting, the Advisory Committee on Policy worked through a series of policy groups, with the parliamentary party providing about half the membership of each,[7] until it was wound up in the 1980s. Under the Maxwell-Fyfe reforms, members of the '22 were also appointed to the National Union Executive Committee. It thus became integrated into the national party organisation, although it was not a body formally constituted by the party. It was created bottom-up by MPs, not top-down by the party leadership.

The 1922's position in the party was formalised as part of the reforms initiated under William Hague's leadership in 1998. The party acquired a formal constitution, under which a Party Board was established 'which shall be the supreme decision-making body in matters of Party organization and management'. It comprises the three parts of the party (voluntary, professional and parliamentary), with the chairman of the '22 serving as a member *ex officio*. The executive of the 1922 Committee may, by resolution, under Schedule 8, initiate a proposal to amend the constitution. The constitution also delineates the role of the 1922 Committee in the election of the party leader:

> Upon the initiation of an election for the Leader, it shall be the duty of the 1922 Committee to present to the Party, as soon as reasonably practicable, a choice of candidates for election as Leader. The rules for deciding the procedure by which the 1922 Committee selects candidates for submission for election shall be determined by the Executive Committee of the 1922 Committee after consultation of the Board. (Schedule 2)

It also stipulates that 'The Chairman of the 1922 Committee, acting on behalf of the Party, shall act as Returning Officer for all stages of the election.'

The 1922 was thus integrated into the party, yet still remains essentially independent of it. Other than covering the role of the 1922 in the election of the leader, the only references to it in the constitution are those already mentioned, plus the inclusion in Schedule 1 (Interpretation) of the statement: '"The 1922 Committee" means a committee comprising all Members of Parliament.' This confuses rather than clarifies. The 1922 does not comprise 'all members of Parliament', or even all Conservative members of Parliament. The party leader is excluded from membership, as are ministers, though they may now attend.

## Relationship with the rest of the party

The relationship between the 1922 Committee and the new Party Board was not problem free. In April 2003, the executive discussed the role of MPs at the party conference. 'The Chairman read the response by the Party board to his letter on this matter, which he said was received with criticism and a display of irritation.'[8] This was followed by a discussion on relations with the Board. It was reported that 'the board saw Members as self-serving terrorists who had the power to bring down the leader that they had elected. The membership through the board saw MPs with suspicion.'[9] The problem was seen as arising from the new rules for electing a leader and it was agreed that the rules and constitution needed to be changed. 'The executive felt that the Party was heading towards a catastrophe, which was not appreciated by the membership.'[10]

Although in the October Iain Duncan Smith was voted out as party leader – criticisms of his leadership being tied up with the view in the executive as to the state of party morale – and in the November it was agreed that the executive should meet the Board three times a year, there were still tensions between the two. Michael Spicer recorded in his diary for 20 June 2005: 'Acrimonious board meeting. I refuse to join discussions about future organization until there is agreement on an end date after we have a new leader.'[11] The following week, he recorded: 'More open discussion of the constitution at '22, most of it firmly anti board's proposals, but sensible. Then Laurence Robertson proposes abolition of the board and gets enough "hear, hears" for me to feel encouraged to bring forward a firm motion next week.'[12] This was at a time when proposals for party reform by Michael Howard generated clear tensions (see Chapter 4) and was exceptional, but is indicative of the independent stance maintained by the '22. The '22 has sought not only to maintain its independent status, but also to protect the position of members in relation both to the activities of the professional section of the party, primarily Central Office, now CCHQ, and the voluntary wing.

At a meeting in December 1953, for example, 'Mr Arbuthnot drew attention to the practice of Central Office in sending division records of Members to their constituencies and to the fact that these records were sometimes inaccurate.'[13] The following week, John Hare reported that he had looked into the complaint and informed the Committee of certain actions that he had taken. What details were being reported to the constituencies is not clear. At that time, MPs, especially Conservative MPs, rarely voted against the party line.[14]

The '22 has been especially robust in relation to candidate selection. This has been an issue of contention over the years, the Committee rallying to the support of candidates under threat. It has sought to establish clear procedures that govern selection as well as pursuing cases where individual members have been deselected as candidates by the local party or prevented from standing by the removal of the whip.

The 1922 submitted a memorandum to the 1970–1 National Union review of party organisation, welcoming the agreement of the party's national executive to include the obligation that a constituency association give a hearing to the sitting MP before deciding whether to open the list to others, 'but we would earnestly request that as a matter of courtesy, a Selection Committee might be expected to allow a sitting Member who so wished to appear again before the Selection Committee after he had been heard by the Association'.[15]

In 1998, the '22 reiterated its opposition to plans for the compulsory re-selection of MPs.[16] In 2001, an attempt by the voluntary wing of the party to enable local associations by a simple majority vote to de-select a sitting MP was 'stymied by an eleventh-hour veto by the Executive of the 1922 Committee'.[17] The '22 resisted attempts by the Party Board to centralise the capacity to determine candidate selection. At a Board meeting in May 2002, Michael Spicer, on behalf of the '22, insisted that constituencies retain sovereignty in the selection of candidates.[18] The following year, the executive reiterated its 'unanimous view that the autonomy of the Associations should remain sacrosanct' in the face of what it saw as attempts by the Board to centralise the running of local campaigns.[19] The executive met the party chairman, Theresa May, and gave her 'a bad time in defence of constituency autonomy'.[20] May spoke at the following week's meeting of the '22 and was given a cool reception: 'A dozen questions, mostly hostile; she seems surprised by this.'[21] In 2005, it was agreed unanimously 'That it be a resolution of the 1922 Committee that "the agreement for being accepted as, and remaining a candidate for the Conservative Party" be rescinded and withdrawn by the Board of Management of the Conservative Party.'[22]

As we have seen, the '22 has also considered the cases of individual MPs under threat. It addressed the issue of Sir Anthony Meyer and his local association, with fears the behaviour of his association may set a precedent. As already noted, the executive was much exercised by the withdrawal of the whip from eight MPs in 1994. At its meeting on 1 December, some members suggested that the whip 'should be restored to those who had recently lost it. Others were against.'[23] However, the following March, by which time the whipless MPs had attracted a great deal of publicity and appeared to be exploiting their status, it was agreed 'to pass on the view of the Executive that those who had the Whip withdrawn should now be offered the opportunity to have it restored'.[24] The position of the 'whipless eight' was discussed in each of the succeeding four weeks and again the following month.

In May 2001, there was a discussion in the executive on the actions of Charles Wardle, MP for Bexhill and Battle, who had lost the whip after criticising the candidate selected to succeed him. The way in which he had lost the whip was raised. 'This developed into a wider discussion about party discipline in the party.'[25] Under Michael Howard's leadership, the '22 was severely exercised by his decision to withdraw the whip from Howard Flight and prevent him being re-selected in his Arundel and South Downs constituency. At one meeting of the '22, Edward Leigh criticised the decision, 'rousing backbenchers to bang their desks in approval'.[26] The stance of the '22 added to conflict with the whips, with the

Chief Whip David Maclean taking the view that it was taking its trade union role of defending members too seriously.[27] Once the decision had been taken, the executive was divided on whether Howard should give way in face of Flight's determination to contest the decision.[28] Subsequently, it was agreed that the 1922 was to have a role in any appeals mechanism for an MP deprived of the whip and before the constituency association adopted a new candidate. The chairman of the '22, or a nominee, was to sit on the tribunal considering the appeal.

The issue arose again in 2014 with moves to de-select two MPs, Anne McIntosh and Tim Yeo. Their situation was raised at the '22 on 7 February, with one backbencher, Sir Peter Tapsell, mounting an impassioned defence of McIntosh and offering £10,000 towards the cost of an open ballot to select the candidate. After several others weighed in to support McIntosh, generally to applause, the chairman, Graham Brady, made clear that the executive had got the message.

The executive has also addressed other aspects of candidate selection, including the use of all-women shortlists. At the beginning of 2003, one member, Robert Walter, introduced the issue: he was in favour, as was another member, Bill Wiggin, but the majority was opposed. If a constituency wished to adopt an all-women shortlist, it could have one, but the executive was against foisting one on them or any element of compulsion.[29] Its opposition was conveyed to the party chairman, Theresa May, when it met her two weeks later.

The executive was also concerned on occasion with the issue of what support MPs could give financially to their local parties. A result of the 1948 Maxwell-Fyfe reforms was to cap the amount a candidate could donate to the local party (£25, or £50 in the case of MPs), a limit designed to prevent the parliamentary party being dominated by wealthy landowners and businessmen who could make substantial donations. The issue was to come up again in later years, not least as to whether and to what extent

MPs could use constituency allowances to help defray the cost of running their local association. At an executive committee meeting in January 1993, it was reported that the chairman of the party's National Union, Sir Basil Feldman, had written to the chairs of local associations for details of MPs' contributions to associations and asking that the letter should not be seen by MPs.[30] The chairman was deputed to check with Sir Basil if this was true. The issue arose again in 2003, when it was reported that Michael Spicer was to be consulted on a letter being sent to constituency chairmen on the issue,[31] and again in late 2007, when it was reported that a member had been asked to pay £10,000 a year to his local association as a pre-condition for being re-selected.[32] The following January, the executive sought clarification as to the amount that could be given: 'John Whittingdale had talked to Lord Norton about the Maxwell-Fyfe rules and Sir Michael Spicer to the Party Chairman on the same subject.'[33]

As we shall see in Chapter 11, the need for the '22 to speak for Tory MPs as Tory MPs has been especially marked at times when the party has formed a government in coalition with other parties. The '22 has been the authentic voice of the Conservative parliamentary party when the government is Conservative-led, but not exclusively Conservative.

In 2003, the '22 also sought to develop links with the party in the European Parliament and the devolved legislatures. As already recorded in Chapter 6, MEPs and members of the devolved assemblies could attend '22 meetings as observers. In June of that year, the executive heard from both the Scottish party chairman, David Mitchell, and the chair of the Welsh Conservative Party, Carol Hyde, and in November it travelled to Brussels to meet Conservative MEPs and 'sister party' members, for what was viewed as a successful gathering. These meetings, though, were not pursued and in event the European Parliament party ceased to exist with the UK's withdrawal from the European Union.

## House matters

There are various issues, covering particularly procedure, facilities and pay, that are regarded as matters for the House, with members able to decide free of the dictates of party.

Such issues are variously discussed by the 1922. Some may be raised by members, but the '22 may be approached by the whips, the business managers or the House authorities. In 1993, it was reported that the House catering committee required official evidence from the 1922.[34] Some of the issues related to the chamber itself. For example, on 5 March 1951, the Chief Whip asked the views of members as to desirability of using the annunciator to give the names of speakers to the public galleries. 'The Committee was against the suggestion.'[35] The reasons for members rejecting the idea are not recorded. In December 2002, it was agreed that the chairman should write to Keith Hill, the chairman of the Joint Committee on Security, 'opposing the proposal to erect a glass screen in front of the public gallery in the House of Commons'.[36] In the event, the view of the executive was trumped by security considerations.

Discussion has also covered conduct in the chamber. During the Speakership of John Bercow, complaints were raised over his willingness to let numerous questions be asked of the Prime Minister, especially, as already noted, when Theresa May was at the despatch box defending her decision to commit to air strikes in Syria. Members also vented their anger at rulings of the Speaker during the chamber battles over Brexit in 2019.

The executive in particular has been exercised by domestic issues, be they affecting relations with the party or in relation to the House. Its agenda has sometimes been a mix of the two. At its meeting on 18 November 1993, after discussing arrangements for the election of the Prime Minister, the principal items on the agenda were rather disparate domestic issues:

> The new Police Superintendent is to be approached to behave himself.

The Speaker is to be asked about the conduct of proceedings during the closing stages of the Railways Bill.

Norman Fowler [Party Chairman] is to be approached about what is happening to Agents.

Additional voluntary contributions to Members' pensions were discussed.[37]

The minutes are silent as to what misbehaviour had been attributed to the Police Superintendent.

Some apparently minor matters can have wider consequences for government. In November 1991, the Prime Minister's PPS, Graham Bright, 'reported that too many Members were asking the Prime Minister to sign bottles of whiskey. It was taking up too much time.'[38] Not having any obvious impact on government, the minutes for the meeting of the executive on 6 June 1996 merely record: 'Lady Astor's bust was discussed.'

Mostly, the domestic matters discussed have tended to be specific and isolated cases, not generating great controversy. However, there has been one issue that has emerged throughout the Committee's existence and which has not always produced a harmonious conclusion and that has been MPs' pay. It has aroused notable conflict, sometimes between members and at other times between members and the government.

Pay was discussed by the Committee in July 1952. It returned to the subject in two successive meetings in March 1954. The following month, the Chancellor of the Exchequer attended to open a discussion on the subject. The issue aroused such strong feelings that it was not just the Chancellor who spoke. The Prime Minister also addressed the meeting. At another meeting on 20 May, the Chancellor and Prime Minister were again present, this time for a discussion on members' allowances (being debated in the House the following Monday). The meeting, attended by 170 MPs, lasted almost two hours. Pay was further considered on 27 May and the chairman and executive met the Prime Minister and certain Cabinet ministers to discuss the issue, reporting back to the

Committee the following week. The House agreed to a recommendation to increase pay from £1,000 to £1,500 a year, but the proposal was not popular with most Conservative MPs. Bob Boothby, who supported the increase, was almost physically attacked when he spoke: 'There was a moment when I hardly dared face the 1922 Committee, and addressed it with my hand on the door, in case immediate escape became necessary.' He described it as 'the roughest treatment I ever got from the Tory Party'.[39]

The Committee returned to the issue, albeit briefly, in July 1957 and again, more substantially, in July 1979 when the executive considered the matter. In 1980, a report (the Boyle report) recommended a significant increase in members' pay. As Kenneth Baker recalled, 'As a member of the 1922 Executive I attended a meeting in February 1980 about the Boyle Report when it was clear that the backbenchers wanted all of their recommended pay increase.'[40] They resisted the pressure of the Prime Minister, Margaret Thatcher, and the whips and got their way. The report absorbed much time of the '22 and especially the executive.

Pay and pensions continued, and continues, to exercise members. Sir John Butterfill, who served as treasurer of the 1922 from 2001 to 2005, was chair of the trustees of MPs' pension fund and provided members with regular updates. After the Independent Parliamentary Standards Authority (IPSA) was created to determine and administer MPs' pay, Charles Walker, vice-chairman of the 1922 from 2010 to 2021, who served on the Speaker's Committee on IPSA (SCIPSA), acted as the 1922 spokesperson in challenging IPSA in the way it was operating. He regularly regaled the 1922 about the inequities of the Authority and members took the opportunity to complain vehemently about the way it handled their claims for expenses, not least the time it took to process them. Some members were notably belligerent in their attitudes.

The criticisms of IPSA were not confined to Tory MPs and Michael Spicer invited the chair of the PLP, Tony Lloyd, to attend a meeting of the '22 executive with the chief executive of IPSA: 'He does (this probably a "first"). In the end both his appearance and the holding of the meeting turn out to be productive. IPSA agrees to discuss policy matters on a regular basis with '22 Executive (and, by implication, PLP).'[41] The agreement reduced some of the pressures, though the chairman of IPSA, Sir Ian Kennedy, reported some difficult meetings initially with the executive of the '22 as well as with Liberal Democrat MPs and (even more so) the PLP.[42] Kennedy, who had a reputation for being confrontational, developed a working relationship with Graham Brady, who, he reported, made the claim for MPs to have greater freedom in deploying the money they spent, but recognised that there was no likelihood of going back. 'He had said his piece and it was important for him to do so. But he was also a pragmatist and knew what was what. The meetings were always cordial.'[43]

Members not only turned their fire on IPSA, but also at the end of 2013 on the Prime Minister after he waded in to comment on proposals from IPSA for members to have a pay rise. When one MP said the PM should shut up speaking about it, he received loud applause.

On matters affecting the House, the 1922 may also have an input. These include the issue of who is to be Speaker. Until a move to election by MPs, with different candidates putting their names forward, the choice of Speaker was usually agreed by the government after consulting the opposition and backbenchers. In 1943, the 1922 decided that the Deputy Speaker, Douglas Clifton-Brown, should be elected Speaker following the death of the incumbent. Churchill apparently favoured another candidate, but the 1922's preference prevailed.[44]

In 1951, following Clifton-Brown's retirement, the government, after discussion through the usual channels, put forward the name of W. S. Morrison to be Speaker, but the Labour Liaison Committee had then decided, the day before the election, that it favoured Labour MP James Milner, an existing Deputy Speaker. He was proposed by a Labour member and supported by opposition leader Clem Attlee. There was no time for the 1922 to consider the matter, but there was probably little need anyway: Morrison was a former chairman of the 1922 and was proposed by his successor as chairman, Sir Hugh O'Neill. Furthermore, Milner's name had been discussed when the 1922 considered who should be selected in 1943. Some members, recalled Cuthbert Headlam, 'did not like the idea of Milner becoming Chairman of Ways and Means – and of course he is not the right type of man for the job'.[45]

The vote was on party lines. Only one Tory voted for Milner and that was Morrison: Milner voted for Morrison. Morrison was elected by 318 votes to 251.[46]

In 1970, the two front benches agreed on the choice of former Chancellor and Leader of the House, Selwyn Lloyd, to succeed Dr Horace King as Speaker. However, the choice generated some controversy as another senior Conservative, John Boyd-Carpenter, had also been sounded out and had been keen to be considered. When Lloyd's name was put to the House, Liberal MP John Pardoe, supported by Tory MP Robin Maxwell-Hyslop and Labour MP William Hamilton, objected on the grounds that, as far as he was aware, neither the Parliamentary Labour Party nor the 1922 Committee, or even the executive of the 1922, had been consulted.[47] 'How this emergence has come about', declared Maxwell-Hyslop, 'either nobody knows except this who were involved in it, or no one is prepared to say. But what we do know is that the House of Commons as a whole has had no opportunity of participating in it.'[48]

The process of election later changed, enabling members to vote for a preferred choice from a range of candidates. There was no party line, but rather the parliamentary parties providing an opportunity to hear from candidates. In the election of a new Speaker in 2019, all the candidates were invited individually to speak to the 1922. Labour MP Chris Bryant made a notably effective speech. He was perhaps assisted by the fact that he followed a Conservative candidate who made a somewhat lacklustre presentation. There was some discussion in the '22 as to whether it was time for a Conservative to be chosen. One member attracted murmurs of support when he suggested that perhaps members should vote for the candidate who they thought would make the best Speaker.

## Speaking for the members

The descriptions of the '22 highlighted in opening the chapter thus appear a fairly accurate characterisation of the '22. It is in effect the trade union body for the workers of the parliamentary party – the backbenchers – and it has a works committee in the form of the executive and a shop steward in its chairman. The chairman is the principal individual who makes representations on behalf of the members to those in authority, be it the party leader, the professional or voluntary wings of the party, and the House authorities. The executive, as we have seen, has been responsible for discussing a range of domestic (party or House) matters that have concerned members. However, the analogy with a trade union is now deficient in one important respect, in that most trade unions do not elect the company boss and the boss is not dependent for continuing in office on the workers.

# Chapter 11

# Us versus them: maintaining the integrity of the party

Anthony King, as recorded in the opening chapter, identified different modes of executive–legislative relations.[1] The opposition mode is the dominant one in the UK, two sides facing one another in adversarial combat. The emphasis, as King argued, is not accommodation, but domination. It is a core feature of the Westminster system of government.[2] Parliamentary rules are largely premised on the existence of two principal parties, forming the government and an official opposition, each enjoying particular roles and privileges. The official opposition is the party designated by the Speaker as the party able to take over the reins of office in the event of the existing administration being unable to carry on.

However, while the opposition mode is the most visible, it is not the only one. The intra-party mode (the relationship between the executive and its own parliamentary party) is usually the most significant, the government being dependent on its own backbenchers to deliver its programme. However, in exceptional times, the opposition mode may go into abeyance and the cross-party mode (members working across party lines) come to the fore.

This characterised the period of national government from 1940 to 1945. At other times, the intra-party mode may compete with the inter-party mode (the relationship between the executive and other parties, not least in a coalition). This marked the period of coalition government from 2010 to 2015, the Prime Minister having to balance the demands of his own supporters against the need to keep on board another party.

Each occasion created conditions that gave a distinct role to the 1922 Committee, that of wartime being especially important as the public voice of party was largely muted. In both, the '22 was key to maintaining a distinct Conservative presence in a government that was not exclusively a Conservative one.

## Wartime coalition

There was a national government from 1931 to 1940, but it was effectively in all but name a Conservative government. (The Conservatives in 1931 had 475 seats out of the 554 held by the government.) There was a Labour opposition. The situation was very different in 1940 when the principal parties combined to form a truly national government. The '22 was not a moving force in the collapse of the Chamberlain government in 1940, but, as we have seen in Chapter 3, it benefitted from the resulting formation of a coalition government. Indeed, it transformed its fortunes. The parties came together to form a united front in facing a common enemy. There was no need for bargaining to agree a compromise programme. There was one core aim. If there was any disagreement within government or between the parties to it, it was over means. The parliamentary rules had to be adapted to the new situation. The system functioned with a Leader of the Opposition, so a Labour backbencher was designated as acting Leader of the Opposition, even though he was a supporter of the government.[3] During the period of war, three Labour backbenchers served unpaid in the role. The last of these, Arthur Greenwood, had been a notably vocal supporter of Churchill in 1940.

The creation of a national government had implications not only for how the parties operate in Parliament, but also in the country. Party competition was put on hold. The life of the Parliament was extended. The parties did not compete against one another in the event of a by-election. As a result, party organisation, both nationally and locally, was wound down.[4] Conservative Central Office lost four-fifths of its staff.[5] The Conservative Research Department went into hibernation.[6] The one body that continued to operate fully and as a distinctive Conservative voice was the 1922 Committee. As Tim Bale recorded, 'Backbenchers continued to meet together in the 1922 Committee and often played an important part (as did activists) in geeing up the activists back in the constituencies.'[7]

As we have seen in Chapter 3, the '22 continued to meet regularly, with meetings often well attended. The election in December 1940 of Alec Erskine Hill – Alec Erskine-Hill from 1943 – as chairman in succession to William Spens resulted in a new form of leadership. He played, as his entry in the *Oxford Dictionary of National Biography* records, 'a pivotal role between the footsoldiers of the Conservative Party in the House of Commons and the coalition government led by Winston Churchill'.[8] He was notably energetic, seeing ministers and hosting dinners (see Chapter 8). He led in ensuring that the voice of the '22 was heard.

He was core to ensuring that a distinct Conservative voice was heard, not only by government, but also in the country. There was a feeling, almost from the beginning of the formation of the national government that, although the parties were united in prosecuting the war, the Labour Party was making the running in articulating Socialist views and in promoting legislation that was viewed by Tory MPs as being in line with those views.[9] As John Charmley noted, 'As early as 1941, members of the 1922 Committee were complaining to Eden about the amount of "socialistic legislation … passed under the guise of war needs".'[10] One MP also told the '22, to general approval, that 'all over the country the Conservative cause was being allowed to go by default'.[11]

Erskine Hill was active in protecting the position of the '22. He was part of a liaison committee formed in March 1941 with what remained of Central Office to ensure that Conservative speakers

were included on Ministry of Information and BBC radio plat-
forms.[12] Criticism had been raised in the '22 of the ministry and the
content of some of the material it disseminated.[13] There were also
calls in the '22 to ensure that Tories got a fair share of time in the
Commons. That remained a concern throughout the war years.
On 1 November 1944, Reginald Manningham-Buller 'wanted
more Conservative adjournment debates, as they seemed all to be
raised by the other side and received a good deal of publicity'.[14]

Erskine Hill articulated backbenchers' opposition to pressure
from Labour to put certain utilities in public ownership. He saw
ministers to stress Tory opposition to coal rationing. The disagreement went public, the abandoning of the scheme, demonstrat-
ing the strength of the '22, in essence its new-found strength. As
we saw in Chapter 3, and as A. J. P. Taylor put it, 'though there
was no hostile vote, the government ran away'.[15] As we have seen,
Churchill's PPS became a regular attender at meetings of the '22.
Despite his personal dislike of Erskine Hill, Churchill made time
to see him.

There was no question of the commitment of the '22 to ensuring victory (though one antisemitic Tory MP, Captain Archibald
Ramsay, was interned), but it held unprecedented leverage given
the government's need to maintain a united House. It needed to
heed any sounds of unrest over the conduct of the war. Criticisms
were voiced over setbacks and there was clear unease at Churchill's
attempts to conduct the war almost single-handedly. As Channon
observed of one of the dinners organised by Erskine Hill, held on
9 January 1942, 'Anthony Eden was present, and seemed upset
when every MP present told him that the Government was doomed
… The Government must be reformed, and that soon.'[16] As Stuart
Ball recorded, the '22 not only induced the government to abandon policies it thought too influenced by the other party, 'it also
played a part in the reconstruction of the government in February
and September 1942'.[17] The restructuring did not still disquiet in
the '22. In October 1942, the '22 discussed 'The Position of the

Party'. Every MP that spoke took a pessimistic line. Oliver Stanley said that the party did not know what its policy was. 'It had to say what it was aiming to do after the war. The party could not regain its place in the House of Commons without reorganization (a clear rebuke for the Whips) and there had never been such a gulf between the party and its leaders.'[18] The following week, a deputation was appointed to discuss with ministers, the Chief Whip and the party chairman the issues raised by Stanley. 'But the moment had passed.'[19] The improving military situation took the sting out of the '22's move and it later retracted its demands. It did not still its concerns. The '22 raised issues of strategy and military supplies.[20]

It remained significant, not only for ensuring a Conservative voice during the war, but also for taking a Conservative view of what should follow once peace was achieved. As hostilities began to swing in the allies' favour, it was possible to start envisaging life in a post-war Britain. Churchill did not have the time, or the inclination, to develop a clear Conservative programme to put before electors. As Chief Whip David Margesson commented, the PM wasn't interested in civil or social problems – his whole interest was in war organisation.[21] The '22 did engage in some forward thinking. The Report of Sir William Beveridge, *Social Insurance and Allied Services*, proposing a form of welfare state with social insurance 'from cradle to grave', was made public on 1 December 1942 and the following day Beveridge addressed the '22. About 140 MPs were present. Although the party generally was to prove 'lukewarm and cautious' about the report,[22] primarily wary of the costs involved of implementing his recommendations,[23] he was reported to have made a 'brilliant speech', winning over many MPs.[24] 'From the talk in the lobbies afterwards the members present had evidently been impressed by his advocacy', reported *The Times*.[25] After a sub-committee considered the issue, its report was debated at the 1922 and some MPs pressed the government to establish a Ministry of Social Security.[26] By 1945, according to

Geoffrey Lewis, 'Beveridge had for the most part been accepted by the Conservative hierarchy.'[27]

The same month that Beveridge spoke to the '22, it heard from Leo Amery, over 100 MPs attending to hear him advocate various constitutional changes once peace was achieved, including the introduction of proportional representation for elections in larger boroughs, the creation of life peers, the appointment of a standing conference on employers' organisations and regular broadcasting of parliamentary proceedings 'so as to create that interest in Parliament without which it cannot live'.[28] Amery judged that the members were keenly interested: 'The idea of broadcasting seems to have gone down particularly well.'[29] He returned two years later, this time arguing for imperial preference and control. He deemed the 60 or more MPs attending to be enthusiastic. He was less sure about the party leader. 'I spoke very strongly and I wonder what kind of report Harvie Watt who was taking notes all the time will give to Winston.'[30] Although Amery's assessment of the reaction of members may have been overly optimistic, the 1922 provided a bespoke party forum for airing ideas for post-war Britain.

## The Con–Lib Dem coalition

The imperative of maintaining a distinct Conservative voice was also present when a coalition government was formed following the indecisive outcome of the 2010 general election. The situation, though, was distinct from that of 1945. As Harold Laski observed in 1950, there is a distinction 'between coalition governments in war-time, when they emphasise the national determination to unify its striking-power, and coalition governments in peace time, which usually represent the effort of politicians to compromise principles in the hope of retaining power'.[31] The situation in 2010 was unique in that it was the first time in modern British politics that a coalition resulted from the electoral arithmetic of a general election.[32] There was post-election bargaining between party leaders with David Cameron seeking and getting the acquiescence of Conservative MPs in the formation of a coalition government. It was an executive coalition, not an electoral coalition. The parties continued as distinct entities in the country, both contesting by-elections. Calls by some Tory MPs for an electoral pact were disavowed by the '22 Committee chairman, Graham Brady, and by the Liberal Democrat leader, Nick Clegg.[33]

Creating a minimal winning coalition provided a basis for some stability in government,[34] but there was the potential for policy tensions. A Coalition Agreement was agreed between the leaders. According to one study, 75 per cent of the Liberal Democrat manifesto found its way into the agreement, as against 60 per cent of the Conservative manifesto.[35] 'Overall', in the estimation of Ruth Fox, 'the Conservatives got the better of the deal in the economic arena, and the Liberal Democrats the political and constitutional reform agenda.'[36]

There was thus the potential for conflict between the party leader and the '22. Although David Cameron became Prime Minister, he lacked the usual powers of a Tory Prime Minister. Liberal Democrat leader Nick Clegg had a veto over policies. Ministerial appointments had to be shared with Liberal Democrats. There was a large number of new Tory MPs – they comprised 48 per cent of the parliamentary party – some of whom attributed their success to their own efforts and not Cameron's leadership.[37] Cameron was not seen as adhering to a clear strand of Conservative thought, but driven instead by a sense of public service.[38] This may have made it easier for him to reach agreement with the Liberal Democrats, but it created the potential for tension at times with backbenchers, tensions that in the event were realised.

These tensions were most pronounced on constitutional issues, not least the two 'red line' issues for the Liberal Democrats, electoral and House of Lords reform. There was regular dissent by Tory MPs in the division lobbies – in the first ten months of the coalition, a quarter of all Conservative MPs cast one or more votes against the government[39] – but not enough to threaten the government's majority. Where dissent found a more notable, and at times crucial, outlet was in the 1922 Committee. Tory backbenchers were sceptical about the commitment to a referendum on the use of the alternative vote as well as about House of Lords reform.

The government included members of both parties committed to the Coalition Agreement. The 1922 comprised members who were prepared, if at times unwillingly, to go into the lobbies in support of the government, but who were also able to look at issues from a purely party perspective. A notable contrast with the position in 1940 was that the 1922 executive decided at the start of the Parliament that no ministers from their coalition partner should be invited to the address the Committee.[40]

The '22 provided an outlet for disagreement with the government's direction of travel. Although MPs voted for the Parliamentary Voting Systems and Constituencies Bill, which provided for a referendum on the alternative vote, there was agitation in the '22 to ensure that the party was active in mobilising a 'no' vote in the referendum. Initially, the party leadership adopted a 'hands-off' approach, leaving the initial work on mounting a 'no' campaign to a cross-party First Past the Post group. When it appeared that the 'no' side may lose, pressure mounted for the Prime Minister to front the campaign. As we have seen, Baroness Warsi, the party chairman, had a bruising meeting with the '22. MPs wanted the party to commit more resources. The mood of the meeting was picked up by the whips. The '22 executive saw David Cameron to press on him the need to be more active in the campaign, stressing the implications of losing. As Matthew d'Ancona observed, 'Defeat in the referendum would make a scratchy mood positively poisonous. The fractious Tory tribe would become openly seditious.'[41] Cameron decided to go with his backbenchers at the expense of assuaging his coalition partner. He campaigned publicly for a 'no' vote. The '22 executive had got its way.

After the 'no' campaign triumphed, Cameron spoke at a packed meeting of the '22 and stressed the role he had played in getting donors to support the campaign. The emphasis in the confines of Committee Room 14 was on the party leader addressing the one body in the House that was confined to Tory MPs. Without the '22 as the authentic and exclusive party body operating to voice Tory interests, Cameron was unlikely to have departed from his detached position, privileging the need to keep the coalition together over the interests of the party. By reacting to the mood of the '22, he strengthened his position within the party. When he gave his end-of-year talk to the '22 in December, he received a loud cheer.

Although the principal opposition to the 2012 House of Lords Reform Bill came from a group of Conservative MPs, self-styled 'The Sensibles', led by Jesse Norman, the MP for Hereford and South Herefordshire,[42] there was tension again between the party leader and members of the '22. Since 1997, successive party leaders had advocated an elected or part-elected second chamber. This brought them into conflict with the executive of the '22 which, whenever it considered the issue, supported retaining an appointed House. In July 2007, all members bar one were opposed to a wholly elected House and only two were against a wholly appointed House.[43] At a meeting with the executive at the start of that year, David Cameron 'recognised that the mood of the Party was moving away from his own viewpoint on this which was for a partially elected House'.[44] He subsequently made clear, including in a meeting with Tory peers the following week, that it would not figure in the programme of a newly elected Conservative government. He later characterised it as constituting a 'third term' issue, in effect, one on which he proposed to take no action.

The Coalition Agreement changed the terms of trade between leader and backbenches. Cameron was committed to a policy that attracted little enthusiasm on the part of the '22 and indeed encountered growing resistance as the Parliament progressed. Speaking for the '22 executive to the Association of Conservative

Peers (ACP) in June 2011, Gavin Barwell said the proposals for Lords reform were about as popular in the Commons as they were in the Lords. The following February, Tracey Crouch reported that opposition to them was growing. When Leader of the Lords, Lord Strathclyde, addressed the '22 at the end of February 2012, enthusiasm for reform was notably lacking among the 30 or so MPs present: four put in questions, all hostile; notably, Strathclyde did not demur from the points they were making. In March, the executive met with the Prime Minister: according to one of those present, he appeared tired and gave the impression that he wished the subject of Lords reform would go away.[45] When the ACP chairman, Lord MacGregor, spoke to the '22 in June and stressed the need to maintain the primacy of the Commons, the 50 MPs present gave him a sustained round of applause.

The House of Lords Reform Bill, once introduced, engendered opposition even from Tory MPs who favoured an elected second chamber, finding fault with the method of election and especially with the provision that members could only serve one non-renewable term, thus removing any accountability to electors. Lobbying by the Prime Minister and the whips for the Bill was more formulaic than enthusiastic and they were out-performed by the energetic and military-style campaign mounted by the Sensibles. When the Bill came before the House for Second Reading, Tory opponents dominated the debate. It encountered the biggest post-war Tory dissenting lobby, with 91 Tory MPs voting against it and a further 19 abstaining. The Opposition supported it at Second Reading, ensuring it achieved a majority, but it was committed to opposing the programme motion. Realising there was no majority for the motion, the government did not move it. Attempts by David Cameron to see if a compromise with backbench dissidents was possible proved fruitless. Recognising that opponents would use the opportunity for endless debate in committee, the government accepted defeat and withdrew the Bill. Senior ministers conceded privately that the issue was dead for the rest of the Parliament.

David Cameron had agreed to a Bill on Lords reform as part of the coalition deal, but notably cooled on the idea as the Parliament progressed. He had no emotional commitment to the issue and was increasingly conscious of the impact on the party. When a small delegation from the ACP met him in late July 2012, the members stressed the need to avoid a fractious party. According to one of those present, he was very much in tune with the message.

The other major issue of contention during the Parliament was an in/out referendum on membership of the EU. This split the two parties to the coalition, though it also divided the '22. However, pressure built up during the Parliament for a referendum, proponents using meetings of the '22 to press their case. As we have seen in Chapter 5, demands for a referendum were taken beyond the confines of private meetings to the floor of the Commons and the division lobbies. David Cameron conceded the case, first for a referendum and then for it to be held before the end of 2017. Opposition from the Liberal Democrats ensured that it was not adopted as government policy. It became Conservative policy, pursued through the medium of a Private Member's Bill. The Prime Minister thus sought, as on Lords reform, to square the circle between the stance of his coalition partner and his backbenchers. The outcome in both cases was determined by the actions of his backbench supporters.

Meetings of the '22 were not the sole means of ensuring a distinctive Conservative voice was heard. The policy groups set up in the Parliament (see Chapter 7) fulfilled a similar role. They worked to ensure that the Conservative elements of the Coalition Agreement were honoured. As one group chairman told Hazell and Yong: 'It is extremely important that ministers, whilst they're working with Liberal Democrats and in a coalition, still have a very, very keen focus on what the Conservative Party, the Conservative voter in the country, thinks and feels.'[46] The groups thus complemented the full '22 in ensuring a Conservative voice throughout the Parliament.

## The exclusive forum

The key point for our purposes is the extent to which the '22 provided the means for Conservative MPs to gather as Conservative MPs to ensure that their distinct voice was heard within a government that was Conservative dominated, but that was not exclusively Conservative. The party leadership had to broker deals with the other party or parties to the government. The '22 ensured that the leader heard, if necessary, a clear party voice in considering whether to concede a policy or compromise on one with another party. It served as a conduit for a clear expression of a party view. However, it also aided the government in that meetings could absorb disquiet without it then necessarily being made public. Ministers could hear and respond to concerns expressed by backbenchers, explaining why a decision had been taken without necessarily committing to a change of policy. Their explanation may have sufficed to prevent opposition being pursued publicly.

The '22 also served a purpose in simply existing. Even if backbenchers did not raise concerns at a meeting, the fact that they knew they could do so helped assuage their fears about the coalition. If they felt a Conservative voice, or at least their voices, were not being heard, there was a mechanism through which their concerns could be raised. The '22 thus served to the benefit of both backbenchers and ministers.

## Chapter 12

# 'May I have a word, minister?' Influencing policy, challenging ministers

Most Tory ministers will not run into trouble with the 1922 Committee. Indeed, the Committee may not even appear on their radar. Some former senior ministers, when interviewed, not only had no recollection of encountering difficulties with the '22, they also could not recall addressing it. (One noted that she must have done, but could not bring to mind when she did so.) When ministers are invited to speak, it is usually to explain current policies or their stewardship of their departments. The exercise is very much one, as discussed in Chapter 9, of exchanging information. This is the norm, not the exception. However, on occasion ministers may face a critical or even hostile audience and have to work hard to carry the meeting with them. The '22 may serve to put a shot across a minister's bows or to induce the minister to introduce, change or abandon a policy. On occasion, a minister may be fighting not just to protect a policy, but also their own position. Not all have been successful, some facing such a hostile reception from the 1922 that they felt that they have had no option but to resign.

The mood of backbenchers carried especial weight in the Second World War, given the need of government to maintain a united House. Sensitivity to how members viewed the conduct of the war appeared a significant factor in the reorganisation of government in 1941. However, it was in post-war years that the impact of the '22 in inducing the resignation of ministers became apparent. The importance of the '22 lay not only in the fact of some ministers going because of pressure from, or their performance before, the '22, but also in the potential for the '22 to turn against a minister who has pursued a failing or unpopular policy or encountered scandal. Some ministers, including the Prime Minister, may appear before the '22 in order to fight for their political lives and may survive. They may also leave the meeting realising that their time is up. On occasion, that fact is conveyed to them by the chairman of the 1922.

## Policy influence

The 1922 has consequences for public policy in that it can have an input into party policy, being part of the process for producing policy advice to the leader. It may press the leader or ministers for new policies or act as a block, or at least send a warning signal, on some that are put forward by the leadership. This matters for citizens because party policy may be translated into public policy when the party is in power, which, for the Conservative Party, is more frequently the case than not.

Most backbench influence has not been exercised through the regular meetings of the '22, but rather through the '22 executive and, until the end of the twentieth century, the backbench committees. If concerns are raised by members, ministers may be invited to discuss a policy with the executive. This is when they need to justify what they plan. As we have seen in Chapter 8, some ministers have had difficult meetings with the executive or been advised of the executive's concerns over a policy. Similarly, some policies have run into trouble at backbench committee meetings, the meetings serving to put a shot across a minister's bows or inducing a change of policy.

Mostly, pressure from a backbench committee affected policy, not the fate of the minister. However, as we have seen in Chapter 7, in 1935, opposition in the Foreign Affairs Committee to the Hoare–Laval Pact was such as to contribute to the government deciding to sacrifice Foreign Secretary Sir Samuel Hoare. However, once the '22 became a key player after 1940, the focus, in terms of ministerial survival, shifted largely, though not completely, to meetings of the '22. Not completely, in that the resignation of another Foreign Secretary, Lord Carrington, followed a meeting of a backbench committee.

Pressure from the '22 may induce action, be it in the form of the leader, or other frontbenchers, attending to defend their position or in a policy change. The leader may attend to rally support, but may not necessarily succeed.

> If the Prime Minister senses strong disapproval, or if he is especially anxious to enlist sympathy for a piece of policy, he will personally attend a 1922 Committee meeting (having engineered an invitation to do so) and will address that meeting, answer questions, mingle with the members, and as a rule manage to get his way. If he fails to do so he must amend his policy.[1]

The '22 may have an influence through being sounded out on policy by ministers or front benchers, or by having a representation on bodies advising on policy. It may have an impact as a result of members being proactive, promoting a particular policy, or being reactive, members raising concerns or leading opposition to a particular policy.

## Sounding board

It is not unusual to see the '22 described as a sounding board. The recognition of the role is longstanding. As *The Times* reported in 1928, 'it has come to be recognized as an accepted channel through which the Government are able to gather the views of the rank-and-file'.[2] It was a point reiterated by Bernard Crick almost 50 years later. 'The 1922 Committee', he wrote, 'does not challenge the right of their Party Leader alone to determine policy, but it is a most effective sounding-board as to whether he is likely to be followed if he leads, or does not lead, in a particular direction.'[3]

The '22 thus serves as a body to be consulted and for leaders to determine whether they will be able to proceed with a policy, where one has been decided, or to gauge backbench opinion before deciding what to do on an issue. This role, as a sounding board, was again one fulfilled until the end of the twentieth century more frequently by the backbench committees than by the 1922. The '22 came into its own in respect of the stance taken by the party leader and when policies became so contentious as to require being rehearsed before the full '22.

Soundings may be taken on substantial issues of policy. To take various illustrative examples, in 1942 the '22 held a special meeting to discuss the situation in India, ahead of an anticipated government statement. Leo Amery, the Secretary of State for India, attended. The meeting 'provided a means of sounding-out back-bench opinion in view of the 1940 pledge to India of full Dominion status after the war'.[4] What emphasised the nature of the meeting as a sounding board was the fact that instead of Amery addressing the meeting, 'many of its members addressed Mr Amery, and he took note of their views'.[5] Although there were concerns about conceding too much to the Congress party, there appeared a greater willingness to accept change than had been apparent in the 1930s. A decade later, it was used to determine a dispute between the backbench Fuel and Power Committee and the minister. The committee chairman raised the issue at the '22. 'There both the Minister and members of the Fuel and Power Committee presented their points of view, with the result that the 1922 Committee endorsed the views of the Minister and rejected those of the Fuel and Power Committee.'[6] In November 1961, Colonial Secretary Iain Macleod came to the Committee to discuss the Commonwealth Immigration Bill,[7] a measure that proved highly contentious.

On occasion, there have been attempts to institutionalise the means of sounding out the '22. Under Margaret Thatcher's leadership, a small party coordinating committee was established, including the Chief Whip, party chairman, deputy leader of the party and the chairman of the '22. 'The committee may occasionally discuss strategy but is mainly used as a sounding board for opinions and as a channel of communication.'[8]

## Policy input

The effect on policy of the '22 became more notable in the years from 1940 and, as we have seen, was facilitated by Churchill as leader presiding rather than leading as party leader. The impact of the '22 was apparent once the party was returned to power in 1951. As we have seen, pressure from MPs in the '22 resulted in changes in policy throughout periods of Conservative government. The extent of '22 influence was variously picked up by the media. Following the resignation of the Minister of Agriculture, Thomas Dugdale, in 1954 following a meeting of the '22, the political correspondent of the *Birmingham Daily Post* reported, 'This is one of several recent instances in which the 1922 Committee has influenced Government policy. Others were the decisions on M.P.s salaries, the Judges' Remuneration Bill, and teachers' pensions.'[9] Labour MP and former Cabinet minister Patrick Gordon Walker also weighed in to argue that Britain was being run by the 'hidden hand' of the 1922 Committee, having had important victories on commercial television, MPs' pay and the Suez base. The 1922 Committee, he said, had exploited the government's small majority and 'has taken policy-making into its own hands'.[10] The influence of the '22 continued under Churchill's successors: 'backbench opinion often undoubtedly influences the Prime Minister – as it seems to have influenced Mr Macmillan in his African and European policy'.[11]

Whereas some issues arise as discrete items of contention, some engage backbench disquiet, sometimes opposition, on a continuing basis. Two prominent examples are European integration – a fault line of British politics since 1945, encountering bruising conflict under Conservative governments from that of Macmillan onwards – and House of Lords reform. As we have seen, John Major struggled to mobilise support in the '22 for his European policy. Backbench pressure led David Cameron to do a U-turn and embrace a referendum on the UK's membership of the EU. The issue of European integration effectively ended both the Cameron and May governments, the origins traceable to stances taken by Conservative backbenchers.

Backbench opposition led to the demise of the 2012 House of Lords Reform Bill, though that was not the first occasion when members of the '22 had influenced the party's stance on the second chamber. In 1968, when the Labour government introduced the Parliament (No. 2) Bill to reform the House of Lords, backbench dissent tended to outweigh the lukewarm support for the Bill offered by the Conservative front bench. Reginald Maudling outlined the stance of the front bench at a meeting of the 1922 attended by 180 members: 'this was followed by a lively discussion, indicating that a large number of those present would vote against the Bill on Second Reading'.[12]

In the event, although the front bench advised voting for the Bill, Tory MPs were allowed a free vote: more voted against the Bill than voted for (105 to 58).[13] The government proposed to guillotine the Bill. As John Boyd-Carpenter recalled, 'with a substantial section of the Conservative Party fighting the Bill hard, the leadership would have got into a lot of trouble if it had not voted against a Guillotine. This was made very plain at the 1922 Committee...'.[14] The party made clear it would oppose a guillotine motion. Given the scale of opposition on its own benches, the government decided not to move the motion; opponents used the opportunity for protracted debate on amendments and the government dropped the Bill.

Even large government majorities, most notably under Margaret Thatcher, were not sufficient to protect all government

policies from the effects of pressure from members of the '22.[15]
Thus, for example, 'Keith Joseph … was forced to abandon the
idea of making parents contribute to university tuition fees in
December 1984 after coming under fire from massed ranks of
backbenchers in the Chamber and then later on that same day in
the 1922 Committee.'[16] The '22 meeting was actually a meeting of
the backbench Education Committee, but over 200 MPs attended.
When one MP told Joseph to scrap the proposal, there was cheering.[17] Of 33 speakers, only three offered the minister guarded support. The Thatcher government was also the first government in
the twentieth century with a working majority to lose a Bill on
Second Reading, when Conservative backbenchers joined with the
Opposition to defeat the 1986 Shops Bill on Sunday trading.[18]

The government of John Major encountered conflict not only
over European integration, but also over a range of other issues.
As we have seen, Environment Secretary Michael Heseltine had
meetings with the 1922 executive over his Bill to reform local government – conceding that a provision for local referendums should
be scrapped – and the policy of pit closures. He agreed to widen
a review into pit closures. The issue of European integration,
as already recorded, was a running issue of contention, leading
David Cameron to concede an in/out referendum on membership
of the European Union, and essentially ending Theresa May's
premiership after she failed to make changes to the Withdrawal
Agreement that garnered enough support for its passage.

Both Boris Johnson and Liz Truss modified or changed policies
under pressure from the 1922. In the case of the former, it was
largely in respect of ending lockdown and requiring mask-wearing
towards the end of the COVID-19 pandemic and in the case of
the latter the government's economic strategy.

The '22 thus influences policies introduced by ministers.
However, influence can be more institutionalised and consistent,
with the 1922 having an input into the formation of party policy
through having members serve on policy groups. In the lead-up to

the 1955 general election, a group of ministers and members of the party's Research Department formed a research study group (RSG), producing a skeleton draft manifesto. It kept in touch with progress of policy work through dinners at the Commons, to which all chairmen of party committees were invited. 'Finally, in September 1954, Sir Derek Walker-Smith, chairman of the 1922 Committee, was coopted onto the RSG for the run up to the election, so as to keep it in touch with opinion on the back bench.'[19] As we have seen, members of the '22 formed about half the membership of policy groups established under Heath's period of opposition from 1965 to 1970.[20] Margaret Thatcher encouraged ministers to meet with the officers of backbench committees. She initially saw them on a rota basis. Members of the '22 engaged in the policy groups established by David Cameron.

## Ministers under fire

However, where the '22 comes into its own on occasion, and attracts the attention of the media, is when criticism of policies or a minister's actions put the minister's future in doubt. On occasion, concerns are raised privately with the Prime Minister by the chairman of the '22. Macmillan recorded John Morrison voicing disquiet over the performance of two party chairmen, Lord Hailsham[21] and Iain Macleod.[22] A minister may appear before the 1922 to fight for political survival. Some do emerge at least still in post. Others have not always been successful. The occasions when ministers resign because of a bruising meeting with the 1922 are rare, but are salutary in reminding others of their political fragility.

## Survival

There have been various instances of ministers, or frontbenchers, pursuing unpopular policies and having to appear before the '22 to justify their position and in effect their political survival.

Sometimes, it has been a case of the party leader apologising for a minister's stance and trying to calm the situation.

The history of the '22, recounted in Part I, is marked by ministers attending to defend their policies, ranging from Home Secretary William Joynson-Hicks in 1929 on the Shop Hours Bill to party leader Michael Howard in 2004 on identity cards. In most cases, although they may be bruising encounters, the future of the speaker is not in doubt. At other times, it is not so clear, and a minister may be having to justify their own continuance in office as much as their policy. The key indication that they are in trouble is when they are effectively summoned to appear before the '22.

Various ministers came under pressure in the 1950s. Other than Agriculture Minister Thomas Dugdale, the Minister of Fuel and Power, Geoffrey Lloyd, managed to see off criticism of his handling of the coal industry. 'He has had to face severe criticism from his own Party and although he is now proud of the way he handled the 1922 Committee when it was clamouring for his blood it was touch and go at the time.'[23] Another vulnerable figure was Education Minister Florence Horsbrugh in 1954 'who has incurred the displeasure of the Committee for her support of a plan to increase teachers' contribution to a pension fund. It is significant that a Bill designed to implement the higher payments has still not been given a second reading.'[24] Though not going as a result directly of pressure from the 1922, she resigned that October.

Another minister coming under fire was Postmaster-General Reginald Bevins in 1963 after he gave a press interview about his policy for television, a policy that was unpopular with some backbenchers. The ensuing story attracted criticism from MPs, a number suggesting that the Prime Minister should dismiss him.

> That evening I saw the Chief Whip, Martin Redmayne, and the Chairman of the 1922 Committee, John Morrison at their request. I readily agreed to attend the 1922 Committee on the following day. There I explained the circumstances in which the interview took place. I justified many of the comments in the article ... I ended

by emphasising that my one wish was to hack my way through the television jungle and to emerge for the party's sake with an honest solution. The meeting accepted my explanation.[25]

Macmillan in 1961 recorded that his Minister of Agriculture 'went to the 1922 Committee and was not very successful. He was in great difficulty and perhaps told them too little or too much. But he has courage and vigour and will recover from this slight set-back.'[26] Given Macmillan's propensity for understatement, the minister may have been in a situation where the outcome was not that clear.

In November 1973, Chancellor Tony Barber was summoned to justify his emergency credit squeeze. He appealed for a 'blank cheque' in terms of the measures that needed to be taken, but he faced criticism from the 18 or 19 members who spoke.[27] He survived the experience.

Employment Secretary Jim Prior in 1981 was similarly summoned and survived. He took the view that the majority would want reassurance that the government's approach was the right one, that he had his brief under control and that his judgement was sound. 'They did not want a discursive analysis on the detailed arguments. So I kept my comments short and to the point, and tried to sound as crisp and confident as possible. It did the trick. There were a few criticisms from predictable quarters, but I had won the Parliamentary Party's support.'[28]

In 2006, Shadow Education Secretary David Willetts made a speech arguing that academic selection was no longer the way to transform the life chances of bright poor pupils, but rather served to entrench advantage. He was immediately challenged by some backbenchers. The party leader, David Cameron, was persuaded that Willetts should explain his speech at a meeting of the '22. 'Far from allowing for a managed deflation, the meeting in Committee Room 14 turned into a ritual humiliation … Dangerously, his critics came from all sections of the party.'[29]

Only two spoke in his support; otherwise, he faced a string of denunciations.[30] In the event, he managed to hang on, but the situation was touch and go. He had a searing experience in appearing before his critics.

Not all ministers are quite so successful. Ministers in the Commons had the advantage of knowing the parliamentary party and often how to handle it. Ministers in the Lords were not always so fortunate. One MP recalled two ministers, Lord Young of Graffham and Lord Bellwin, encountering difficult meetings of the '22, having to contend with personal insults as well as criticisms.[31] It was a senior minister in the Lords who was to prove a notable casualty.

Most significantly, as we have seen in Part I, there have been instances of the party leader appearing before the '22 in order to fight for their political lives, not least Theresa May, on more than one occasion. We return to the position of the leader in the next chapter. Our concern here is ministers. Not all have managed to stay in post once they have come under fire from the '22.

## Resignation

The reputation of the '22 as a powerful body, not least in the perception of the media, comes not so much from ministers surviving bruising meetings – though that can make headlines – but from the occasions when ministers or frontbenchers have realised they do not have the confidence of the '22 and have fallen on their swords.

The most prominent example of this in the 1950s is that of Agriculture Minister Thomas Dugdale. Other high-profile cases were to follow in later periods of Tory government, the most notable, but not the only, resignations being those of Foreign Secretary Lord Carrington over the Falkland Islands, Trade and Industry Secretary Sir Leon Brittan over the Westland crisis, National Heritage Secretary David Mellor over personal scandal, Trade and Industry Secretary Nicholas Ridley over an interview about Germany, and Chief Whip Andrew Mitchell over an alleged altercation at the gates of Downing Street.

Crichel Down in 1954 was a celebrated case that has been popularly portrayed as an instance of a minister resigning because he accepted responsibility for errors made by officials in his department. However, the minister, Thomas Dugdale, supported the position of his department (to retain Crichel Down, taken for war use, as one unit rather than sell it to its original owners); Conservative MPs disagreed with the policy. At a meeting on 15 July 1954, attended by 140 members, the Home Secretary, Sir David Maxwell-Fyfe, opened a discussion on Crichel Down.[32] A dozen or more members spoke. Dugdale attended, but did not speak; Maxwell-Fyfe responded to the comments. In a debate in the House, Dugdale announced a reversal of the policy as well as his own resignation. Herbert Morrison, speaking from the Opposition despatch box, declared 'Now the 1922 Committee has the scalp of a minister.'[33] As S. E. Finer observed, the opposition seemed more sympathetic to the minister than his own backbenchers. 'It is a fair inference from the distribution and tenor of the speeches on the Conservative side that Sir Thomas has lost the confidence of at least the farmers' MPs … Evidently his back-benchers disliked the policy of his department as well as his administration.'[34]

As the political correspondent of the *Birmingham Daily Post* reported, Dugdale, 'I understand, made up his mind to resign after attending a meeting of the 1922 Committee last Thursday.'[35]

That the pressure came from backbenchers was clear from Churchill's letter reluctantly accepting his resignation. As the *Yorkshire Post and Leeds Intelligencer* reported, 'Sir Winston's warm response will inevitably be read as an implied rebuke to those Conservative Backbench MPs – and they formed the majority of the party – who have so persistently attacked Sir Thomas.'[36]

However, the most significant period for resignations was in the period of Conservative governments under Margaret Thatcher and John Major. Since then, the most significant casualties have not been ministers, but the party leader.

In 1982, as already recorded in Chapter 4, Foreign Secretary Lord Carrington faced a hostile reception when he appeared before the backbench Defence Committee – but which was, in effect, a meeting of the '22 – to defend the government's stance on the Falkland Islands and, taken aback by the scale of the hostility, decided to resign. As Defence Secretary John Nott recorded, 'It seemed to me then – and still does now – that it was the party meeting that did him in, not the newspapers that called for his resignation.'[37] Carrington was not used to facing a critical audience of MPs and the bruising experience left him feeling unable to carry on.

The Westland crisis of 1986, involving a dispute between Cabinet ministers over whether to favour an American or European bid for the Westland helicopter company, led to the resignation of Trade and Industry Secretary Leon Brittan after he was accused of leaking an extract of a confidential letter from the Solicitor General. He came under fire when he appeared before the '22. 'The savagery of the personal attacks', recalled one MP, 'was quite extraordinary.'[38] 'On 23 January', wrote Ian Gilmour, 'Brittan, who despite his intelligence had never gained a parliamentary following and was widely regarded as Mrs Thatcher's creation, was savaged by the 1922 Committee in one of its ugliest moods. He loyally resigned the next day.'[39] The Prime Minister was unable to save him. 'She ever afterwards maintained the position that she had wanted Brittan to stay while the 1922 Committee forced him to go.'[40]

In 1988, a junior health minister, Edwina Currie, said that 'most of the egg production in this country, sadly, is now affected with salmonella'. This was followed by a 60 per cent drop in egg sales and the destruction of about 4 million hens. The minister was widely criticised by the poultry industry and by Tory MPs. Pressure from members of the '22 meant that her position was untenable and she resigned. 'The final blow fell when Cranley Onslow, chairman of the Tory back bench 1922 Committee, called on Mrs Thatcher to express the outrage of MPs.'[41] Currie recounted that she was told by one member of the 1922 executive that some members had spoken up for her, but Onslow had nonetheless gone to the Prime Minister to say they were unanimous that she had to go.[42]

In 1990, the *Spectator* published an interview with Trade and Industry Secretary Nicholas Ridley, in which he attacked Germany, describing economic and monetary union as a 'German racket' designed to take over the whole of Europe. 'The Chief Whip, Tim Renton, conveyed to Mrs Thatcher the view of the executive of the 1922 Committee that, if Ridley did not resign, his views would be taken to be hers (which, to a large extent, they were). The writing was on the wall'.[43] Ridley resigned. As one of his Cabinet colleagues noted: 'He was in effect drummed out by the reaction of a broad majority of Conservative MPs.'[44]

In 1993, junior minister Michael Mates resigned because of his association with a controversial businessman, Asil Nadir, who had fled the country. 'Senior Tory MPs', reported *The Independent*, 'complained that Mr Major appeared to be waiting for the Tory backbench 1922 Committee to deliver the *coup de grâce* at its weekly meeting last night. "He should either have stood by Mates, or sacked him. There is complete lack of command," said one of Mr Major's former leadership campaign team.'[45] National Heritage Secretary David Mellor was seen as a competent minister, but he too fell because of a scandal. He was the subject of tabloid interest after a former mistress published a 'kiss and tell' story about their relationship, but what did for his political career was the discovery that he had accepted a month-long family holiday in Marbella from the daughter of the finance director of the Palestine Liberation Organisation (PLO). He received a telephone call from the chairman of the '22, Sir Marcus Fox. 'Sir Marcus telephoned Mellor this morning and gave him the black spot. It's all over bar the "personal statement".'[46] John Major indicated that Fox had got in ahead of him. 'I was inclined towards asking for David's resignation', he recalled, 'but what finally led to it was the response of the backbench 1922 Committee, who were determined that David should go.'[47]

It was some years before another minister was to go because of losing the support of the '22. In October 2012, Chief Whip Andrew Mitchell endured a media storm after an altercation with police officers in Downing Street. His position appeared under threat. His future was discussed at the 1922 Committee. According to Mitchell: 'Twelve colleagues spoke about the position of the Chief Whip. While most were supportive, four were not.'[48] This is a somewhat optimistic interpretation. At the crowded meeting – there were over 100 MPs present – the first to support him drew muted applause; if anything, applause was louder for the members saying he should go. The critics included a former whip and members of the 2010 intake. Most MPs remained silent. 'At the Chief Whip's usual private meeting with the officers of the 1922 Committee', Mitchell recorded, 'I asked for a supportive statement, which the Chairman and his colleagues, while personally sympathetic, felt they could not give. During the course of that day, I decided I needed their clear backing to remain in post.'[49] The following day, after consulting some trusted colleagues, he resigned.

An article on Mitchell's resignation, by Sue Cameron in the *Daily Telegraph*, summed up the perceived impact of the 1922: 'When the 1922 committee comes calling, it's time to go.'[50] Occasions when the 1922 have called, deciding whether to issue a black spot or not, are rare, but the very fact that they do happen serves as a lesson to ministers. There is always the prospect that a policy, or a single statement or action, may generate disquiet or fierce opposition on the part of backbenchers. A crowded meeting of the '22 may result in a minister, or the whips, realising that the minister's position is tenuous or, at worst, untenable. For most ministers, the '22 will not impinge notably on their consciousness or activity. But it can. And in recent years, for the occupant of one ministerial office, that of Prime Minister, it has.

# Chapter 13

# 'The men in grey suits': choosing a leader

The executive of the 1922 has been portrayed as the body that told a party leader when it was time to go.[1] 'Often described as "the men in grey suits", the officers of the 1922 would be responsible for telling the Prime Minister when he or she had lost the confidence of the party and should exit No. 10 as swiftly as possible,' wrote one joint secretary of the Committee. 'Such influence was partially diminished when the Conservative Party started electing their leaders in 1965.'[2]

This, though, is a popular myth. No Tory leader was ousted by a visit by 'the men in grey suits'.[3] The changes of 1965 empowered the 1922, not limited it. Prior to then, some party leaders had been under pressure to retire, but they went more because of visits by the equivalent of men in white coats (their doctors) than by the executive of the 1922. That applied to Eden and Macmillan. Churchill eventually gave way to age and Douglas-Home to the feeling he had had enough: his announcement to the 1922 in 1965 that he was retiring took members by surprise. Before Churchill's premiership, the 1922, as we have seen in Chapter 2, was largely supportive of the party leader and lacked the political clout to determine his departure.

The 1922 was nonetheless important after 1940 in a way it had not been before in relation to the leadership. Its involvement was more in the choice of a leader than in dispatching one. It had some input into deliberations over the succession in 1957, but it was not the decisive influence: the important soundings were those taken of Cabinet ministers. The chairman of the 1922, John Morrison, was consulted; according to Robert Blake, he 'assessed backbench opinion with surprising confidence from the Isle of Islay'.[4]

In 1963, it played a greater role. The 1922 executive did endorse the process developed by Macmillan to ensure party views were canvassed and considered in identifying a successor. There was, though, wariness of anything that may smack of interfering with the prerogative of the monarch. Macmillan, according to Rab Butler, 'wants to preserve a proper degree of the Queen's choice and does not want a diktat from the 1922 Committee'.[5] Insofar as the 1922 had an impact, it was in terms of the officers persuading Lord Home to let his name be put forward and in conveying to Butler that he was not acceptable. As we have seen in Chapter 3, John Morrison told Butler, 'The chaps won't have you.'[6] Morrison was a much-underrated influence, his impact overlooked in Randolph Churchill's study of the fight for the leadership.[7] Notably when the Chief Whip and Morrison saw Macmillan in hospital, the Prime Minister spent some minutes alone with the chairman of the 1922.[8]

## Electing the leader

In 1965, Douglas-Home installed a method of election for his successors. To be elected, a candidate had to achieve an overall majority and the majority had to represent at least 15 per cent of the votes cast; if no candidate achieved that, a second ballot took place which new candidates could enter, with the winner requiring only an overall majority. If no candidate achieved that, the top three candidates went through to a third ballot with the alternative vote method of election being utilised.

Since then, there have been changes to the rules,[9] the 1922 moving when problems have appeared with the process. The first major, indeed, fundamental change took place in 1975, when the leadership moved, in the terminology of one backbench MP, from being freehold to leasehold. Party leader Edward Heath conceded the case for the leader to be subject to re-election and, as recorded in Chapter 4, established a committee under Lord Home – with members drawn from different parts of the party (1922 Committee, National Union, party chairman, Chief Whip and two peers) – to devise the rules. As Home's biographer noted, 'if Heath thought Home's committee would produce an anodyne revision, he was in for a rude awakening'.[10] The principal concern of the recommendations was to ensure that a leader who had lost the support of the party could be challenged. If a ballot showed that MPs wanted a change, then subsequent ballots would determine the candidate most likely to unite the party.[11] There was discussion as to whether the franchise should extend beyond the parliamentary party, but the Committee decided against it,[12] though agreeing that the party outside Parliament should be consulted.

It also recommended that the leader should be subject to annual election, within four weeks of the start of a session and within three to six months of the start of a Parliament. This provision did not distinguish between when the party was in government or opposition, so a Conservative Prime Minister could be subject to challenge. Though this is sometimes viewed as an oversight, Douglas-Home was apparently aware that such a challenge was possible.[13]

The Committee moved promptly and produced its report within three weeks. Heath, as we have seen (in Chapter 4), was voted out of the leadership, to be replaced by Margaret Thatcher.

The provisions for electing the leader vested major power in the hands of the 1922 Committee and especially the chairman. From 1965 to 1997, leaders were elected by the party's MPs and since 1975 have served at the pleasure of the party's MPs. Four have gone because of the actions of electors. Major, Hague and Howard resigned because of leading the party to defeat in a general election and Cameron because of losing the referendum on leaving the European Union. The other leaders – Heath, Thatcher, Duncan Smith, May, Johnson and Truss – have gone because they have lost the confidence of their MPs, most removed or wounded, more or less fatally, by votes triggered by members of the '22 dissatisfied with their leadership. Since 1998, in order to gain election, leaders have had to appeal to a substantial number of the party's MPs as well as a majority of the party membership, but their continuance in post rests on the confidence of the party's MPs.

The rules agreed in 1975 and in 1998 each generated the conditions for instability. The problem with the 1975 rules, as we have noted, is that the leader was subject to annual election. Threat of a challenge, even if it emanated from a few disgruntled backbenchers, could generate media stories that undermined the party leader. The issue became acute when Margaret Thatcher was Prime Minister and backbench critics raised the possibility of her being challenged for the leadership. This occurred early on in her premiership, not least in 1981 over the government's economic policy, with reports of a possible backbench challenge to her leadership in the autumn. It became reality in 1989 when Sir Anthony Meyer mounted his leadership challenge. Although he was not deemed a serious candidate, rather a 'stalking horse' for a more serious challenger who never came forward, his actions prompted the '22 executive to appoint a sub-committee to look again at the rules.

In the wake of Meyer's challenge, the 1922 modified the rules, requiring the names of the proposer and seconder of a candidate to be made public. A more substantial change was made after Thatcher's loss of the leadership in 1990, with the requirement being introduced that an election could only be triggered if 10 per cent of Tory MPs wrote to the chairman of the 1922 requesting one.

This change did not affect the operation of the rules governing the ballots. Margaret Thatcher in 1990 fell four votes short of reaching the super-majority imposed by the requirement for the overall majority to represent 15 per cent of the MPs voting. She got 204 votes. In subsequent ballots, the requirement for a super-majority no longer pertained. In the second ballot, John Major got 185 votes. The failure to hold a third ballot meant that there was no opportunity for him to gain a larger vote share. He was thus elected with a smaller number of votes than Thatcher had obtained in the first ballot.[14]

Under William Hague, further changes occurred. Hague's preference was for a relatively high percentage of 25 per cent of MPs to request a confidence vote. The 1922 executive pressed for a lower threshold and got its way. On 22 January 1998, the leader met the executive and effectively agreed their proposal, hammered out earlier in the day, for a 15 per cent threshold, with the leader not able to stand for re-election if no confidence was carried by a simple majority. 'It would have been a bad day for the parliamentary party', recorded one member of the executive, 'if he had rolled over us. In the event he doesn't.'[15]

The executive, sometimes the chairman, has also on occasion taken unilateral action. In 1995, John Major reached agreement with '22 chairman Sir Marcus Fox that, following the leadership contest triggered by Major, there would be no further elections during the lifetime of the Parliament.[16] The decision was taken, as Norman Lamont noted, without the executive consulting anyone.[17] Other decisions are within the discretion of the chairman, such as deciding, usually after consultation with the leader, how soon a vote of confidence will take place.

It is also in the gift of the '22 as to how many MPs are required to nominate a leadership contender. When elections were first held, it was two. This was increased to eight in 2019 and 20 in the first leadership election in 2022. As we have seen, following the resignation of Liz Truss, the executive decided it would be 100. The chairman also agrees the length of an election campaign and the '22 arranges hustings for leadership candidates. In 2016, each candidate had a 15-minute slot, names being pulled out of a hat to determine the speaking order. Andrea Leadsom recalled speaking at the first of two hustings: 'And I really messed up.' She had not had time to prepare properly. 'Big mistake. This was perhaps the toughest electorate on the planet; cynical and many openly hostile.'[18]

## Removing leaders

Before 1965, backbenchers could make their views known, and may have influenced the leader's decision to go, but the occasions were exceptional. As we saw in Chapter 3, there was frequent disquiet expressed about Churchill's leadership after 1945, but it was not sufficient to ease him out of the leadership. There was dissatisfaction with Eden's leadership almost from the point he entered No. 10. He was seen, not least by some colleagues, as not up to the task. Douglas-Home was the subject of pressure from some backbenchers, who had pressed the executive of the '22 for a debate on his leadership. He told his Chief Whip, Willie Whitelaw, that he would stand down unless Whitelaw persuaded him it was in the best interests of the party to stay. Whitelaw apparently took the view that his reputation would be enhanced if he went, rather than waiting for the pressure to become irresistible.[19]

The '22 has become a major actor because of the introduction of leadership elections. The decision in 1998 to enlarge the electorate limited the power of the '22, in that the MPs narrowed the candidates down to two and the final decision was handed to party members, but the way in which the process operates enhances the potential for the leader to be removed by a vote of no confidence or, less formally, by a visit by the chairman of the '22 – in every instance so far, it has been Graham Brady – telling the leader that she or he has lost the confidence of the party's MPs. Surviving a vote of confidence is not sufficient to keep the leader in office. In practice, expectations, both under the old and the new rules, were such that an incumbent had not only to clear the formal hurdle, but also win 'convincingly'.[20] Failure to do so could result in a leader being seriously, if not fatally, wounded. May and Johnson failed to win 'convincingly' and Major was close to falling below the hurdle, not least the one he set himself, of such a win.[21] As Gyles Brandreth noted of the Major result, 'The truth is it's good enough, just.'[22]

In December 2018, Theresa May faced a no confidence vote when 15 per cent of Tory MPs had submitted letters. She survived by 200 votes to 117, but the vote was not decisive and meant most backbenchers had voted against her. Continuing controversy over the EU withdrawal agreement led to calls for her to resign. As we have seen, at a meeting of the 1922 on 27 March 2019, she failed to commit to a date for her departure if the agreement was passed by the House. On 24 April 2019, the executive discussed changing the rule that a further confidence vote could not take place for another year. This followed two former chairs of the 1922, Archie Hamilton and Michael Spicer, having written an article for the *Daily Telegraph* arguing that the rules could be changed. A proposal that an early additional vote could take place was narrowly defeated. On 16 May, the executive met Theresa May in her office in the Commons and told her that it was time for her to go. After a failed attempt to bolster support for the withdrawal agreement, May, as already noted (see Chapter 5), succumbed to the inevitable and, on the morning of 24 May, after seeing Graham Brady, stood outside No. 10 and announced her resignation.

Her successor, Boris Johnson, although achieving an absolute majority of MPs in the final ballot, never had a notably secure base in the parliamentary party. Like May, he was not one for mixing in the Palace and utilising informal space to rally support. He was described by one journalist as a loner at heart and 'strangely unclubbable'.[23] However, his enforced departure from No. 10 – less than three years after Theresa May's resignation – was triggered not by the 1922 Committee but by somewhat different 'men (and women) in grey suits', in this case, members of his own government. However, as with Margaret Thatcher's departure in 1990 and Theresa May's in 2019, this followed a vote by the party's MPs that effectively meant that it was a case of when, rather than if, the leader gave up the reins of office. As we have recorded (see Chapter 5), May, Johnson and Truss resigned following a meeting with the chairman of the '22.

Central to any analysis of leadership elections is the role of the 1922 Committee and especially the chairman. Before 1965, the '22 was not formally, nor in practice, the body that determined who became leader. Since then, it has been the core player. Since 1998, it has shared the role with the party membership, but the very nature of the election contests has enhanced the likelihood of the '22 taking central stage not so much as the maker, but rather the slayer, of party leaders.

The key point here was encapsulated in Thomas Quinn's discussion of Iain Duncan Smith's loss of the party leadership: 'The fact that there was an eviction mechanism enabled backbenchers to play the principal role in ousting Duncan Smith.'[24] It is the backbenchers that are now the key actors and the way the rules work facilitate them moving against a leader chosen by a method that does not rest on establishing, as had been the case under the Douglas-Home rules, the overwhelming endorsement of the party's MPs.[25] And as Quinn's study concluded, one of the institutional features that make it easiest for intra-party actors to evict leaders is anonymity for those who wish to instigate a vote.[26] Letters sent to the chairman of the 1922 Committee calling for a vote of confidence remain confidential, unless the letter writer wishes to confirm that they have written. How MPs vote in a leadership ballot is secret, as is the identity of those forcing it. 'More than any other institutional device', wrote Quinn, 'the secret ballot reduces the risks to those who want to evict the leader. In doing so, it solves the rebels' collective-action problem for them and reduces the costs to those leading the rebellion of mobilising opposition.'[27] As we noted in Chapter 1, institutions and processes are not neutral in their effect.

## 'Uneasy lies the head that wears the crown'

The Douglas-Home rules were designed to produce a leader who was in the strongest position to unite the party. The rules agreed in 1998 ended that principle. As the rules operate, if there are more than two candidates, eliminating ballots are held, or one ballot if there are only three candidates, but the mischief lies in the fact that there are three candidates in the final ballot, with the top two going through to election by the party membership. A candidate may thus be in the last two having gained the support of a low percentage of the party's MPs. This was demonstrated when the rules were applied for the first time in 2001, Duncan Smith being elected as leader by the membership, having gained the votes of only one-third of the parliamentary party. It was also marked in 2022, when Liz Truss got 32 per cent of MPs' votes in the final ballot, just edging ahead of Penny Mordaunt. Indeed, of the five contested elections since the rules were introduced in which there were three or more candidates, three (2001, 2005 and 2022) resulted in a leader being elected who did not gain an absolute majority in the final ballot. Only Theresa May in 2016 and Boris Johnson in 2019 received an absolute majority in the final ballot of MPs, though, as we have seen, their premierships were to fall foul of other developments, leading to them facing votes of confidence.

The problem inherent in this process has been recognised both by some of the candidates as well as by the 1922 executive. As we noted in Chapter 5, Andrea Leadsom was conscious she did not enjoy the confidence of backbenchers and this induced her withdrawal from the race. As she recalled: 'There was a real worry that if I was elected by the membership in the face of resistance from the parliamentary party, I could face a vote of no confidence within days of taking office, causing serious turmoil in the party.'[28]

It is an issue that has exercised the executive as well as the full '22. The problem was clearly apparent following the vote of no confidence in Iain Duncan Smith. In November 2003, the executive was unanimous in the view that the 1922 should seek to return to the practice of the 1922 electing the leader.[29] In 2005, new party chairman Francis Maude produced a consultation paper criticising the 1998 rules. It argued that it was wrong in principle for one set of electors to have the power to choose the leader and a different group to have the power to remove him or her. Party members, it contended, could not know the candidates as well as MPs.[30] As we have seen, as part of the Howard reforms discussed in 2005, the '22 wanted to return to the election of the leader by MPs. Various proposals were considered, initially that the party Convention should rank candidates' names and with MPs then having the final vote.[31] Michael Howard's proposal that candidates nominated by 10 per cent of the party would be voted on, with the candidate supported by the party Convention being guaranteed a place in each round, was rejected as a recipe for an MPs versus membership conflict.[32] The executive pressed for a compromise whereby local associations would be informed of the candidates and send back their two preferences listed in order. MPs could then consider these when voting in a final elimination ballot.[33] None of the proposals was agreed. As we have seen in Chapter 4, Howard's proposals were rejected at several meetings of the '22: 'as Howard scanned the room for support on one occasion he could only find two MPs who were prepared to speak up in his support'.[34] There was a bad-tempered meeting between the executive and Howard and his team.[35] In 2006, the executive discussed a paper from Sir John Stanley on leadership election rules and agreed to press for MP-only elections when in government, facilitating a rapid election.[36]

The instability inherent in the leadership election rules has generated conflict within the party, with the 1922 Committee and the Party Board taking opposing positions. The '22 argues the case for a reversion to election by MPs, while the Board will not give up the power of the party membership to have the final say. When the '22 introduced the requirement in the second leadership election of 2022 for a candidate to be nominated by 100 MPs and only one candidate, Rishi Sunak, was nominated, a group of party activists, including party donor Lord Cruddas, sought to take legal action challenging the process.

This situation limits the '22 in the choice of party leader while at the same time creating conditions where it may be more prone to exercise the power that does rest exclusively with it, that is, to remove a leader. The method of removing the leader may be clean and sharp by passing a vote of no confidence. It may be messy by holding a confidence vote that is not carried, but with the minority being so sizeable as to indicate a limited tenure. Or it may be the consequence of the threat of a vote. As we have seen, the executive has variously discussed changing the rule that prohibits the leader facing a no confidence vote within a year of one being held or within a year of being elected leader. It has done so under successive premierships since that of Theresa May, up to and including that of Rishi Sunak. Early in 2023, there were reports that the '22 would consider a rule change if the party did badly in the May local elections.

The rules for electing the leader have thus created what amounts to an invitation to struggle, a leader who has gained election through the votes of the party membership having to maintain the confidence of a parliamentary party that may not have voted for him or her to be leader. The skills necessary to appeal to party members may not be the same as those required for effective leadership of a parliamentary party and of government. Leaders have been vulnerable since the power to vote them out was introduced and that vulnerability has been most potent since 1998. Since then, as we have noted, national votes – two general elections and a referendum – have ended the premiership of three party leaders, not as many as ended by the party's MPs and the same number as those brought to an end following a visit by 1922 Committee chairman Graham Brady. The 1922 Committee has come a long way since 1923, when a request from the chairman of the '22 to see the Prime Minister held no particular fears for the occupant of No. 10. Since 2010, when a leader has been under attack by their own MPs, the message that 'the chairman of the 1922 Committee would like to see you' is akin to being offered a cigar and a revolver.

## Chapter 14

# Conclusion: the 1922 in British politics

We end as we began. The 1922 Committee, a century after it came into being, remains little known, and, as Arthur Evans MP put it in his letter to *The Times* in 1942, 'much abused and sadly misunderstood'.[1] There are two principal reasons for a general lack of awareness, and some misrepresentation, of its activity.

The first, and most important, explaining why it is little known, is that it is not at the forefront of British politics and policy making. That role is fulfilled by the government. A basic feature of the Westminster system of government is that it is executive-centric.[2] Cameras focus on 10 Downing Street. Ministers appear at the despatch box in the two Houses to explain and justify their policies. They trawl the television studios to justify their actions. The government's conduct of economic policy and of other issues attracts the headlines. Tory governments rely on their capacity to convey that they are competent in statecraft and handling the affairs of the nation, especially public finance.[3]

By comparison, the 1922 Committee is seen as a minor player. For most of its history, it has not been much in the public eye. When it has been, it has suffered from the second reason for being little understood. That is its name. Its counterpart, the Parliamentary Labour Party, has a name that conveys what it is. The name 'the 1922 Committee' confuses rather than enlightens. As we observed in the introduction, some scholars and political commentators – and at times even members of the 1922 Committee executive – have been unaware of when, and why, it was formed. References to it in some politics texts and in media stories get either or both the year of its foundation, and the reasons for it coming into being, wrong. Even in 2022, some senior past and present Tory MPs tried to link its formation to the Carlton Club meeting of October 1922. Even when informed that its name did not derive from that famous gathering, some still sought to suggest a connection, such as the meeting leading to a more independent environment on the Conservative benches that was conducive to the formation of the 1922. There is no evidence to sustain these assertions. As we have seen, the motivation was more parochial and practical.

The 1922 Committee has, however, come to play a role, sometimes a critical one, in British politics. It matters because Parliament matters. Parliament is the authoritative arena in which the battle between competing parties takes place. It retains the power to say no to the executive. This coercive power gives it leverage.[4] Members may persuade, may influence, the executive because it rests on the House to enact its measures and to sustain it in office. As we recounted in Chapter 1, and it bears repetition, that activity takes place not just in the formal space – the proceedings in the chamber and committee rooms – but also the informal space, where members meet to chat and exchange information,[5] and also, and at times crucially, private space, where members gather in organised form, be it private advocacy groups or parliamentary parties. Constitutionally, a government rests on the confidence of the House.[6] The political reality is that this means usually relying on the confidence of its own MPs – Anthony King's intra-party mode of executive–legislative relations (see Chapter 11). Prime ministers thus need to ensure the support of their backbenchers. The means of doing so is through the parliamentary party. If that support is withdrawn, they cannot survive.

The 1922 Committee is now the body that determines, jointly with the party's membership, who is the Conservative leader and

# Conclusion

has the independent capacity to decide who remains the leader. That makes it a key player in the politics of the Conservative Party. As the party, more often than not over the past century, has been the party in government, that has consequences for the governance of the UK. Since 1965, the 1922 has elected, alone or in conjunction with the party membership, the party leader and by its actions has removed or facilitated the removal of six leaders (Heath, Thatcher, Duncan Smith, May, Johnson and Truss), a far greater number than has been removed by the actions of electors. This role attracts the headlines. But the 1922 Committee, on a more regular basis, has various consequences. As we have seen, these consequences are not usually headline grabbing. Months may elapse in which the 1922 attracts no attention from journalists and indeed little interest or attention from its own members. The activities are not newsworthy, nor do they impinge on the work of ministers, who may at most during their ministerial careers make a few appearances before the 1922 to explain their policies. Some pen autobiographies that make no reference to the '22. The same applies to some memoirs from backbench MPs. They may not have regularly attended 1922 meetings or, if they did, the experience has not impinged on their consciousness, or at least not figured in their priorities when penning their tomes. Yet, despite this, the '22 matters politically and on an increasingly significant basis.

It has attracted media interest on a notable scale, initially for a period during the Second World War, and then more continuously since the 1970s, in effect since Tory MPs gained the power to elect the party leader. It has peaked at times when a leader is struggling to survive. It was to the fore throughout 2022, the chairman of the '22, Sir Graham Brady, becoming a public figure despite his stance being one of enigmatic silence. The question most frequently posed to him by journalists ('How many letters have you received?') was the one he was never going to answer. The members of the '22 mattered – they were the ones submitting the letters – and Sir Graham was the one counting them. His significance extended beyond this formal process in that he had to assess whether conditions were such that it was feasible for a leader to continue, even without a formal vote of no confidence. He delivered the *coup de grâce* to three leaders (May, Johnson, Truss) when, even without a formal vote by MPs, it was apparent their time was up. In each case, a visit to No. 10 by the chairman of the '22 was followed by a lectern being erected in Downing Street and the Prime Minister striding out to announce, be it emotionally or with obvious resentment, that she or he would be visiting the sovereign to resign.

The 1922 has clearly come a long way since Gervais Rentoul invited some fellow newly elected MPs to gather in a committee room to decide what to do to render more understandable the parliamentary environment that they now occupied. It is now regularly referred to in the media as the 'powerful' or 'influential' 1922 Committee whenever a crisis erupts – it is not in the interests of the media to describe it at such times as weak and insignificant – but it suffers from the fact that the coverage is confined to periods of political turmoil and often from garbled or simply wrong descriptions of what it is and when it was formed. In its centenary year, some progress was made in enlightening various media as to when and why it was formed, but it was at times an uphill struggle, not least given those requiring enlightenment extended in some cases to senior figures in the '22.

Ironically, the 1922 Committee has largely become what some thought was its purpose when first established. It was not formed as a means of keeping the leadership in check. It was formed to enable new MPs to play a more active part in parliamentary life. It has largely ceased to fulfil its founding purpose – induction is largely left to the whips, David Maclean as Chief Whip introducing at the start of the twenty-first century a structured programme of induction – and has moved to engage with and keep under scrutiny the party leadership. It holds the power that was exercised de facto by Conservative MPs gathered in the Carlton Club in 1922. That meeting had no causal link to the formation of the 1922, but because of the way the 1922 has developed – the result of critical junctures over the course of the century – it has become an embedded form of that meeting. At its formation, the only power it had was persuasive. It now has a coercive capacity.

In short, it is difficult if not impossible to make sense of contemporary British politics without reference to the 1922 Committee. There has been over the years, and especially in the period of Tory government from 2015, greater public awareness of its political significance, even if that awareness far outstrips a grasp of the history and precise nature of the body. The contrast is stark when one considers the number of Tory leaders toppled by the 1922 Committee in recent years against the fact that this volume constitutes only the second full-length book written exclusively about the Committee. It is a powerful body, but one that has been largely hidden in plain sight.

# Notes

## Preface: what is 'the 1922'?

1  The 1922 Committee continues to use the term chairman, rather than chair, so this term is followed in the text.

2  See, e.g., I. Bulmer-Thomas, *The Party System in Great Britain* (London: Phoenix House, 1953): 119; I. Jennings, *Parliament*, 2nd edn (Cambridge: Cambridge University Press, 1957): 140; F. W. G. Benemy, *The Elected Monarch* (London: George G. Harrap & Co., 1965): 104; R. M. Punnett, *British Government and Politics* (London: Heinemann, 1968): 111; M. Beloff and G. Peele, *The Government of the UK* (London: Weidenfeld & Nicolson, 1980): 188–9; N. Forman, *Mastering British Politics* (Basingstoke: Macmillan, 1985): 61; M. Thatcher, *The Downing Street Years* (London: HarperCollins, 1993): 33–4.

3  P. Haigh and A. Gaudion, 'What Is the 1922 Committee, Who Is on It and What Do They Do?' *Metro*, 21 July 2022, www.msn.com/en-gb/news/world/what-is-the-1922-committee-who-is-on-it-and-what-do-they-do/ar-AAZPgAy

4  John Osborn MP to Sir Harry Legge-Bourke KBE DL MP, 4 May 1971. Letter in Conservative Party archives. Cited in P. Norton, *The Voice of the Backbenchers: The 1922 Committee: The First 90 Years, 1923–2013* (London: Conservative History Group, 2013): 7.

5  1922 Committee, *Minutes*, 21 May 1992.

6  Norton, *The Voice of the Backbenchers*.

7  P. Norton, *Governing Britain* (Manchester: Manchester University Press, 2020).

## 1 Setting the scene

1  Lord Bryce, *Modern Democracies*, Vol. 2 (London: Macmillan, 1921): 367–77. See P. Norton, 'General Introduction', in P. Norton (ed.), *Legislatures* (Oxford: Oxford University Press, 1990): 47–56.

# Notes

2 G. Loewenberg (ed.), *Modern Parliaments: Change or Decline?* (Chicago: Aldine-Atherton, 1971): 7.

3 B. Crick, *The Reform of Parliament*, revised 2nd edn (London: Weidenfeld & Nicolson, 1970): 3.

4 A. King, 'Modes of Executive–Legislative Relations: Great Britain, France and West Germany', *Legislative Studies Quarterly*, 1 (1976): 11–34.

5 See S. Sieberer, 'Party Unity in Parliamentary Democracies: A Comparative Analysis', *The Journal of Legislative Studies*, 22 (2006): 150–78.

6 P. Cowley, 'Unbridled Passions? Free Votes, Issues of Conscience and the Accountability of British Members of Parliament', *The Journal of Legislative Studies*, 4 (1998): 70–88; P. Cowley and M. Stuart, 'Party Rules, OK: Voting in the House of Commons on the Human Fertilisation and Embryology Bill', *Parliamentary Affairs*, 63 (2010): 173–81; A. Plumb, 'Research Note: A Comparison of Free Vote Patterns in Westminster-Style Parliaments', *Commonwealth & Comparative Politics*, 51 (2013): 254–66.

7 P. Norton, 'Cohesion without Discipline: Party Voting in the House of Lords', *The Journal of Legislative Studies*, 9 (2003): 57–72.

8 See C. Kam, 'Party Discipline', in S. Martin, T. Saalfeld and K. Strøm (eds), *The Oxford Handbook of Legislative Studies* (Oxford: Oxford University Press, 2014): 399–417.

9 R. Carroll and K. Poole, 'Roll-Call Analysis and the Study of Legislatures', in Martin, Saalfeld and Strøm (eds), *The Oxford Handbook of Legislative Studies*: 103–25.

10 See House Democratic Cloakroom, https://democraticcloakroom.house.gov/about

11 See P. Norton, 'The Organization of Parliamentary Parties', in S. A. Walkland (ed.), *The House of Commons in the Twentieth Century* (Oxford: Clarendon Press, 1979): 22.

12 C. R. Attlee, *The Labour Party in Perspective* (London: Gollancz, 1937): 109.

13 Benemy, *The Elected Monarch*: 105.

14 See S. Smith, J. M. Roberts and R. J. Vander Wielen, *The American Congress*, 6th edn (Cambridge: Cambridge University Press, 2009).

15 K. Heidar and R. Koole (eds), *Parliamentary Party Groups in European Democracies* (London: Routledge, 2000).

16 D. Schindler and O. Kannenberg, 'Elite Domination or Participatory Democracy? Comparing the Rules of the Game within Parliamentary Party Groups', paper delivered at the 15th Workshop of Parliamentary Scholars and Parliamentarians, Wroxton, UK, 31 July 2022.

17 See C. Close, S. Gherghina and V. Sierens, 'Prompting Legislative Agreement and Loyalty: What Role for Intra-Party Democracy?', *Parliamentary Affairs*, 72 (2019): 387–405.

18 T. Saalfeld and K. Strøm, 'Political Parties and Legislatures', in Martin, Saalfeld and Strøm (eds), *The Oxford Handbook of Legislative Studies*: 392.

19 S. Ball, 'The 1922 Committee: The Formative Years 1922–1945', *Parliamentary History*, 9 (1990): 129–57. See also S. Ball, *Portrait of a Party: The Conservative Party in Britain 1918–1945* (Oxford: Oxford University Press, 2013): 381–4.

20 P. Norton, 'The Parliamentary Party and Party Committees', in A. Seldon and S. Ball (eds), *Conservative Century* (Oxford: Oxford University Press, 1994); Norton, *The Voice of the Backbenchers*.

21 P. Goodhart, *The 1922* (London: Macmillan, 1973).

22 S. Lukes, *Power: A Radical View*, 2nd revised edn (Basingstoke: Palgrave Macmillan, 2004); P. Norton, *Parliament in British Politics*, 2nd edn (Basingstoke: Palgrave Macmillan, 2013): 4–7.

23 P. Bachrach and M. Baratz, 'Two Faces of Power', *American Political Science Review*, 56 (1962): 947–52; Lukes, *Power*.

24 The power elite thesis developed in C. W. Mills, *The Power Elite* (New York: Oxford University Press, 1956).

25 P. Norton, 'Playing by the Rules: The Constraining Hand of Parliamentary Procedure', *The Journal of Legislative Studies*, 7 (2001): 13–33.

26 L. P. Stark, *Choosing a Leader* (Basingstoke: Macmillan, 1996): 133.

27 R. Packenham, 'Legislatures and Political Development', in A. Kornberg and L. D. Musolf (eds), *Legislatures in Developmental Perspective* (Durham, NC: Duke University Press, 1970): 522.

28 *Ibid.*: 523.

29 *Ibid.*: 536.

30 *Ibid.*: 536–46; L. Allmark, 'More than Rubber Stamps: The Consequences Produced by Legislatures in Non-Democratic States beyond Latent Legitimation', *The Journal of Legislative Studies*, 18 (2012): 184–202; W. Chen, 'Is the Label "Minimal Legislature" Still Appropriate? The Role of the National People's Congress in China's Political System', *The Journal of Legislative Studies*, 22 (2016): 257–75.

31 Schindler and Kannenberg, 'Elite Domination'.

32 E. Crewe, *House of Commons: An Anthropology of the Work of MPs* (London: Haus Publishing, 2015): 1.

33 *Ibid.*

34 T. Ingold, *Making: Anthropology, Archaeology, Art and Architecture* (London: Routledge, 2013), cited in E. Crewe, *The Anthropology of Parliaments* (London: Routledge, 2021): 10 (italics in the original text).

35 *Ibid.*

36 Crewe, *Anthropology of Parliaments*: 10.

37 Benemy, *The Elected Monarch*: 105.

38 M. Spicer, *The Spicer Diaries* (London: Biteback, 2012): 455.

39 P. Rawlinson, *A Price Too High* (London: Weidenfeld & Nicolson, 1989): 72.

40 Thatcher, *The Downing Street Years*: 33–4.

41 J. Critchley, *A Bag of Boiled Sweets* (London: Faber & Faber, 1994): 84.

42 *Ibid.*

43 *Ibid.*

44 P. Norton, 'Power behind the Scenes: The Importance of Informal Space in Legislatures', *Parliamentary Affairs*, 72 (2019): 245–66.

45 See N. W. Polsby, 'The Institutionalisation of the U.S. House of Representatives', *American Political Science Review*, 62 (1968): 145; S. C. Patterson, 'Legislative Institutions and Institutionalisation in the United States', *The Journal of Legislative Studies*, 1 (1995): 16.

46 Polsby, 'Institutionalisation of the U.S. House of Representatives': 145, 153–60.

47 Norton, 'Power behind the Scenes': 249–50.

## 2 Modest beginnings

1 See R. Blake, *The Conservative Party from Peel to Churchill* (London: Eyre & Spottiswoode, 1970): 2; P. Norton, 'History of the Party I: Tory to Conservative', in P. Norton (ed.), *The Conservative Party* (London: Prentice-Hall/Harvester Wheatsheaf, 1996): 17–18.

2 P. Norton, 'History of the Party II: From a Marquess to an Earl', in Norton (ed.), *The Conservative Party*: 31.

3 See A. L. Lowell, *The Government of England*, Vol. 1 (London: Macmillan, 1908): 455–6.

4 A. Aspinall, 'English Party Organisation in the Early Nineteenth Century', *English Historical Review*, 41 (1926): 393.

5 Lord Barnby to author, 1977, cited in Norton, 'Organization of Parliamentary Parties': 27. As Francis Willey, he was the Conservative MP for Bradford South from 1918 to 1922.

6 See the sources cited in the Preface n. 2.

7 Ball, 'The 1922 Committee': 131.

8 See P. Norton, 'Learning the Ropes: Training MPs in the United Kingdom', in C. Lewis and K. Coghill (eds), *Parliamentarians' Professional Development* (Cham: Springer, 2016): 187–8.

9 See the comments of Sir Guy Gaunt, in *The Yield of the Years*, cited in Goodhart, *The 1922*: 19.

10 G. Rentoul, *Sometimes I Think* (London: Hodder & Stoughton, 1940): 232.

11 *The Times*, 7 February 1927.

12 See Ball, *Portrait of a Party*: 381–4.

13 1922 Committee, *Minutes*, 18 April 1923.

14 1922 Committee, *Minutes*, 30 April 1923.

15 Rentoul, *Sometimes I Think*: 233.

16 1922 Committee, *Minutes*, 30 July 1923.

17 Ball, *Portrait of a Party*: 375.

# Notes

18  Rentoul, *Sometimes I Think*: 233.
19  1922 Committee, *Minutes*, 11 February 1924.
20  Rentoul, *Sometimes I Think*: 234.
21  1922 Committee, *Minutes*, 13 February 1924.
22  1922 Committee, *Minutes*, 27 February 1924.
23  Rentoul, *Sometimes I Think*: 234.
24  *Ibid*.
25  1922 Committee, *Minutes*, 27 February 1924.
26  1922 Committee, *Minutes*, 10 March 1924.
27  Rentoul, *Sometimes I Think*: 235.
28  1922 Committee, *Minutes*, 6 March 1925; *The Times*, 7 March 1925.
29  1922 Committee, *Minutes*, 26 February 1926.
30  *Manchester Evening News*, 22 February 1926.
31  For example, *Dundee Courier*, 23 February 1926; *The Scotsman*, 23 February 1926; *Westminster Gazette*, 23 February 1926; *Gloucester Citizen*, 24 February 1926; *Taunton Courier and Western Advertiser*, 24 February 1926; *Western Mail*, 25 February 1926.
32  1922 Committee, *Minutes*, 1 March 1926.
33  *The Times*, 12 March 1929.
34  Rentoul, *Sometimes I Think*: 238.
35  *Western Gazette*, 11 May 1928; *Staffordshire Sentinel*, 22 May 1928; *Gloucester Citizen*, 23 May 1928.
36  1922 Committee, *Minutes*, 12 May 1930; S. Ball, *Baldwin and the Conservative Party: The Crisis of 1929–1931* (New Haven, CT: Yale University Press, 1988): 79–80.
37  1922 Committee, Circular from the Chairman, 7 June 1928.
38  Ball, 'The 1922 Committee': 140.
39  Ball, *Baldwin and the Conservative Party*.
40  1922 Committee, *Minutes*, 7 December 1936.
41  A. Lexden, *Neville Chamberlain: Redressing the Balance* (London: Conservative History Group, 2018): 30.
42  Ball, *Baldwin and the Conservative Party*: 145.
43  Goodhart, *The 1922*: 73.
44  Ball, 'The 1922 Committee': 145
45  1922 Committee, *Minutes*, 13 June 1932.
46  Rentoul, *Sometimes I Think*: 242.
47  Summarised in *The Times*, 17 November 1932.
48  *Leeds Mercury*, 29 November 1932.
49  'Westminster Whispers', *The Bystander*, 1 February 1933.
50  1922 Committee, *Minutes*, 14 November 1932.
51  *The Times*, 16 November 1932.
52  1922 Committee Executive, *Minutes*, 1 May 1933.
53  *Leeds Mercury*, 29 November 1932.

# Notes

54 *The Times*, 6 December 1932.

55 J. M. McEwen, 'Unionist and Conservative Members of Parliament', unpublished PhD thesis, University of London, 1959; Norton, 'Organization of Parliamentary Parties': 33–4; Ball, *Portrait of a Party*: Ch. 5.

56 Ball, *Portrait of a Party*: 353.

57 Ball, *Baldwin and the Conservative Party*: 21–4.

58 Ball, *Portrait of a Party*: 342–52.

59 N. C. Fleming, *Britannia's Zealots*, Vol. 1 (London: Bloomsbury, 2019): Ch. 4.

60 Jennings, *Parliament*: 380.

61 Ball, *Baldwin and the Conservative Party*: 91.

62 Viscount Templewood, *Nine Troubled Years* (London: Collins, 1954): 376.

63 *Ibid.*

64 *Henry 'Chips' Channon: The Diaries 1918–38*, ed. S. Heffer (London: Hutchinson, 2021): 93.

65 *The Times*, 31 March 1939.

66 Ball, *Portrait of a Party*: 383.

67 Jennings, *Parliament*: 375.

68 *The Times*, 1 June 1938.

69 G. Rentoul, *This Is My Case* (London: Hutchinson, 1944): 111.

70 C. Ponsonby, *Ponsonby Remembers* (Oxford: The Alden Press, 1965): 70.

71 Ball, *Portrait of a Party*: 383.

# 3 Speaking truth to power

1 J. Colville, *The Fringes of Power: Downing Street Diaries, Volume One: September 1939–October 1941* (London: Sceptre, 1986): 140.

2 J. Eaves, *Emergency Powers and the Parliamentary Watchdog: Parliament and the Executive in Great Britain 1939–51* (London: Hansard Society, 1957).

3 S. King-Hall, 'Foreword', in J. Eaves, *Emergency Powers*: 2.

4 R. Butt, *The Power of Parliament* (London: Constable, 1967): 175; P. Norton, 'Winning the War but Losing the Peace: The British House of Commons during the Second World War', *The Journal of Legislative Studies*, 4:3 (1998): 39.

5 A. Roberts, *Eminent Churchillians* (London: Weidenfeld & Nicolson, 1994): 183.

6 J. Schneer, *Ministers at War* (London: OneWorld Publications, 2015): 47.

7 A. Roberts, *The Holy Fox: The Life of Lord Halifax* (London: Weidenfeld & Nicolson, 1991): 281. Owen ascribes the observation to Spens. D. Owen, *Cabinet's Finest Hour* (London: Haus Publishing, 2017): 91.

8 *Channon Diaries 1918–38*: 408.

9 1922 Committee Executive, *Minutes*, 17 January 1940.

# Notes

10  Letter, *The Times*, 29 October 1942.

11  *Channon Diaries 1918–38*: 773–4.

12  *Henry 'Chips' Channon: The Diaries 1938–43*, ed. S. Heffer (London: Hutchinson, 2021).

13  *Henry 'Chips' Channon: The Diaries 1943–57*, ed. S. Heffer (London: Hutchinson, 2022).

14  Goodhart, *The 1922*: 104.

15  *The Times*, 16 October 1940.

16  *Ibid.*

17  *The Times*, 27 March 1941.

18  *Edinburgh Evening News*, 9 March 1942.

19  Schneer, *Ministers at War*: 146–7.

20  M. Lee, *The Churchill Coalition, 1940–1945* (London: Batsford, 1980): 41.

21  *Daily Herald*, 15 June 1942.

22  *Channon Diaries 1938–43*: 602.

23  *Daily Mirror*, 1 May 1942.

24  *The Times,* 7 May 1942.

25  *The Times*, 14 May 1942.

26  Earl Winterton, *Orders of the Day* (London: Cassell, 1953): 280.

27  House of Commons Debates (*Hansard*), 9 February 1943, cols 1279–82; Ball, 'The 1922 Committee': 149.

28  *Gloucester Citizen*, 26 January 1945.

29  House of Commons Debates (*Hansard*), 20 April 1943, col. 1576.

30  House of Commons Debates (*Hansard*), 13 February 1945, col. 161.

31  G. Harvie-Watt, *Most of My Life* (London: Springwood Books, 1980): 79.

32  See J. Barnes and D. Nicholson (eds), *The Leo Amery Diaries 1929–1945* (London: Hutchinson, 1988): 776.

33  Ball, *Portrait of a Party*: 383–4.

34  Harvie-Watt, *Most of My Life*: 55.

35  Schneer, *Ministers at War*: 149.

36  Harvie-Watt, *Most of My Life*: 55.

37  Ball, *Portrait of a Party*: 384.

38  A. Scott-James, 'What Does an MP Do for His Money?' *Picture Post*, 12 December 1942: 16.

39  J. Charmley, *A History of Conservative Party Politics, 1900–1996* (Basingstoke: Macmillan Press, 1996): 124.

40  *Parliament and Politics in the Age of Churchill and Attlee: The Headlam Diaries 1935–1951*, ed. S. Ball (Cambridge: Cambridge University Press, 1999): 576.

41  Lord Boothby to author, 30 January 1973.

42  *Harold Nicolson: Diaries and Letters, 1945–62*, ed. N. Nicolson (London: Fontana, 1971): 32.

43  *Daily Herald*, 21 November 1945; *Sunday Pictorial*, 25 November 1945.

# Notes

44 *CHIPS: The Diaries of Sir Henry Channon*, ed. R. Rhodes James (London: Weidenfeld & Nicolson, 1967): 412; *Channon Diaries 1943–57*, ed. S. Heffer: 300.
45 H. Macmillan, *Tides of Fortune, 1945–1955* (London: Macmillan, 1969): 287.
46 Former Conservative MP to author, 1973.
47 J. Stuart, *Within the Fringe* (London: The Bodley Head, 1967): 144–7; R. Harris, *The Conservatives: A History* (London: Bantam Press, 2011): 375; also Lord Moran, *Winston Churchill: The Struggle for Survival, 1940–1965* (London: Constable, 1966): 308.
48 *Headlam Diaries 1935–1951*: 576.
49 *Channon Diaries 1943–57*: 538.
50 J. D. Hoffman, *The Conservative Party in Opposition 1945–51* (London: MacGibbon & Kee, 1964): 187.
51 *Ibid.*: 185.
52 K. Theakston, *Winston Churchill and the British Constitution* (London: Politico's, 2003): 150–1.
53 Goodhart, *The 1922*: 143.
54 A. Cooke and S. Parkinson, 'Rab Butler's Golden Era?' in A. Cooke (ed.), *Tory Policy-Making* (London: Conservative Research Department, 2009): 27–53.
55 A. Howard, *RAB: The Life of R. A. Butler* (London: Jonathan Cape, 1987): 166.
56 *Headlam Diaries 1935–1951*: 623.
57 E. Heath, *The Course of My Life* (London: Hodder & Stoughton, 1998): 142.
58 1922 Committee, *Minutes*, 7 June 1951.
59 1922 Committee, *Minutes*, 14 June 1951.
60 *Channon Diaries 1943–57*: 726.
61 1922 Committee, *Minutes*, 28 June 1951.
62 1922 Committee, *Minutes*, 9 May 1951.
63 Harris, *The Conservatives*: 387.
64 H. H. Wilson, *Pressure Group* (London: Secker & Warburg, 1961): 89.
65 *Daily Telegraph*, 10 April 1952, cited in Jackson, *Rebels and Whips*: 104–5.
66 See *Channon Diaries 1943–57*: 924.
67 S. Onslow, *Backbench Debate within the Conservative Party and its Influence on British Foreign Policy, 1948–57* (Basingstoke: Macmillan Press, 1997): 181.
68 *Channon Diaries 1943–57*: 769.
69 *Ibid.*: 806.
70 See P. Norton, 'Votes of Confidence and the Fixed-Term Parliaments Act', in A. Horne, L. Thompson and B. Yong (eds), *Parliament and the Law*, 3rd edn (Oxford: Hart Publishing, 2022): 383–8.
71 1922 Committee, *Minutes*, 13 September 1956.
72 Howard, *RAB*: 241.
73 *Channon Diaries 1943–57*: 1082.
74 *Belfast Telegraph*, 19 December 1956.

# Notes

75  N. Fisher, *Iain Macleod* (London: Andre Deutsch, 1973): 116.

76  Goodhart, *The 1922*: 175; D. Walters, *Not Always with the Pack* (London: Constable. 1989): 120–1; S. Heffer, *Like the Roman: The Life of Enoch Powell* (London: Phoenix, 1998): 210.

77  C. Williams, *Harold Macmillan* (London: Phoenix, 2009): 269.

78  M. Jago, *Rab Butler: The Best Prime Minister We Never Had?* (London: Biteback, 2015): 305. See also P. Cosgrave, *The Lives of Enoch Powell* (London: Pan Books, 1990): 150

79  Rawlinson, *A Price Too High*: 72.

80  Jago, *Rab Butler*: 305.

81  *Channon Diaries 1943–57*: 1071.

82  Earl of Kilmuir, *Political Adventure* (London: Weidenfeld & Nicolson, 1962): 285.

83  Goodhart, *The 1922*: 176.

84  *The Macmillan Diaries*, Vol. 2, ed. P. Catterall (London: Macmillan, 2011): 29, 399, 446, 487, 557, 581.

85  *Ibid.*: 367, 522, 532.

86  Lord Hailsham, *The Door Wherein I Went* (London: Collins, 1978): 155.

87  A. Horne, *Macmillan 1957–1986, Vol. II of the Official Biography* (London: Macmillan, 1989): 158.

88  Goodhart, *The 1922*: 177.

89  R. Blake, *The Conservative Party from Peel to Major* (London: Arrow, 1998): 289.

90  Sir Peter Tapsell to author, 2013.

91  R. Shepherd, *Iain Macleod* (London: Hutchinson, 1994): 268.

92  *Birmingham Daily Post*, 28 April 1962.

93  R. Lamb, *The Macmillan Years 1957–1963: The Emerging Truth* (London: John Murray, 1995): 451.

94  Butt, *The Power of Parliament*: 246.

95  *Birmingham Daily Post*, 18 July 1962.

96  Heffer, *Like the Roman*: 313.

97  Rawlinson, *A Price Too High*: 98.

98  Blake, *The Conservative Party*: 290.

99  *Birmingham Daily Post*, 18 June 1963.

100  J. Ramsden, *The Winds of Change: Macmillan to Heath, 1957–1975* (London: Longman, 1996): 192. See also *Sunday Mirror*, 21 July 1963.

101  Heffer, *Like the Roman*: 317.

102  Lamb, *The Macmillan Years*: 13; also 476. *Daily Mirror*, 21 June 1963.

103  See Horne, *Macmillan 1957–1986*: 484.

104  Critchley, *A Bag of Boiled Sweets*: 85. See also Horne, *Macmillan 1957–1986*: 529.

105  A. Clark, *The Tories: Conservatives and the Nation State* (London: Weidenfeld & Nicolson, 1998): 322.

# Notes

106  *Belfast Telegraph*, 25 July 1963.
107  D. R. Thorpe, *Alec Douglas-Home* (London: Sinclair-Stevenson, 1996): 293.
108  *Ibid.*: 293; Shepherd, *Iain Macleod*: 305.
109  Lamb, *The Macmillan Years*: 494.
110  Goodhart, *The 1922*: 195.
111  Shepherd, *Iain Macleod*: 323.
112  V. Bogdanor, 'The Selection of the Party Leader', in A. Seldon and S. Ball (eds), *Conservative Century* (Oxford: Oxford University Press, 1994): 77; Goodhart, *The 1922*: 191.
113  G. Nabarro, *Portrait of a Politician* (Oxford: Robert Maxwell, 1969): 45.
114  J. Bruce-Gardyne and N. Lawson, *The Power Game* (London: Macmillan, 1976): 102.
115  E. du Cann, *Two Lives* (Upton upon Severn: Images Publishing, 1995): 88. See also R. Findley, 'The Conservative Party and Defeat: The Significance of Resale Price Maintenance and the General Election of 1964', *Twentieth Century British History*, 12 (2001): 327–53.
116  See J. E. Schwarz and G. Lambert, 'The Voting Behavior of British Conservative Backbenchers', in S. C. Patterson and John C. Wahlke (eds), *Comparative Legislative Behavior: Frontiers of Research* (New York: Wiley-Interscience, 1972): 73.
117  Thorpe, *Alec Douglas-Home*: 378–83.
118  Stark, *Choosing a Leader*: 33–5.
119  *Ibid.*: 35.
120  R. Shepherd, *The Power Brokers* (London: Hutchinson, 1991): 163.

## 4 Wielding the sword

1  Shepherd, *The Power Brokers*: 161; Shepherd, *Iain Macleod*: 400.
2  K. Young, *Sir Alec Douglas-Home* (London: J. M. Dent, 1970): 232.
3  Thorpe, *Alec Douglas-Home*: 387.
4  P. Cosgrave, *Carrington: A Life and a Policy* (London: J. M. Dent, 1985): 78. D. Butler and M. Pinto-Duschinsky, *The British General Election of 1970* (London: Macmillan, 1971): 67. See also J. Campbell, *Edward Heath: A Biography* (London: Jonathan Cape, 1993): 217; J. Ramsden, *The Making of Conservative Party Policy* (London: Longman, 1980): 241.
5  Butler and Pinto-Duschinsky, *The British General Election*: 67.
6  Ramsden, *Making of Conservative Party Policy*: 238.
7  *Ibid.*
8  P. Norton, 'Party Management', in A. S. Roe-Crines and T. Heppell (eds), *Policies and Politics under Prime Minister Edward Heath* (Cham: Palgrave Macmillan, 2021): 245–56; P. Norton, *Conservative Dissidents* (London: Temple Smith, 1978).

# Notes

9 M. McManus, *Edward Heath: A Singular Life* (London: Elliott and Thompson, 2016): 133.

10 *Ibid.*: 313.

11 Ramsden, *Winds of Change*: 336.

12 Detailed note, with no attribution of authorship, in the 1922 Committee files.

13 Norton, *Conservative Dissidents*: Ch. 3.

14 *Ibid.*: Ch. 4.

15 N. Fisher, *The Tory Leaders* (London: Weidenfeld & Nicolson, 1977): 141.

16 Richard Body MP to author; cited in Norton, *Conservative Dissidents*: 230.

17 *Ibid.*: 229.

18 P. Norton, *Dissension in the House of Commons 1945–1974* (London: Macmillan Press, 1975): 609–10; Norton, *Conservative Dissidents*: Ch. 8.

19 Norton, *The Voice of the Backbenchers*: 21.

20 Du Cann, *Two Lives*: 194.

21 P. Ziegler, *Edward Heath* (London: HarperPress, 2010): 431.

22 J. Aitken, *Margaret Thatcher: Power and Personality* (London: Bloomsbury, 2013): 163.

23 G. Gardiner, *Margaret Thatcher: From Childhood to Leadership* (London: William Kimber, 1975): 147.

24 *The Times*, 19 October 1973.

25 R. Behrens, *The Conservative Party from Heath to Thatcher* (Farnborough: Saxon House, 1980): 24.

26 *The Times*, 10 May 1974.

27 C. Moore, *Margaret Thatcher: The Authorized Biography*, Vol. 1 (London: Allen Lane, 2015): 251, 252.

28 *Daily Mirror*, 14 June 1974.

29 Stark, *Choosing a Leader*: 27.

30 Aitken, *Margaret Thatcher: Power and Personality*: 149; Behrens, *The Conservative Party*: 29; Moore, *Margaret Thatcher*, Vol. 1: 267.

31 Moore, *Margaret Thatcher*: 268.

32 *The Times*, 15 November 1974.

33 Norton, 'Power behind the Scenes': 258.

34 D. Butler and D. Kavanagh, *The British General Election of 1979* (London: Macmillan, 1980): 62.

35 H. Stephenson, *Mrs Thatcher's First Year* (London: Jill Norman, 1980): 94.

36 Butler and Kavanagh, *The British General Election*: 67.

37 J. Critchley, *Westminster Blues* (London: Futura, 1986): 126.

38 M. Burch, 'Approaches to Leadership in Opposition: Edward Heath and Margaret Thatcher', in Z. Layton-Henry (ed.), *Conservative Party Politics* (London: Macmillan, 1980): 175.

39 Butler and Kavanagh, *The British General Election*: 68.

40 Stephenson, *Thatcher's First Year*: 94.

# Notes

41 J. Ramsden, *An Appetite for Power* (London: HarperCollins, 1998): 424.

42 Du Cann, *Two Lives*: 210.

43 E. Du Cann, 'Formidable', in I. Dale (ed.), *Memories of Maggie* (London: Politico's, 2000): 287.

44 Gow to Thatcher, 1 August 1980. Thatcher MSS, THCR 2/6/2/ 114 pt 2 (9).

45 Gow to Thatcher, 10 December 1982. Thatcher MSS, THCR 2/6/2/ 114 pt 4 f6.

46 Gow to Thatcher, note of meeting of 31 January 1980. Thatcher MSS, THCR 2/6/2/114 pt 2 (60).

47 *Ibid.*

48 Norton, *The Voice of the Backbenchers*: 23.

49 1922 Committee Executive, *Minutes*, 12 March 1981.

50 1922 Committee Executive, *Minutes*, 26 March 1981.

51 Gow to Thatcher, 20 November 1981. Thatcher MSS, THCR 2/6/2/ 60 pt 2 f14.

52 C. Lee, *Carrington: An Honourable Man* (London: Viking, 2018): 429.

53 J. Nott, *Here Today, Gone Tomorrow* (London: Politico's, 2002): 269.

54 N. Wapshott and G. Brock, *Thatcher* (London: MacDonald & Co., 1983): 247.

55 *Ibid.*: 210.

56 Gow to Thatcher, 18 June 1981. Thatcher MSS, THCR 2/6/2/114 pt 3 f9.

57 1922 Committee Executive, *Minutes*, 18 June 1981.

58 Nigel Fisher MP to Thatcher, 9 February 1983. Thatcher MSS, THCR 1/3/10 f126.

59 Senior Conservative parliamentarian to author. Norton, *The Voice of the Backbenchers*: 22.

60 Aitken, *Margaret Thatcher: Power and Personality*: 517.

61 1922 Committee Executive, *Minutes*, 17 May 1984.

62 1922 Committee Executive, *Minutes*, 7 June 1984.

63 Officer of the 1922 Committee to author, interview. Norton, *The Voice of the Backbenchers*: 22.

64 J. Campbell, *Margaret Thatcher, Vol. 2: The Iron Lady* (London: Jonathan Cape, 2003): 454.

65 A. Clark, *Diaries* (London: Weidenfeld & Nicolson, 1993): 83.

66 Alison to Thatcher, 11 November 1985. Thatcher MSS, THCR 2/6/3/ 114(ii) f14.

67 *Ibid.*

68 Thatcher notes, 16 July 1987. Thatcher MSS, THCR 5/1/4/136 f17.

69 Aitken, *Margaret Thatcher: Power and Personality:* 537.

70 *Ibid.*

71 Note of meeting by Mark Lennox-Boyd, 11 July 1989. Thatcher MSS, THCR 2/6/4/67 pt 2 f235.

# Notes

72  1922 Committee Executive, *Minutes*, 13 July 1989.

73  Lennox-Boyd to Thatcher, 13 July 1989. Thatcher MSS, THCR 2/6/4/ 67 pt 2 f230.

74  Attached to Lennox-Boyd to Thatcher, 13 July 1989. Thatcher MSS, THCR 2/6/4/67 pt 2 f230.

75  K. Baker, *The Turbulent Years* (London: Faber & Faber, 1993): 135.

76  1922 Committee Executive, *Minutes*, 14 December 1989.

77  C. Moore, *Margaret Thatcher: The Authorized Biography*, Vol. 3 (London: Allen Lane, 2019): 557.

78  E. Pearce, *The Quiet Rise of John Major* (London: Weidenfeld & Nicolson, 1991): 137.

79  G. Gardiner, 'A Cell of Revolutionaries', in I. Dale (ed.), *Memories of Maggie* (London: Politico's, 2000): 46.

80  *Sandwell Evening Mail*, 29 July 1989.

81  *Dundee Courier*, 2 March 1990.

82  Thatcher to Cranley Onslow, 21 July 1990. Thatcher MSS, THCR 3/2/ 291 f35.

83  A. Watkins, *A Conservative Coup* (London: Duckworth, 1991): 179; N. Ridley, *'My Style of Government': The Thatcher Years* (London: Fontana, 1992): 241.

84  Baker, *The Turbulent Years*: 390.

85  *The Independent*, 28 November 1990, cited in R. M. Punnett, *Selecting the Party Leader* (Hemel Hempstead: Harvester Wheatsheaf, 1992): 68.

86  P. Norton, 'The Conservative Party: "In Office but Not in Power"', in A. King (ed.), *New Labour Triumphs: Britain at the Polls* (Chatham, NJ: Chatham House Publishers, 1998): 79–82.

87  G. Gardiner, *A Bastard's Tale* (London: Aurum Press, 1999): 17–18.

88  1922 Committee Executive, *Minutes*, 11 June 1992.

89  1922 Committee Executive, *Minutes*, 24 September 1992.

90  1922 Committee Executive, *Minutes*, 28 January 1993.

91  1922 Committee Executive, *Minutes*, 10 June 1993.

92  *The Times*, 26 November 1993.

93  See H. Williams, *Guilty Men: Conservative Government, 1992–97* (London: Aurum Press, 1998): 146.

94  Norton, 'In Office but Not in Power': 88.

95  A. Seldon, *Major: A Political Life* (London: Weidenfeld & Nicolson, 1997): 438.

96  T. Bale, *The Conservative Party from Thatcher to Cameron* (Cambridge: Polity, 2010): 58.

97  1922 Committee Executive, *Minutes*, 29 June 1995.

98  *Ibid.*

99  Seldon, *Major*: 663.

100  1922 Committee Executive, *Minutes*, 12 December 1996.

# Notes

101 P. Cowley, 'Chaos or Cohesion? Major and the Parliamentary Conservative Party', in P. Dorey (ed.), *The Major Premiership: Politics and Policies under John Major, 1990–97* (Basingstoke: Palgrave, 1999): 1.

102 P. Dorey, 'Despair and Disillusion Abound: The Major Premiership in Perspective', in P. Dorey (ed.), *The Major Premiership: Politics and Policies under John Major, 1990–97* (Basingstoke: Palgrave, 1999): 222–3.

103 1922 Committee Executive, *Minutes*, 22 May 1997.

104 *Ibid.*

105 C. Gill, *Cracking the Whip* (Epsom: Bretwalda Books, 2012): 11–13, 32–3.

106 P. Norton, 'The Conservative Party: Is There Anyone Out There?' in A. King (ed.), *Britain at the Polls, 2001* (Chatham, NJ: Chatham House Publishers, 2002): 68–94.

107 Bale, *The Conservative Party*: 87–8.

108 *Ibid.*: 82.

109 *Ibid.*: 93.

110 Gill, *Cracking the Whip*: 53.

111 *Ibid.*: 58.

112 N. Fletcher, 'William Hague', in T. Heppell (ed.), *Leaders of the Opposition* (Basingstoke: Palgrave Macmillan, 2012): 189.

113 *Ibid.*: 93.

114 Norton, 'The Conservative Party: Is There Anyone Out There?': 79–80.

115 See A. Denham and K. O'Hara, *Democratising Conservative Leadership Selection* (Manchester: Manchester University Press, 2008): 53–64.

116 R. Hayton and T. Heppell, 'The Quiet Man of British Politics: The Rise, Fall and Significance of Iain Duncan Smith', *Parliamentary Affairs*, 63 (2010): 432.

117 *Ibid.*: 439.

118 P. Cowley and M. Stuart, 'Still Causing Trouble: The Conservative Parliamentary Party', *Political Quarterly*, 75 (2004): 357.

119 Cowley and Stuart, 'Still Causing Trouble': 357; Hayton and Heppell, 'The Quiet Man': 432.

120 Cowley and Stuart, 'Still Causing Trouble': 357–9.

121 Spicer, *The Spicer Diaries*: 471, 473, 479, 497, 500, 506.

122 Personal observation. See also *ibid.*: 468.

123 *Ibid.*: 473.

124 *Ibid.*: 476.

125 *Ibid.*

126 Hayton and Heppell, 'The Quiet Man': 431.

127 1922 Committee Executive, *Minutes*, 8 and 15 January 2003.

128 1922 Committee Executive, *Minutes*, 26 February 2003.

129 Spicer, *The Spicer Diaries*: 495–6.

130 *Ibid.*: 510.

131 Hayton and Heppell, 'The Quiet Man': 435.

# Notes

132  Bale, *The Conservative Party*: 192.
133  P. Norton, 'The Conservative Party: The Politics of Panic', in J. Bartle and A. King (eds), *Britain at the Polls, 2005* (Washington, DC: CQ Press, 2006): 40–1; Spicer, *The Spicer Diaries*: 516.
134  P. Snowdon, *Back from the Brink* (London: HarperPress, 2010): 119.
135  See Norton, 'The Politics of Panic': 41.
136  D. Cameron, *For the Record* (London: William Collins, 2019): 62.
137  M. Crick, *In Search of Michael Howard* (London: Simon & Schuster, 2005): 462, 467.
138  Spicer, *The Spicer Diaries*: 547.
139  *Ibid.*: 538, 539.
140  *Ibid.*: 546.
141  The Rt Hon. Lord Howard of Lympne to author, 2023.
142  Spicer, *The Spicer Diaries*: 561, see also 552.
143  *Ibid.*: 562–3.
144  Snowdon, *Back from the Brink*: 174.
145  F. Elliott and J. Hanning, *Cameron: The Rise of the New Conservative* (London: HarperPress, 2007): 256–90.

## 5 The maker and slayer of leaders

1  P. Norton, 'Cameron and Conservative Success: Architect or By-stander?' in S. Lee and M. Beech (eds), *The Conservatives under David Cameron: Built to Last?* (Basingstoke: Palgrave Macmillan, 2009): 39–40; Bale, *The Conservative Party*: 381–2; Hayton and Heppell, 'The Quiet Man': 439–40; R. Hayton, *Reconstructing Conservatism? The Conservative Party in Opposition, 1997–2010* (Manchester: Manchester University Press, 2012): 142–3.
2  Norton, 'Cameron and Conservative Success': 42–3.
3  Snowdon, *Back from the Brink*: 250–1.
4  F. Elliott and J. Hanning, *Cameron: Practically a Conservative* (London: Fourth Estate, 2012): 318.
5  Snowdon, *Back from the Brink*: 357.
6  *Ibid.*: 367.
7  D. Seawright, 'The Conservative Election Campaign', in T. Heppell and D. Seawright (eds), *Cameron and the Conservatives* (Basingstoke: Palgrave Macmillan, 2012): 32–43.
8  R. Wilson, *5 Days to Power* (London: Biteback, 2010): 219.
9  A. Seldon and P. Snowdon, *Cameron at 10: The Inside Story 2010–2015* (London: William Collins, 2015): 26–7.
10  P. Norton, 'The Coalition and the Conservatives', in A. Seldon and M. Finn (eds), *The Coalition Effect 2010–2015* (Cambridge: Cambridge University Press, 2015): 471–3.

# Notes

11 Harris, *The Conservatives*: 516.
12 P. Norton, 'Coalition Cohesion', in T. Heppell and D. Seawright (eds), *Cameron and the Conservatives* (Basingstoke: Palgrave Macmillan, 2012): 184–6.
13 Seldon and Snowdon, *Cameron at 10*: 117.
14 Norton, 'The Coalition and the Conservatives': 480–1.
15 K. Fall, *The Gatekeeper* (London: HQ, 2020): 179.
16 M. d'Ancona, *In It Together* (London: Viking, 2013): 245.
17 Norton, 'The Coalition and the Conservatives': 483.
18 Norton, *The Voice of the Backbenchers*: 31.
19 Cited in P. Cowley and D. Kavanagh, *The British General Election of 2015* (Basingstoke: Palgrave Macmillan, 2016): 48.
20 Fall, *The Gatekeeper*: 179.
21 A. Leadsom, *Snakes and Ladders* (London: Biteback, 2022): 104–6.
22 A. Seldon, *May at 10* (London: Biteback, 2019): 58–9.
23 G. Barwell, *Chief of Staff* (London: Atlantic Books, 2021): 24.
24 Seldon, *May at 10*: 284–7.
25 *Ibid.*: 287.
26 Barwell, *Chief of Staff*: 305.
27 *Daily Telegraph*, 13 December 2018.
28 Norton, 'Power behind the Scenes': 245–66; P. Norton, 'Theresa May and the Constitution: A Failure of Statecraft', in A. Roe-Crines and D. Jeffery (eds), *Policies and Politics under Prime Minister Theresa May: A Question of Statecraft* (Cham: Palgrave Macmillan, 2023).
29 T. Bower, *Boris Johnson – The Gambler* (London: W. H. Allen, 2020): 376.
30 The Rt Hon. Theresa May to author, 2023.
31 1922 Committee Executive member to author, 2023.
32 Sir Graham Brady to author, 2022.
33 The Rt Hon. Theresa May to author, 2023.
34 *The Independent*, 25 September 2020.
35 *The Guardian*, 25 September 2020.
36 S. Payne, *The Fall of Boris Johnson* (London: Macmillan, 2022): 127.
37 *ITV News*, 6 June 2022; Payne, *The Fall of Boris Johnson*: 138, Note of PM's comments circulated after the meeting.
38 *The Economist*, 6 June 2022.
39 Payne, *The Fall of Boris Johnson*: 205.
40 *Ibid.*: 208–9.
41 *The Times*, 4 October 2022.
42 H. Cole and J. Heale, *Out of the Blue* (London: HarperCollins, 2022): 291.
43 *The Guardian* (online), 12 October 2022.
44 Cole and Heale, *Out of the Blue*: 308.
45 *The Times*, 21 October 2022.

# Notes

## 6 Who and when

1  1922 Committee Executive, *Minutes*, 2 May 1923.
2  1922 Committee, *Minutes*, 24 March 1924.
3  *Yorkshire Post and Leeds Intelligencer*, 24 March 1934.
4  See P. Norton, 'Conservative Politics and the Abolition of Stormont', in P. Catterall and S. McDougall (eds), *The Northern Ireland Question in British Politics* (London: Macmillan, 1996): 129–42.
5  See N. Watson, *Robin Chichester-Clark* (London: Profile Books, 2020): 103.
6  1922 Committee, *Minutes*, 27 February 1969.
7  1922 Committee Executive, *Minutes*, 6 February 2002.
8  Gill, *Cracking the Whip*: 97–8.
9  1922 Committee Executive, *Minutes*, 12 February 2014.
10  1922 Committee Executive, *Minutes*, 13 July 1989.
11  Former MEP to author, 2023.
12  1922 Committee Executive, *Minutes*, 25 June 2003.
13  1922 Committee Executive, *Minutes*, 9 July 2003.
14  1922 Committee, *Minutes*, 24 February 1943, 10 March 1943.
15  *The Times*, 11 March 1943.
16  1922 Committee, *Minutes*, 3 February 1943.
17  Derek Walker-Smith MP to the Rt Hon. Patrick Buchan-Hepburn, 11 July 1952. Letter in 1922 Committee files.
18  1922 Committee, *Minutes*, 6 December 1956.
19  1922 Committee, *Minutes*, 23 July 1964.
20  Ian Gow MP to the Prime Minister, 29 July 1982. Thatcher MSS, THCR 2/6/2/114 pt 4 f24.
21  1922 Committee, *Minutes*, 18 March 1971.
22  William van Straubenzee MP to Rt Hon. Edward du Cann MP, 5 March 1975. Letter in 1922 Committee files.
23  1922 Committee Executive, *Minutes*, 17 January 2007.
24  N. de Bois, *Confessions of a Recovering MP* (London: Biteback, 2018): 79.
25  *Ibid.*: 79; see Bale, *The Conservative Party*: 401.
26  Cameron, *For the Record*: 238.
27  Elliott and Hanning, *Cameron: Practically a Conservative*: 418.
28  B. Cash, 'Composition Controversy', *The House*, 36:1452 (17 May 2013): 11.
29  Harris, *The Conservatives*: 533.
30  Elliott and Hanning, *Cameron: Practically a Conservative*: 418.
31  Norton, *The Voice of the Backbenchers*: 40.
32  Elliott and Hanning, *Cameron: Practically a Conservative*: 418.
33  Cameron, *For the Record*: 239.
34  1922 Committee, *Minutes*, 23 November 1950.
35  1922 Committee Executive, *Minutes*, 14 November 1996.

36 A. Mitchell, *Beyond a Fringe: Tales from a Reformed Establishment Lackey* (London: Biteback, 2021): 268.

37 Two former Chief Whips to author, 2023; G. Brandreth, *Breaking the Code* (London: Phoenix, 2000): 437.

38 *Ibid.*

39 1922 Committee Executive, *Minutes*, 5 May 2004.

40 1922 Committee, *Minutes*, 25 April 2007.

41 1922 Committee, *Minutes*, 22 November 2000.

42 1922 Committee, *Minutes*, 15 March 1926.

43 As in, e.g. 1922 Committee, *Minutes*, 22 July 1976, 21 July 1977, 27 July 1978.

44 1922 Committee, *Minutes*, 28 April 1983.

45 1922 Committee, *Minutes*, 7 July 1983.

46 Memorandum of points raised at the 1922 Committee Executive, 26 July 1984.

47 Senior MP to author, 2023.

48 J. Critchley, *Palace of Varieties* (London: John Murray, 1989): 127.

49 Sir Peter Bottomley to author, 2023.

## 7 Engaging members' interests

1 Norton, 'Organization of Parliamentary Parties': 34–41; P. Norton, 'Party Committees in the House of Commons', *Parliamentary Affairs*, 36 (1983): 7–27.

2 H. Macmillan, *Winds of Change* (London: Macmillan, 1966): 159.

3 Jennings, *Parliament*: 374.

4 *The Times*, 10 March 1927.

5 *The Times*, 24 February 1937.

6 *The Times*, 18 June 1937; House of Commons, *Hansard*, 29 June 1937, cols 1801–7.

7 See Chapter 2 and *The Times*, 12 June 1934, 27 November 1934.

8 See, for example, Barnes and Nicholson, *The Leo Amery Diaries 1929–45*: 411 and *passim*.

9 Cited in Jennings, *Parliament*: 380.

10 Lord Turton to author. Norton, 'Organization of Parliamentary Parties': 35.

11 *The Times*, 21 November 1928.

12 *The Scotsman*, 21 March 1933, *Belfast Telegraph*, 21 March 1933.

13 *Aberdeen Press and Journal*, 16 February 1937.

14 *The Times*, 12 July 1938.

15 *The Times*, 30 November 1938; *Western Daily Press*, 30 November 1938; *The Scotsman*, 30 November 1938.

16 *Western Daily Press*, 1 December 1938; Jennings, *Parliament*: 379, n. 3.

17 Ball, *Portrait of a Party*: 380.

# Notes

18 *Ibid.*

19 A. King (ed.), *British Members of Parliament: A Self-Portrait* (London: Macmillan, 1974): 49.

20 Ball, *Portrait of a Party*: 380.

21 Chamberlain letters. R. C. Self (ed.), *The Austen Chamberlain Diary Letters* (Cambridge: Cambridge University Press, 1995): 482. See also *Parliament and Politics in the Age of Baldwin and Macdonald: The Headlam Diaries, 1923–35*, ed. S. Ball (London: The Historians' Press, 1992): 332.

22 K. Middlemas and J. Barnes, *Baldwin* (London: Weidenfeld & Nicolson, 1969): 894.

23 Self, *Austen Chamberlain Diary Letters*: 487.

24 G. Stewart, *Burying Caesar: Churchill, Chamberlain and the Battle for the Tory Party* (London: Phoenix, 2000): 258.

25 *Ibid.*: 288.

26 Winterton, *Orders of the Day*: 317–18.

27 D. Judge, *Backbench Specialisation in the House of Commons* (London: Heinemann, 1981): 129–33.

28 H. Beer, *Modern British Politics* (London: Faber & Faber, 1969): 378.

29 D. Judge, *Parliament and Industry* (Aldershot: Dartmouth, 1990): 202.

30 M. Rifkind, *Power and Pragmatism* (London: Biteback, 2016): 136.

31 NOW!, 'Blue Chips and Guy Fawkes: Mrs Thatcher's Loyal Rebels', 4 January 1980: 44.

32 R. Shepherd, *Enoch Powell* (London: Hutchinson, 1996): 107.

33 Gardiner, *A Bastard's Tale*: 134.

34 J. Brand, *British Parliamentary Parties* (Oxford: Oxford University Press, 1992): 53.

35 Burch, 'Approaches to Leadership': 170.

36 Rawlinson, *A Price Too High*: 82.

37 Ball, *Portrait of a Party*: 80.

38 *Ibid.*: 380.

39 Fisher, *Iain Macleod*: 78.

40 Butler and Pinto-Duschinsky, *The British General Election*: 75.

41 Norton, *Conservative Dissidents*: 220, 241.

42 *Ibid.*: 241.

43 T. Gorman, *The Bastards* (London: Pan Books, 1993): 29.

44 Norton, *Conservative Dissidents*: 268–71.

45 John Biffen MP to author. Norton, *Conservative Dissidents*: 269.

46 Cited in Judge, *Parliament and Industry*: 203.

47 Peter G. Richards, *The Backbenchers* (London: Faber & Faber, 1974): 49.

48 Jennings, *Parliament*: 380.

49 H. Fairlie, *The Life of Politics* (London: Methuen, 1968): 225.

50 Brand, *British Parliamentary Parties*: 127.

51 *Yorkshire Observer*, 22 April 1953.

# Notes

52 R. J. Jackson, *Rebels and Whips* (London: Macmillan, 1968): 105.
53 *The Economist*, 6 April 1957, cited in Beer, *Modern British Politics*: 379.
54 Onslow, *Backbench Debate*: 179.
55 *Ibid.*: 183.
56 C. Mott-Radclyffe, *Foreign Body in the Eye* (London: Leo Cooper, 1975): 222.
57 *Ibid.*
58 Shepherd, *Iain Macleod*: 224.
59 *The Macmillan Diaries*, Vol. 2: 364.
60 Shepherd, *Iain Macleod*: 228.
61 *Ibid.*: 231.
62 Bruce-Gardyne and Lawson, *The Power Game*: 102.
63 P. Norton, 'Intra-Party Dissent in the House of Commons: A Case Study. The Immigration Rules, 1972', *Parliamentary Affairs*, 29 (1976): 407–8.
64 P. Norton, *Conservative Dissidents* (London: Temple Smith, 1978): 131.
65 Burch, 'Approaches to Leadership': 175.
66 Ian Gow MP to the Prime Minister, Note, 28 January 1980. Thatcher MSS, THCR 2/6/2/15 pt 2 (8).
67 Norton, 'Party Committees': 16.
68 N. Lawson, *The View from No. 11* (London: Bantam Press, 1992): 320.
69 *Ibid.*: 843.
70 Brand, *British Parliamentary Parties*: 49.
71 *Ibid.*: 53–4.
72 A. Barker and M. Rush, *The Member of Parliament and His Information* (London: George Allen & Unwin, 1970): 281.
73 1922 Committee, *Minutes*, 13 April 1961.
74 1922 Committee, *Minutes*, 21 October 1982.
75 1922 Committee Executive, *Minutes*, 26 April 1984, 5 July 1984.
76 1922 Committee, *Minutes*, 29 November 1984.
77 1922 Committee, *Minutes*, 14 November 1985.
78 1922 Committee Executive, *Minutes*, 5 March 1992.
79 1922 Committee Executive, *Minutes*, 7 May 1992.
80 1922 Committee, *Minutes*, 21 May 1992.
81 1922 Committee Executive, *Minutes*, 2 February 1995.
82 Norton, 'The Parliamentary Party': 126–8.
83 *Ibid.*: 126.
84 Cited in Judge, *Parliament and Industry*: 202.
85 Junior minister to author. Norton, 'The Parliamentary Party': 129.
86 Confidential source to author. Norton, 'The Parliamentary Party': 129.
87 P. Norton, 'The Constitutional Position of Parliamentary Private Secretaries', *Public Law*, winter (1989): 235.
88 Norton, 'The Parliamentary Party': 127.
89 1922 Committee Executive, *Minutes*, 19 January 2000.
90 1922 Committee Executive, *Minutes*, 20 March 2002.

91  1922 Committee Executive, *Minutes*, 8 May 2002.

92  1922 Committee Executive, *Minutes*, 17 December 2003.

93  1922 Committee Executive, *Minutes*, 21 April 2004.

94  R. Hazell and B. Yong, *The Politics of Coalition* (Oxford: Hart Publishing, 2012): 112.

95  1922 Committee Executive, *Minutes*, 28 June 2017.

96  Sir Graham Brady to author, 2023.

# 8 Transforming or presiding?

1  Critchley, *Palace of Varieties*: 99.

2  Clark, *The Tories*: 373.

3  Sir Graham Brady to author, 2022.

4  *Ibid.*

5  *Belfast Telegraph*, 22 July 1929.

6  *Headlam Diaries, 1923–35*: 305.

7  Harvie-Watt, *Most of My Life*: 72.

8  Goodhart, *The 1922*: 74.

9  *Ibid.*: 96–7.

10  *Ibid.*: 102–3.

11  Schneer, *Ministers at War*: 204.

12  Goodhart, *The 1922*: 103.

13  *Channon Diaries 1938–43*: 557.

14  Roberts, *Eminent Churchillians*: 197.

15  Winterton, *Orders of the Day*: 289.

16  Harvie-Watt, *Most of My Life*: 55.

17  Kilmuir, *Political Adventure*: 63.

18  S. Ball (ed.), *Parliament and Politics in the Age of Churchill and Attlee: The Headlam Diaries 1935–1951* (Cambridge: Cambridge University Press, 1999): 289.

19  Harvie-Watt, *Most of My Life*: 74.

20  *Ibid.*: 131.

21  *Ibid.*

22  T. Bale, *The Conservatives since 1945* (Oxford: Oxford University Press, 2012): 49.

23  The Rt Hon. Sir Peter Tapsell to author, 2013.

24  Aitken, *Margaret Thatcher: Power and Personality*: 158.

25  H. Macmillan, *Riding the Storm 1956–1959* (New York: Harper & Row, 1971): 282.

26  *The Macmillan Diaries*, Vol. 2: 634.

27  As, e.g. Horne, *Macmillan 1957–1986*: 398.

28  Clark, *The Tories*: 376.

29 D. Waddington, *Memoirs* (London: Biteback, 2012): 104.

30 H. Young, *One of Us* (London: Macmillan, 1989): 94.

31 Conservative MP to author, 2023.

32 Shepherd, *The Power Brokers*: 15.

33 Critchley, *Palace of Varieties*: 99.

34 Watkins, *A Conservative Coup*: 149.

35 T. Renton, *Chief Whip* (London: Politico's, 2004): 91.

36 Shepherd, *The Power Brokers*: 37.

37 Renton, *Chief Whip*: 91.

38 Watkins, *A Conservative Coup*: 2; Clark, *Diaries*: 358.

39 1922 Committee Executive, *Minutes*, 22 January 1998.

40 Obituary, *The Guardian*, 6 June 2019.

41 1922 Committee Executive member to author, 2023.

42 Conservative MP to author, 2023.

43 A. Seldon, *May at No. 10: The Verdict* (London: Biteback, 2020): 286–7.

44 *The Times*, 5 June 2021.

45 *The Times*, 7 July 2021.

46 Du Cann, *Two Lives*: 55.

47 Ball, 'The 1922 Committee': 145.

48 1922 Committee, *Minutes*, 17 November 1955.

49 Ball, 'The 1922 Committee': 151.

50 Fisher, *Iain Macleod*: 72.

51 On the unofficial groupings, see L. Grant, 'An Historical Study of Unofficial Parliamentary Party Groupings in the Conservative Party from 1830', unpublished PhD thesis, University of Hull, 2010.

52 Ian Gow MP to the Prime Minister, 29 June 1979. Thatcher MSS, THCR 2/6/2/15.

53 Spicer, *The Spicer Diaries*: 447–8.

54 *Ibid.*: 455.

55 Norton, 'The Parliamentary Party': 118.

56 T. Bale, *The Conservative Party from Thatcher to Cameron*, 2nd edn (Cambridge: Polity Press, 2016): 362.

57 *The Guardian*, 17 May 2012.

58 Fisher, *The Tory Leaders*: 148.

59 *Ibid.*: 148–50; Du Cann, *Two Lives*: 202–3.

60 *Ibid.*: 203.

61 Spicer, *The Spicer Diaries*: 503.

62 I. Gilmour, *The Body Politic*, revised edn (London: Hutchinson, 1971): 272.

63 Bale, *The Conservatives since 1945*: 30.

64 Ziegler, *Edward Heath*: 108.

65 1922 Committee Executive, *Minutes*, 1 December 1994.

66 1922 Committee Executive, *Minutes*, 2 March 1995.

67 Lawson, *The View from No. 11*: 320.

68 1922 Committee Executive, *Minutes*, 25 January 2006.
69 Note of a meeting between Mrs Thatcher and the 1922 Committee executive, on Tuesday, 11 November 1975, to discuss devolution. Thatcher MSS, THCR 2/6/2/14/15.
70 Note prepared by Ian Gow, 1 August 1980. Thatcher MSS, THCR 2/6/2/114 pt 2 (9).
71 *The Macmillan Diaries*, Vol. 2: 367.
72 Shepherd, *The Power Brokers*: 101.
73 Brandreth, *Breaking the Code*: 128.
74 Spicer, *The Spicer Diaries*: 476.
75 Bale, *The Conservative Party*: 44.
76 Seldon, *Major*: 534.
77 Spicer, *The Spicer Diaries*: 495.
78 Bale, *The Conservative Party*: 338–9.
79 Ziegler, *Edward Heath*: 431.
80 Lawson, *The View from No. 11*: 175.
81 *Ibid.*: 369.
82 1922 Committee Executive, *Minutes*, 8 May 2002.
83 1922 Committee Executive, *Minutes*, 14 December 1989.
84 1922 Committee Executive, *Minutes*, 6 July 1995.
85 1922 Committee Executive, *Minutes*, 7 November 2001.
86 1922 Committee Executive, *Minutes*, 14 December 1989.
87 N. Ghani, 'Talking Tech', *The House*, 45:1735 (12 December 2022): 40.

## 9 What's going on?

1 Norton, 'Learning the Ropes': 188–9.
2 Rentoul, *Sometimes I Think*: 232.
3 1922 Committee Executive, *Minutes*, 2 July 2003.
4 1922 Committee Executive, *Minutes*, 21 February 2007.
5 1922 Committee Executive, *Minutes*, 7 January 2004.
6 1922 Committee Executive, *Minutes*, 5 May 2004.
7 1922 Committee Executive, *Minutes*, 25 January 2006.
8 1922 Committee Executive, *Minutes*, 8 February 2006.
9 1922 Committee Executive, *Minutes*, 4 March 2015.
10 See Angela Browning in E. Peplow and P. Pivatto, *The Political Lives of Postwar British MPs* (London: Bloomsbury Academic, 2020): 123.
11 1922 Committee Executive, *Minutes*, 20 July 2011.
12 Lord Hayward to author, 2023.
13 Sir Graham Brady to author, 2022.
14 Member of the 1922 Committee Executive to author, 2023.
15 Sir Graham Brady to author, 2022.

# Notes

16 E. Boyle and A. Crosland, *The Politics of Education* (Harmondsworth: Penguin, 1971): 119.

17 A. J. Davies, *We, the Nation: The Conservative Party and the Pursuit of Power* (London: Little, Brown and Company, 1995): 118.

18 1922 Committee, *Minutes*, 8 November 1962.

19 1922 Committee, *Minutes*, 12 March 1981.

20 1922 Committee, *Minutes*, 3 March 1983.

21 1922 Committee, *Minutes*, 2 December 1976.

22 1922 Committee, *Minutes*, 1 March 1990.

23 1922 Committee, *Minutes*, 4 June 1992.

24 1922 Committee, *Minutes*, 22 October 1992.

25 Personal observation.

26 Member of the 1922 Committee Executive to author, 2023.

27 D. Dilks, 'Baldwin's Second Government', in Lord Butler of Saffron Walden (ed.), *The Conservatives: A History from Their Origins to 1965* (London: George Allen & Unwin, 1977): 314. See also Ramsden, *Appetite for Power*: 287.

28 P. Norton, '"The Lady's Not for Turning": But What about the Rest of the Party? Mrs Thatcher and the Conservative Party 1979–1989', *Parliamentary Affairs*, 43 (1990): 41–58.

29 P. Norton, 'The Conservative Party from Thatcher to Major', in A. King (ed.), *Britain at the Polls 1992* (Chatham, NJ: Chatham House Publishers, 1993): 58–9.

30 *The Scotsman*, 1 December 1945.

31 T. Bale, 'Afterword', in T. Bale, *The Conservative Party from Thatcher to Cameron* (Cambridge: Polity, 2011): 401.

32 Senior backbencher to author. Norton, *The Voice of the Backbenchers*: 61.

33 Ramsden, *Winds of Change*: 361.

34 Former government chief whip to author, 2023.

35 Moore, *Margaret Thatcher*, Vol. 3: 557.

36 1922 Committee, *Minutes*, 7 June 1951.

37 J. Boyd-Carpenter, *Way of Life* (London: Sidgwick & Jackson, 1980): 116.

38 *Ibid.*: 117.

39 Shepherd, *Iain Macleod*: 274.

40 1922 Committee, *Minutes*, 31 October 1974.

41 1922 Committee, *Minutes*, 17 January 2001.

42 Thatcher, *The Downing Street Years*: 130.

43 1922 Committee Executive, *Minutes*, 14 October 2009.

## 10 Collective action

1 De Bois, *Confessions of a Recovering MP*: 77.

2 Cameron, *For the Record*: 11.

# Notes

3 'Who Are the '22?', *BBC Radio 4*, 29 August 2022; Sir Graham Brady to author, 2022.

4 Peplow and Pivatto, *Political Lives*: 122.

5 1922 Committee, *Minutes*, 16 February 1925.

6 C. Patten, 'Policy Making in Opposition', in Z. Layton-Henry (ed.), *Conservative Party Politics* (London: Macmillan Press, 1980): 10–11.

7 P. Norton and A. Aughey, *Conservatives and Conservatism* (London: Temple Smith, 1981): 229–30.

8 1922 Committee Executive, *Minutes*, 9 April 2003.

9 *Ibid.*

10 *Ibid.*

11 Spicer, *The Spicer Diaries*: 562.

12 *Ibid.*: 563.

13 1922 Committee, *Minutes*, 10 December 1953.

14 Norton, *Dissension in the House of Commons*: 609.

15 Memorandum, 1922 Committee to National Union Review, undated, 1922 Committee papers.

16 Gill, *Cracking the Whip*: 37–8.

17 Bale, *The Conservative Party*: 75.

18 Spicer, *The Spicer Diaries*: 475.

19 1922 Committee Executive, *Minutes*, 14 May 2003.

20 Spicer, *The Spicer Diaries*: 505.

21 *Ibid.*: 505.

22 1922 Committee, *Minutes*, 29 June 2005.

23 1922 Committee Executive, *Minutes*, 1 December 1994.

24 1922 Committee Executive, *Minutes*, 2 March 1995.

25 1922 Committee Executive, *Minutes*, 2 May 2001.

26 Snowdon, *Back from the Brink*: 185.

27 Rt Hon. Lord Blencathra to author, 2023.

28 Spicer, *The Spicer Diaries*: 555.

29 1922 Committee Executive, *Minutes*, 22 January 2003.

30 1922 Committee Executive, *Minutes*, 28 January 1993.

31 1922 Committee Executive, *Minutes*, 22 January 2003.

32 1922 Committee Executive, *Minutes*, 12 December 2007.

33 1922 Committee Executive, *Minutes*, 23 January 2008.

34 1922 Committee Executive, *Minutes*, 18 March 1993.

35 1922 Committee, *Minutes*, 1 March 1951.

36 1922 Committee Executive, *Minutes*, 4 December 2003.

37 1922 Committee Executive, *Minutes*, 18 November 1993.

38 1922 Committee Executive, *Minutes*, 7 November 1991.

39 Cited in R. Rhodes James, *Bob Boothby: A Portrait* (London: Hodder & Stoughton, 1991): 374.

40 Baker, *The Turbulent Years*: 261.

# Notes

41 Spicer, *The Spicer Diaries*: 608.
42 I. Kennedy, *Cleaning up the Mess* (London: Biteback, 2019): 103–8.
43 *Ibid.*: 119.
44 Harvie-Watt, *Most of My Life*: 119; *Channon Diaries 1938–43*: 972–3.
45 *Headlam Diaries 1935–1951*: 358.
46 Norton, *Dissension in the House of Commons*: 89.
47 House of Commons, *Hansard*, 12 January 1971, col. 11. See also S. Lloyd, *Mr Speaker, Sir* (London: Jonathan Cape, 1976): 20–4.
48 House of Commons, *Hansard*, 12 January 1971, col. 16.

# 11 Us versus them

1 King, 'Modes of Executive–Legislative Relations': 11–34.
2 P. Norton, 'Is the Westminster System of Government Alive and Well?' *Journal of Comparative and International Law*, 9 (2022): 10–12, 16–18.
3 Eaves, *Emergency Powers*: 21.
4 Roberts, *Eminent Churchillians*: 187.
5 Bale, *The Conservatives since 1945*: 17.
6 Ramsden, *Making of Conservative Party Policy*: 95.
7 Bale, *The Conservatives since 1945*: 17.
8 G. F. Millar, 'Hill, Sir Alexander Galloway Erskine-, First Baronet (1894–1947)', *Oxford Dictionary of National Biography* (Oxford: Oxford University Press, online edn 2008, www.oxforddnb.com/display/10.1093/ref:odnb/9780198614128.001.0001/odnb-9780198614128-e-64631 [accessed 5 January 2023].
9 Ball, *Portrait of a Party*: 239.
10 Charmley, *History of Conservative Party Politics*: 115.
11 Roberts, *Eminent Churchillians*: 187.
12 Millar, 'Hill, Sir Alexander Galloway Erskine-'.
13 *Birmingham Mail*, 8 August 1940.
14 Goodhart, *The 1922*: 133.
15 A. J. P. Taylor, '1932–1945', in D. Butler (ed.), *Coalitions in British Politics* (London: Macmillan, 1978): 91.
16 *CHIPS*, ed. R. Rhodes James: 316.
17 Ball, 'The 1922 Committee': 149.
18 Clark, *The Tories*: 233.
19 *Ibid.*: 234.
20 Goodhart, *The 1922*: 111–12.
21 R. Hermiston, *All Behind You, Winston* (London: Aurum Press, 2016): 140.
22 Ball, *Portrait of a Party*: 465.
23 *Ibid.*: 239.
24 Hermiston, *All Behind You*: 236.

# Notes

25 *The Times*, 12 February 1943.
26 *Ibid.*
27 G. Lewis, *Lord Hailsham: A Life* (London: Pimlico, 1998): 114.
28 Barnes and Nicholson, *The Leo Amery Diaries 1929–1945*: 850.
29 *Ibid.*: 967.
30 *Ibid.*
31 H. J. Laski, *Reflections on the Constitution* (Manchester: Manchester University Press, 1950): 57.
32 P. Norton, 'The Politics of Coalition', in N. Allen and J. Bartle (eds), *Britain at the Polls 2010* (London: Sage, 2011): 242.
33 *Ibid.*: 261.
34 M. Laver and N. Schofield, *Multi-Party Government: The Politics of Coalition in Europe* (Ann Arbor, MI: University of Michigan Press, 1998): 150–5.
35 J. Gerard, *The Clegg Coup* (London: Gibson Square, 2011): 157.
36 R. Fox, 'Five Days in May: A New Political Order Emerges', in A. Geddes and J. Tonge (eds), *Britain Votes 2010* (Oxford: Oxford University Press, 2010): 34.
37 Norton, 'The Coalition and the Conservatives': 474.
38 *Ibid.*: 474–5.
39 P. Cowley, 'The Coalition and Parliament', in A. Seldon and M. Finn (eds), *The Coalition Effect 2010–2015* (Cambridge: Cambridge University Press, 2015): 146.
40 1922 Committee Executive, *Minutes*, 16 June 2010.
41 D'Ancona, *In It Together*: 80.
42 Norton, 'The Coalition and the Conservatives': 481.
43 1922 Committee Executive, *Minutes*, 18 July 2007.
44 1922 Committee Executive, *Minutes*, 10 January 2007.
45 Member of the 1922 Committee Executive to author, 2012.
46 Hazell and Yong, *The Politics of Coalition*: 112.

## 12 'May I have a word, minister?'

1 Benemy, *The Elected Monarch*: 105.
2 *The Times*, 1 May 1928.
3 Crick, *The Reform of Parliament*: 102. See also R. McKenzie, *British Political Parties*, 2nd edn (London: Heinemann Educational Books, 1967): 59.
4 Goodhart, *The 1922*: 112–13.
5 *Daily Record*, 6 March 1942.
6 McKenzie, *British Political Parties*: 61.
7 1922 Committee, *Minutes*, 16 November 1961.
8 Burch, 'Approaches to Leadership': 176.
9 *Birmingham Daily Post*, 21 July 1954.

# Notes

10 P. Gordon Walker, 'Danger! Tory Back-Seat Drivers', *Daily Mirror*, 28 July 1954: 2.
11 Benemy, *The Elected Monarch*: 105.
12 1922 Committee, *Minutes*, 30 January 1968.
13 House of Commons, *Hansard*, 3 February 1969, cols 167–72; Norton, *Dissension in the House of Commons*: 313.
14 Boyd-Carpenter, *Way of Life*: 216.
15 See D. Kavanagh, *Thatcherism and British Politics* (Oxford: Oxford University Press, 1987): 267; P. Jenkins, *Mrs Thatcher's Revolution* (London: Pan Books, 1988): 176–7.
16 Bale, *The Conservatives since 1945*: 291.
17 A. Denham and M. Garnett, *Keith Joseph* (London: Routledge, 2002): 392.
18 P. Regan, 'The 1986 Shops Bill', *Parliamentary Affairs*, 41 (1987); 218–35; F. A. Bown, 'The Shops Bill', in M. Rush (ed.), *Parliament and Pressure Politics* (Oxford: Clarendon Press, 1990).
19 Ramsden, *Making of Conservative Party Policy*: 175.
20 *Ibid.*: 238.
21 *The Macmillan Diaries*, Vol. 2: 108.
22 *Ibid.*: 494.
23 *Truth*, 25 February 1955.
24 *Birmingham Gazette*, 22 July 1954.
25 E. Bevins, *The Greasy Pole* (London: Hodder & Stoughton, 1965): 95.
26 *The Macmillan Diaries*, Vol. 2: 383.
27 Norton, *Conservative Dissidents*: 150.
28 J. Prior, *A Balance of Power* (London: Hamish Hamilton, 1986): 163.
29 Elliott and Hanning, *Cameron: Practically a Conservative*: 318.
30 Snowdon, *Back from the Brink*: 250–1.
31 Former MP and Cabinet minister to author, 2023.
32 1922 Committee, *Minutes*, 15 July 1954.
33 House of Commons, *Hansard*, 20 July 1954, col. 1283.
34 S. E. Finer, 'The Individual Responsibility of Ministers', in G. Marshall (ed.), *Ministerial Responsibility* (Oxford: Oxford University Press, 1989): 124.
35 *Birmingham Daily Post*, 21 July 1954.
36 *Yorkshire Post and Leeds Intelligencer*, 21 July 1954.
37 Nott, *Here Today*: 269.
38 The Rt Hon. Sir Peter Tapsell to author, 2013.
39 I. Gilmour, *Whatever Happened to the Tories: The Conservatives since 1945* (London: Fourth Estate, 1998): 332.
40 C. Moore, *Margaret Thatcher: The Authorized Biography*, Vol. 2 (London: Allen Lane, 2015): 481.
41 *Daily Mirror*, 17 December 1988.
42 E. Currie, *Diaries, Vol. II: 1992–1997* (London: Biteback, 2012): 46.
43 Moore, *Margaret Thatcher*, Vol. 3: 552.

44 G. Howe, *Conflict of Loyalty* (London: Macmillan, 1994): 633.

45 *The Independent*, 24 June 1993.

46 G. Brandreth, *Something Sensational to Read on the Train* (London: John Murray, 2009): 541.

47 J. Major, *The Autobiography* (London: HarperCollins, 1999): 553.

48 Mitchell, *Beyond a Fringe*: 303.

49 *Ibid.*

50 S. Cameron, 'When the 1922 Committee Comes Calling, It's Time to Go', *Daily Telegraph*, 17 October 2012.

# 13 'The men in grey suits'

1 As, e.g. Ridley, *The Thatcher Years*: 251.

2 De Bois, *Confessions of a Recovering MP*: 77.

3 P. Norton, 'The Party Leader', in P. Norton (ed.), *The Conservative Party* (London: Prentice-Hall/Harvester Wheatsheaf, 1996): 145–7.

4 Blake, *The Conservative Party*: 278.

5 R. A. Butler, *The Art of the Possible* (London: Penguin, 1973): 238.

6 Goodhart, *The 1922*: 191.

7 R. Churchill, *The Fight for the Tory Leadership* (London: William Heinemann, 1964).

8 *The Macmillan Diaries*, Vol. II: 609.

9 On the rules, see T. Heppell, *Choosing the Tory Leader* (London: I. B. Tauris, 2007).

10 Thorpe, *Alec Douglas-Home*: 446.

11 *Ibid.*

12 *The Times*, 22 November 1974.

13 Thorpe, *Alec Douglas-Home*: 447.

14 See Punnett, *Selecting the Party Leader*: 73.

15 Spicer, *The Spicer Diaries*: 381.

16 K. Alderman, 'The Conservative Party Leadership Election of 1995', *Parliamentary Affairs*, 45 (1996): 321, 327–8.

17 N. Lamont, *In Office* (London: Little, Brown and Company, 1999): 464.

18 Leadsom, *Snakes and Ladders*: 96.

19 M. Garnett and I. Aitken, *Splendid! Splendid!* (London: Jonathan Cape, 2002): 67.

20 P. Cowley, 'The Mystery of the Third Hurdle: Re-electing the Conservative Leader', *Politics*, 16 (1996): 80–3.

21 Norton, 'In Office but Not in Power': 102.

22 Brandreth, *Breaking the Code*: 344. See also T. McMeeking, *The Political Leadership of Prime Minister John Major* (Cham: Palgrave Macmillan, 2021): 153–5.

23  H. Mount, *Summer Madness* (London: Biteback, 2017): 194

24  T. Quinn, *Electing and Ejecting Party Leaders in Britain* (Basingstoke: Palgrave Macmillan, 2015): 125.

25  Denham and O'Hara, *Democratising Conservative Leadership Selection*: 18.

26  Quinn, *Electing and Ejecting Party Leaders*: 179.

27  *Ibid.*

28  Leadsom, *Snakes and Ladders*: 104.

29  1922 Committee Executive, *Minutes*, 19 November 2003.

30  *A 21st Century Party*, cited in Snowdon, *Back from the Brink*: 184.

31  Letter from Sir Michael Spicer to Raymond Monbiot, 4 March 2004.

32  1922 Committee Executive, *Minutes*, 19 May 2005.

33  1922 Committee Executive, *Minutes*, 7 June 2015, 5 July 2005.

34  Snowdon, *Back from the Brink*: 185.

35  *Ibid.*: 185–6.

36  1922 Committee Executive, *Minutes*, 8 March 2006.

## 14 Conclusion

1  Letters, *The Times*, 29 October 1942.

2  Norton, 'Westminster System of Government': 1–24.

3  Norton, 'In Office but Not in Power': 77.

4  Norton, *Parliament in British Politics*: 5.

5  Norton, 'Power behind the Scenes': 245–66.

6  Norton, 'Votes of Confidence': 189.

# Bibliography

Aitken, J., *Margaret Thatcher: Power and Personality* (London: Bloomsbury, 2013).

Alderman, K., 'The Conservative Party Leadership Election of 1995', *Parliamentary Affairs*, 45 (1996), pp. 316–32.

Allmark, L., 'More than Rubber Stamps: The Consequences Produced by Legislatures in Non-Democratic States beyond Latent Legitimation', *The Journal of Legislative Studies*, 18 (2012), pp. 184–202.

Aspinall, A., 'English Party Organisation in the Early Nineteenth Century', *English Historical Review*, 41 (1926), pp. 389–411.

Attlee, C. R., *The Labour Party in Perspective* (London: Gollancz, 1937).

Bachrach, P. and Baratz, M., 'Two Faces of Power', *American Political Science Review*, 56 (1962), pp. 947–52.

Baker, K., *The Turbulent Years* (London: Faber & Faber, 1993).

Bale, T., *The Conservatives Since 1945* (Oxford: Oxford University Press, 2012).

Bale, T., *The Conservative Party from Thatcher to Cameron*, 2nd edn (Cambridge: Polity, 2016).

Ball, S., *Baldwin and the Conservative Party: The Crisis of 1929–1931* (New Haven, CT: Yale University Press, 1988).

Ball, S., 'The 1922 Committee: The Formative Years 1922–1945', *Parliamentary History*, 9 (1990), pp. 129–57.

Ball, S. (ed.), *Parliament and Politics in the Age of Baldwin and Macdonald: The Headlam Diaries, 1923–35* (London: The Historians' Press, 1992).

Ball, S. (ed.), *Parliament and Politics in the Age of Churchill and Attlee: The Headlam Diaries 1935–1951* (Cambridge: Cambridge University Press, 1999).

Ball, S., *Portrait of a Party: The Conservative Party in Britain 1918–1945* (Oxford: Oxford University Press, 2013).

Barker, A. and Rush, M., *The Member of Parliament and His Information* (London: George Allen & Unwin, 1970).

Barnes, J. and Nicholson, D. (eds), *The Leo Amery Diaries 1929–1945* (London: Hutchinson, 1988).

# Bibliography

Barwell, G., *Chief of Staff* (London: Atlantic Books, 2021).

Beer, S. H., *Modern British Politics* (London: Faber & Faber, 1969).

Behrens, R., *The Conservative Party from Heath to Thatcher* (Farnborough: Saxon House, 1980).

Beloff, M. and Peele, G., *The Government of the UK* (London: Weidenfeld & Nicolson, 1980).

Benemy, F. W. G., *The Elected Monarch* (London: George G. Harrap & Co., 1965).

Bevins, E., *The Greasy Pole* (London: Hodder & Stoughton, 1965).

Blake, R., *The Conservative Party from Peel to Churchill* (London: Eyre & Spottiswoode, 1970).

Blake, R., *The Conservative Party from Peel to Major* (London: Arrow, 1998).

Bogdanor, V., 'The Selection of the Party Leader', in A. Seldon and S. Ball (eds), *Conservative Century* (Oxford: Oxford University Press, 1994).

Bower, T., *Boris Johnson – The Gambler* (London: W. H. Allen, 2020).

Bown, F. A., 'The Shops Bill', in M. Rush (ed.), *Parliament and Pressure Politics* (Oxford: Clarendon Press, 1990).

Boyd-Carpenter, J., *Way of Life* (London: Sidgwick & Jackson, 1980).

Boyle, E. and Crosland, A., *The Politics of Education* (Harmondsworth: Penguin, 1971).

Brand, J., *British Parliamentary Parties* (Oxford: Oxford University Press, 1992).

Brandreth, G., *Breaking the Code* (London: Phoenix, 2000).

Brandreth, G., *Something Sensational to Read on the Train* (London: John Murray, 2009).

Bruce-Gardyne, J. and Lawson, N., *The Power Game* (London: Macmillan, 1976).

Bryce, Lord, *Modern Democracies*, Vol. 2 (London: Macmillan, 1992).

Bulmer-Thomas, I., *The Party System in Great Britain* (London: Phoenix House, 1953).

Burch, M., 'Approaches to Leadership in Opposition: Edward Heath and Margaret Thatcher', in Z. Layton-Henry (ed.), *Conservative Party Politics* (London: Macmillan, 1980).

Butler, R. A., *The Art of the Possible* (London: Penguin, 1973).

Butler, D. and Kavanagh, D., *The British General Election of 1979* (London: Macmillan, 1980).

Butler, D. and Pinto-Duschinsky, M., *The British General Election of 1970* (London: Macmillan, 1971).

Butt, R., *The Power of Parliament* (London: Constable, 1967).

Cameron, D., *For the Record* (London: William Collins, 2019).

Cameron, S., 'When the 1922 Committee Comes Calling, It's Time to Go', *Daily Telegraph*, 17 October 2012.

Campbell, J., *Edward Heath: A Biography* (London: Jonathan Cape, 1993).

# Bibliography

Campbell, J., *Margaret Thatcher, Vol. 2: The Iron Lady* (London: Jonathan Cape, 2003).

Carroll, R. and Poole, K., 'Roll-Call Analysis and the Study of Legislatures', in S. Martin, T. Saalfeld and K. Strøm (eds), *The Oxford Handbook of Legislative Studies* (Oxford: Oxford University Press, 2014).

Cash, B., 'Composition Controversy', *The House*, 36:1452 (2013), 17 May, p. 11.

Catterall, P. (ed.) *The Macmillan Diaries*, Vol. 2 (London: Macmillan, 2011).

Charmley, J., *A History of Conservative Party Politics, 1900–1996* (Basingstoke: Macmillan Press, 1996).

Chen, W., 'Is the Label "Minimal Legislature" Still Appropriate? The Role of the National People's Congress in China's Political System', *The Journal of Legislative Studies*, 22 (2016), pp. 257–75.

Churchill, R., *The Fight for the Tory Leadership* (London: William Heinemann, 1964).

Clark, A., *Diaries* (London: Weidenfeld & Nicolson, 1993).

Clark, A., *The Tories: Conservatives and the Nation State* (London: Weidenfeld & Nicolson, 1998).

Close, C., Gherghina, S. and Sierens, V., 'Prompting Legislative Agreement and Loyalty: What Role for Intra-Party Democracy?', *Parliamentary Affairs*, 72 (2019), pp. 387–405.

Cole, H. and Heale, J., *Out of the Blue* (London: HarperCollins, 2022).

Colville, J., *The Fringes of Power: Downing Street Diaries, Volume One: September 1939–October 1941* (London: Sceptre, 1986).

Commission to Strengthen Parliament, *Strengthening Parliament* (London: The Conservative Party, 2000).

Cooke, A. and Parkinson, S., 'Rab Butler's Golden Era?' in A. Cooke (ed.), *Tory Policy-Making* (London: Conservative Research Department, 2009).

Cosgrave, P., *Carrington: A Life and a Policy* (London: J. M. Dent, 1985).

Cosgrave, P., *The Lives of Enoch Powell* (London: Pan Books, 1990).

Cowley, P., 'The Mystery of the Third Hurdle: Re-electing the Conservative Leader', *Politics*, 16 (1996), pp. 79–86.

Cowley, P., 'Unbridled Passions? Free Votes, Issues of Conscience and the Accountability of British Members of Parliament', *The Journal of Legislative Studies*, 4 (1998), pp. 70–88.

Cowley, P., 'Chaos or Cohesion? Major and the Parliamentary Conservative Party', in P. Dorey (ed.), *The Major Premiership: Politics and Policies under John Major, 1990–97* (Basingstoke: Palgrave, 1999).

Cowley, P., 'The Coalition and Parliament', in A. Seldon and M. Finn (eds), *The Coalition Effect 2010–2015* (Cambridge: Cambridge University Press, 2015).

Cowley, P. and Kavanagh, D., *The British General Election of 2015* (Basingstoke: Palgrave Macmillan, 2016).

259

# Bibliography

Cowley, P. and Stuart, M., 'Still Causing Trouble: The Conservative Parliamentary Party', *Political Quarterly*, 75 (2004), pp. 356–61.

Cowley, P. and Stuart, M., 'Party Rules, OK: Voting in the House of Commons on the Human Fertilisation and Embryology Bill', *Parliamentary Affairs*, 63 (2010), pp. 173–81.

Crewe, E., *House of Commons: An Anthropology of the Work of MPs* (London: Haus Publishing, 2015).

Crewe, E., *The Anthropology of Parliaments* (London: Routledge, 2021).

Crick, B., *The Reform of Parliament*, revised 2nd edn (London: Weidenfeld & Nicolson, 1970).

Crick, M., In *Search of Michael Howard* (London: Simon & Schuster, 2005).

Critchley, J., *Westminster Blues* (London: Futura, 1986).

Critchley, J., *Palace of Varieties* (London: John Murray, 1989).

Critchley, J., *A Bag of Boiled Sweets* (London: Faber & Faber, 1994).

Currie, E., *Diaries, Vol. II: 1992–1997* (London: Biteback, 2012).

D'Ancona, M., *In It Together* (London: Viking, 2013).

Davies, A. J., *We, The Nation: The Conservative Party and the Pursuit of Power* (London: Little, Brown and Company, 1995).

De Bois, N., *Confessions of a Recovering MP* (London: Biteback, 2018).

Denham, A. and Garnett, M., *Keith Joseph* (London: Routledge, 2002).

Denham, A. and O'Hara, K., *Democratising Conservative Leadership Selection* (Manchester: Manchester University Press, 2008).

Dilks, D., 'Baldwin's Second Government', in Lord Butler of Saffron Walden (ed.), *The Conservatives: A History from Their Origins to 1965* (London: George Allen & Unwin, 1977).

Dorey, P., 'Despair and Disillusion Abound: The Major Premiership in Perspective', in P. Dorey (ed.), *The Major Premiership: Politics and Policies under John Major, 1990–97* (Basingstoke: Palgrave, 1999).

Du Cann, E., *Two Lives* (Upton upon Severn: Images Publishing, 1995).

Du Cann, E., 'Formidable', in I. Dale (ed.), *Memories of Maggie* (London: Politico's, 2000).

Eaves, J., *Emergency Powers and the Parliamentary Watchdog: Parliament and the Executive in Great Britain 1939–51* (London: Hansard Society, 1957).

Elliott, F. and Hanning, J., *Cameron: The Rise of the New Conservative* (London: HarperPress, 2007).

Elliott, F. and Hanning, J., *Cameron: Practically a Conservative* (London: Fourth Estate, 2012).

Fairlie, H., *The Life of Politics* (London: Methuen, 1968).

Fall, K., *The Gatekeeper* (London: HQ, 2020).

Findley, R., 'The Conservative Party and Defeat: The Significance of Resale Price Maintenance and the General Election of 1964', *Twentieth Century British History*, 12 (2001), pp. 327–53.

# Bibliography

Finer, S. E., 'The Individual Responsibility of Ministers', in G. Marshall (ed.), *Ministerial Responsibility* (Oxford: Oxford University Press, 1989).

Fisher, N., *Iain Macleod* (London: Andre Deutsch, 1973).

Fisher, N., *The Tory Leaders* (London: Weidenfeld & Nicolson, 1977).

Fleming, N. C., *Britannia's Zealots*, Vol. 1 (London: Bloomsbury, 2019).

Fletcher, N., 'William Hague', in T. Heppell (ed.), *Leaders of the Opposition* (Basingstoke: Palgrave Macmillan, 2012).

Forman, N., *Mastering British Politics* (Basingstoke: Macmillan, 1985).

Fox, R., 'Five Days in May: A New Political Order Emerges', in A. Geddes and J. Tonge (eds), *Britain Votes 2010* (Oxford: Oxford University Press, 2010).

Gardiner, G., *Margaret Thatcher: From Childhood to Leadership* (London: William Kimber, 1975).

Gardiner, G., *A Bastard's Tale* (London: Aurum Press, 1999).

Gardiner, G., 'A Cell of Revolutionaries', in I. Dale (ed.), *Memories of Maggie* (London: Politico's, 2000).

Garnett, M. and Aitken, I., *Splendid! Splendid!* (London: Jonathan Cape, 2002).

Gerard, J., *The Clegg Coup* (London: Gibson Square, 2011).

Ghani, N., 'Talking Tech', *The House*, 45:1735 (2022), 12 December, pp. 36–40.

Gill, C., *Cracking the Whip* (Epsom: Bretwalda Books, 2012).

Gilmour, I., *The Body Politic*, revised edn (London: Hutchinson, 1971).

Gilmour, I., *Whatever Happened to the Tories: The Conservatives since 1945* (London: Fourth Estate, 1998).

Goodhart, P., *The 1922* (London: Macmillan, 1973).

Gordon Walker, P., 'Danger! Tory Back-Seat Drivers', *Daily Mirror*, 28 July 1954, p. 2.

Gorman, T., *The Bastards* (London: Pan Books, 1993).

Grant, L., 'An Historical Study of Unofficial Parliamentary Party Groupings in the Conservative Party from 1830', unpublished PhD thesis, University of Hull, 2010.

Haigh, P. and Gaudion, A., 'What Is the 1922 Committee, Who Is on It and What Do They Do?' *Metro*, 21 July 2022. www.msn.com/en-gb/news/world/what-is-the-1922-committee-who-is-on-it-and-what-do-they-do/ar-AAZPgAy

Hailsham, Lord, *The Door Wherein I Went* (London: Collins, 1978).

Harris, R., *The Conservatives: A History* (London: Bantam Press, 2011).

Harvie-Watt, G., *Most of My Life* (London: Springwood Books, 1980).

Hayton, R., *Reconstructing Conservatism? The Conservative Party in Opposition, 1997–2010* (Manchester: Manchester University Press, 2012).

Hayton, R. and Heppell, T., 'The Quiet Man of British Politics: The Rise, Fall and Significance of Iain Duncan Smith', *Parliamentary Affairs*, 63 (2010), pp. 425–45.

Hazell, R. and Yong, B., *The Politics of Coalition* (Oxford: Hart Publishing, 2012).

# Bibliography

Heath, E., *The Course of My Life* (London: Hodder & Stoughton, 1998).

Heffer, S., *Like the Roman: The Life of Enoch Powell* (London: Phoenix, 1998).

Heffer, S. (ed.), *Henry 'Chips' Channon: The Diaries 1918–38* (London: Hutchinson, 2021).

Heffer, S. (ed.), *Henry 'Chips' Channon: The Diaries 1938–43* (London: Hutchinson, 2021).

Heffer, S. (ed.), *Henry 'Chips' Channon: The Diaries 1943–57* (London: Hutchinson, 2022).

Heidar, K. and Koole, R. (eds), *Parliamentary Party Groups in European Democracies* (London: Routledge, 2000).

Heppell, T., *Choosing the Tory Leader* (London: I. B. Tauris, 2007).

Hermiston, R., *All Behind You, Winston* (London: Aurum Press, 2016).

Hoffman, J. D., *The Conservative Party in Opposition 1945–51* (London: MacGibbon & Kee, 1964).

Horne, A., *Macmillan 1957–1986, Vol. II of the Official Biography* (London: Macmillan, 1989).

Howard, A., *RAB: The Life of R. A. Butler* (London: Jonathan Cape, 1987).

Howe, G., *Conflict of Loyalty* (London: Macmillan, 1994).

Ingold, T., *Making: Anthropology, Archaeology, Art and Architecture* (London: Routledge, 2013).

Jackson, R. J., *Rebels and Whips* (London: Macmillan, 1968).

Jago, M., *Rab Butler: The Best Prime Minister We Never Had?* (London: Biteback, 2015).

Jenkins, P., *Mrs Thatcher's Revolution* (London: Pan Books, 1988).

Jennings, I., *Parliament*, 2nd edn (Cambridge: Cambridge University Press, 1957).

Judge, D., *Backbench Specialisation in the House of Commons* (London: Heinemann, 1981).

Judge, D., *Parliament and Industry* (Aldershot: Dartmouth, 1990).

Kam, C., 'Party Discipline', in S. Martin, T. Saalfeld and K. Strøm (eds), *The Oxford Handbook of Legislative Studies* (Oxford: Oxford University Press, 2014).

Kavanagh, D., *Thatcherism and British Politics* (Oxford: Oxford University Press, 1987).

Kennedy, I., *Cleaning up the Mess* (London: Biteback, 2019).

Kilmuir, Earl of, *Political Adventure* (London: Weidenfeld & Nicolson, 1964).

King, A. (ed.), *British Members of Parliament: A Self-Portrait* (London: Macmillan, 1974).

King, A., 'Modes of Executive–Legislative Relations: Great Britain, France and West Germany', *Legislative Studies Quarterly*, 1 (1976), pp. 11–34.

King-Hall, S., 'Foreword', in J. Eaves, *Emergency Powers and the Parliamentary Watchdog: Parliament and the Executive in Great Britain 1939–51* (London: Hansard Society, 1957).

Lamb, R., *The Macmillan Years 1957–1963: The Emerging Truth* (London: John Murray, 1995).

# Bibliography

Lamont, N., *In Office* (London: Little, Brown and Company, 1999).

Laski, H. J., *Reflections on the Constitution* (Manchester: Manchester University Press, 1950).

Laver, M. and Schofield, N., *Multi-Party Government: The Politics of Coalition in Europe* (Ann Arbor, MI: University of Michigan Press, 1998).

Lawson, N., *The View from No. 11* (London: Bantam Press, 1992).

Leadsom, A., *Snakes and Ladders* (London: Biteback, 2022).

Lee, C., *Carrington: An Honourable Man* (London: Viking, 2018).

Lee, M., *The Churchill Coalition, 1940–1945* (London: Batsford, 1980).

Lewis, G., *Lord Hailsham: A Life* (London: Pimlico, 1998).

Lexden, A., *Neville Chamberlain: Redressing the Balance* (London: Conservative History Group, 2018).

Lloyd, S., *Mr Speaker, Sir* (London: Jonathan Cape, 1976).

Loewenberg, G. (ed.), *Modern Parliaments: Change or Decline?* (Chicago: Aldine-Atherton, 1971).

Lowell, A. L., *The Government of England*, Vol. 1 (London: Macmillan, 1908).

Lukes, S., *Power: A Radical View*, 2nd revised edn (Basingstoke: Palgrave Macmillan, 2004).

McEwen, J. M., 'Unionist and Conservative Members of Parliament', unpublished PhD thesis, University of London, 1959.

McKenzie, R., *British Political Parties*, 2nd edn (London: Heinemann Educational Books, 1967).

McManus, M., *Edward Heath: A Singular Life* (London: Elliott and Thompson, 2016).

McMeeking, T., *The Political Leadership of Prime Minister John Major* (Cham: Palgrave Macmillan, 2021).

Macmillan, H., *Winds of Change* (London: Macmillan, 1966).

Macmillan, H., *Tides of Fortune, 1945–1955* (London: Macmillan, 1969).

Macmillan, H., *Riding the Storm 1956–1959* (New York: Harper & Row, 1971).

Major, J., *The Autobiography* (London: HarperCollins, 1999).

Middlemas, K. and Barnes, J., *Baldwin* (London: Weidenfeld & Nicolson, 1969).

Millar, G. F., 'Hill, Sir Alexander Galloway Erskine-, First Baronet (1894–1947)', *Oxford Dictionary of National Biography*, online edn (Oxford: Oxford University Press, 2008), www.oxforddnb.com/display/10.1093/ref:odnb/9780198614128.001.0001/odnb-9780198614128-e-64631 [accessed 5 January 2023].

Mills, C. Wright, *The Power Elite* (New York: Oxford University Press, 1956).

Mitchell, A., *Beyond a Fringe: Tales from a Reformed Establishment Lackey* (London: Biteback, 2021).

Moran, Lord, *Winston Churchill: The Struggle for Survival, 1940–1965* (London: Constable, 1966).

Moore, C., *Margaret Thatcher: The Authorized Biography*, Vol. 1 (London: Allen Lane, 2015).

# Bibliography

Moore, C., *Margaret Thatcher: The Authorized Biography*, Vol. 2 (London: Allen Lane, 2015).

Moore, C., *Margaret Thatcher: The Authorized Biography*, Vol. 3 (London: Allen Lane, 2019).

Mott-Radclyffe, C., *Foreign Body in the Eye* (London: Leo Cooper, 1975).

Mount, H., *Summer Madness* (London: Biteback, 2017).

Nabarro, G., *Portrait of a Politician* (Oxford: Robert Maxwell, 1969).

Nicolson, N. (ed.), *Harold Nicolson: Diaries and Letters, 1945–62* (London: Fontana, 1971).

Norton, P., *Dissension in the House of Commons 1945–1974* (London: Macmillan Press, 1975).

Norton, P., 'Intra-Party Dissent in the House of Commons: A Case Study. The Immigration Rules, 1972', *Parliamentary Affairs*, 29 (1976), pp. 404–20.

Norton, P., *Conservative Dissidents* (London: Temple Smith, 1978).

Norton, P., 'The Organization of Parliamentary Parties', in S. A. Walkland (ed.), *The House of Commons in the Twentieth Century* (Oxford: Clarendon Press, 1979).

Norton, P., 'Party Committees in the House of Commons', *Parliamentary Affairs*, 36 (1983), pp. 7–27.

Norton, P., 'The Constitutional Position of Parliamentary Private Secretaries', *Public Law* (winter 1989), pp. 232–6.

Norton, P., 'General Introduction', in P. Norton (ed.), *Legislatures* (Oxford: Oxford University Press, 1990).

Norton, P. '"The Lady's Not for Turning": But What about the Rest of the Party? Mrs Thatcher and the Conservative Party 1979–1989', *Parliamentary Affairs*, 43 (1990), pp. 41–58.

Norton, P., 'The Conservative Party from Thatcher to Major', in A. King (ed.), *Britain at the Polls 1992* (Chatham, NJ: Chatham House Publishers, 1993).

Norton, P., 'The Parliamentary Party and Party Committees', in A. Seldon and S. Ball (eds), *Conservative Century* (Oxford: Oxford University Press, 1994).

Norton, P., 'Conservative Politics and the Abolition of Stormont', in P. Catterall and S. McDougall (eds), *The Northern Ireland Question in British Politics* (London: Macmillan, 1996).

Norton, P., *The Conservative Party* (London: Prentice-Hall/Harvester Wheatsheaf, 1996).

Norton, P., 'The Conservative Party: "In Office but Not in Power"', in A. King (ed.), *New Labour Triumphs: Britain at the Polls* (Chatham, NJ: Chatham House Publishers, 1998).

Norton, P., 'Winning the War but Losing the Peace: The British House of Commons during the Second World War', *The Journal of Legislative Studies*, 4:3 (1998), pp. 43–51.

Norton, P., 'Playing by the Rules: The Constraining Hand of Parliamentary Procedure', *The Journal of Legislative Studies*, 7 (2001), pp. 1–33.

# Bibliography

Norton, P., 'The Conservative Party: Is There Anyone Out There?' in A. King (ed.), *Britain at the Polls, 2001* (Chatham, NJ: Chatham House Publishers, 2002).

Norton, P., 'Cohesion without Discipline: Party Voting in the House of Lords', *The Journal of Legislative Studies*, 9 (2003), pp. 57–72.

Norton, P., 'The Conservative Party: The Politics of Panic', in J. Bartle and A. King (eds), *Britain at the Polls, 2005* (Washington, DC: CQ Press, 2006).

Norton, P., 'Cameron and Conservative Success: Architect or By-stander?' in S. Lee and M. Beech (eds), *The Conservatives under David Cameron: Built to Last?* (Basingstoke: Palgrave Macmillan, 2009).

Norton, P., 'The Politics of Coalition', in N. Allen and J. Bartle (eds), *Britain at the Polls 2010* (London: Sage, 2011).

Norton, P., 'Coalition Cohesion', in T. Heppell and D. Seawright (eds), *Cameron and the Conservatives* (Basingstoke: Palgrave Macmillan, 2012).

Norton, P., *Parliament in British Politics*, 2nd edn (Basingstoke: Palgrave Macmillan, 2013).

Norton, P., *The Voice of the Backbenchers. The 1922 Committee: The First 90 Years, 1923–2013* (London: Conservative History Group, 2013).

Norton, P., 'The Coalition and the Conservatives', in A. Seldon and M. Finn (eds), *The Coalition Effect 2010–2015* (Cambridge: Cambridge University Press, 2015).

Norton, P., 'A Temporary Occupant of No 10? Prime Ministerial Succession in the Event of the Death of the Incumbent', *Public Law* (January 2016), pp. 18–33.

Norton, P., 'Learning the Ropes: Training MPs in the United Kingdom', in C. Lewis and K. Coghill (eds), *Parliamentarians' Professional Development* (Cham: Springer, 2016).

Norton, P., 'Is the House of Commons Too Powerful? The 2019 Bingham Lecture in Constitutional Studies, University of Oxford', *Parliamentary Affairs*, 72 (2019), pp. 996–1013.

Norton, P., 'Power behind the Scenes: The Importance of Informal Space in Legislatures', *Parliamentary Affairs*, 72 (2019), pp. 245–66.

Norton, P., *Governing Britain* (Manchester: Manchester University Press, 2020).

Norton, P., 'Sir Anthony Eden (1955–7)', in I. Dale (ed.), *The Prime Ministers* (London: Hodder & Stoughton, 2020).

Norton, P., 'Party Management', in A. S. Roe-Crines and T. Heppell (eds), *Policies and Politics under Prime Minister Edward Heath* (Cham: Palgrave Macmillan, 2021).

Norton, P., 'Is the Westminster System of Government Alive and Well?' *Journal of Comparative and International Law*, 9 (2022), pp. 1–24.

Norton, P., 'Votes of Confidence and the Fixed-Term Parliaments Act', in A. Horne, L. Thompson and B. Yong (eds), *Parliament and the Law*, 3rd edn (Oxford: Hart Publishing, 2022), pp. 189–207.

# Bibliography

Norton, P., 'Theresa May and the Constitution: A Failure of Statecraft', in A. Roe-Crines and D. Jeffery (eds), *Policies and Politics under Prime Minister Theresa May: A Question of Statecraft* (Cham: Palgrave Macmillan, 2023).

Norton, P. and Aughey, A., *Conservatives and Conservatism* (London: Temple Smith, 1981).

Nott, J., *Here Today, Gone Tomorrow* (London: Politico's, 2002).

NOW!, 'Blue Chips and Guy Fawkes: Mrs Thatcher's Loyal Rebels', 4 January 1980.

Onslow, S., *Backbench Debate within the Conservative Party and its Influence on British Foreign Policy, 1948–57* (Basingstoke: Macmillan Press, 1997).

Owen, D., *Cabinet's Finest Hour* (London: Haus Publishing, 2017).

Packenham, R., 'Legislatures and Political Development', in A. Kornberg and L. D. Musolf (eds), *Legislatures in Developmental Perspective* (Durham, NC: Duke University Press, 1970).

Patten, C., 'Policy Making in Opposition', in Z. Layton-Henry (ed.), *Conservative Party Politics* (London: Macmillan Press, 1980).

Patterson, S. C., 'Legislative Institutions and Institutionalisation in the United States', *The Journal of Legislative Studies*, 1 (1995), pp. 10–29.

Payne, S., *The Fall of Boris Johnson* (London: Macmillan, 2022).

Pearce, E., *The Quiet Rise of John Major* (London: Weidenfeld & Nicolson, 1991).

Peplow, E. and Pivatto, P., *The Political Lives of Postwar British MPs* (London: Bloomsbury Academic, 2020).

Plumb, A., 'Research Note: A Comparison of Free Vote Patterns in Westminster-Style Parliaments', *Commonwealth & Comparative Politics*, 51 (2013), pp. 254–66.

Polsby, N. W., 'The Institutionalisation of the U.S. House of Representatives', *American Political Science Review*, 62 (1968), pp. 144–68.

Ponsonby, C., *Ponsonby Remembers* (Oxford: The Alden Press, 1965).

Prior, J., *A Balance of Power* (London: Hamish Hamilton, 1986).

Punnett, R. M., *British Government and Politics* (London: Heinemann, 1968).

Punnett, R. M., *Selecting the Party Leader* (Hemel Hempstead: Harvester Wheatsheaf, 1992).

Quinn, T., *Electing and Ejecting Party Leaders in Britain* (Basingstoke: Palgrave Macmillan, 2015).

Ramsden, J., *The Making of Conservative Party Policy* (London: Longman, 1980).

Ramsden, J., *The Winds of Change: Macmillan to Heath, 1957–1975* (London: Longman, 1996).

Ramsden, J., *An Appetite for Power* (London: HarperCollins, 1998).

Rawlinson, P., *A Price Too High* (London: Weidenfeld & Nicolson, 1989).

Regan, P., 'The 1986 Shops Bill', *Parliamentary Affairs*, 41 (1987), pp. 218–35.

Renton, T., *Chief Whip* (London: Politico's, 2004).

Rentoul, G., *Sometimes I Think* (London: Hodder & Stoughton, 1940).

Rentoul, G., *This Is My Case* (London: Hutchinson, 1944).

# Bibliography

Rhodes James, R. (ed.), *CHIPS: The Diaries of Sir Henry Channon* (London: Weidenfeld & Nicolson, 1967).

Rhodes James, R., *Bob Boothby: A Portrait* (London: Hodder & Stoughton, 1991).

Richards, P. G. (1974), *The Backbenchers* (London: Faber & Faber, 1974).

Ridley, N., *'My Style of Government': The Thatcher Years* (London: Fontana, 1992).

Rifkind, M., *Power and Pragmatism* (London: Biteback, 2016).

Roberts, A., *The Holy Fox: The Life of Lord Halifax* (London: Weidenfeld & Nicolson, 1991).

Roberts, A., *Eminent Churchillians* (London: Weidenfeld & Nicolson, 1994).

Saalfeld, T. and Strøm, K., 'Political Parties and Legislatures', in S. Martin, T. Saalfeld and K. Strøm (eds), *The Oxford Handbook of Legislative Studies* (Oxford: Oxford University Press, 2014).

Schindler, D. and Kannenberg, O., 'Elite Domination or Participatory Democracy? Comparing the Rules of the Game within Parliamentary Party Groups', paper delivered at the 15th Workshop of Parliamentary Scholars and Parliamentarians, Wroxton, UK, 31 July 2022.

Schneer, J., *Ministers at War* (London: OneWorld Publications, 2015).

Schwarz, J. E. and Lambert, G., 'The Voting Behavior of British Conservative Backbenchers', in S. C. Patterson and J. C. Wahlke (eds), *Comparative Legislative Behavior: Frontiers of Research* (New York: Wiley-Interscience, 1972).

Scott-James, A., 'What Does an MP Do for His Money?' *Picture Post*, 12 December 1942.

Seawright, D., 'The Conservative Election Campaign', in T. Heppell and D. Seawright (eds), *Cameron and the Conservatives* (Basingstoke: Palgrave Macmillan, 2012).

Seldon, A., *Major: A Political Life* (London: Weidenfeld & Nicolson, 1997).

Seldon, A., *May at 10* (London: Biteback, 2019).

Seldon, A., *May at No. 10: The Verdict* (London: Biteback, 2020).

Seldon, A. and Snowdon, P., *Cameron at 10: The Inside Story 2010–2015* (London: William Collins, 2015).

Self, R. C. (ed.), *The Austen Chamberlain Diary Letters* (Cambridge: Cambridge University Press, 1995).

Shepherd, R., *The Power Brokers* (London: Hutchinson, 1991).

Shepherd, R., *Iain Macleod* (London: Hutchinson, 1994).

Shepherd, R., *Enoch Powell* (London: Hutchinson, 1996).

Sieberer, S., 'Party Unity in Parliamentary Democracies: A Comparative Analysis', *The Journal of Legislative Studies*, 22 (2006), pp. 150–78.

Smith, S. S., Roberts, J. M. and Vander Wielen, R. J., *The American Congress*, 6th edn (Cambridge: Cambridge University Press, 2009).

Snowdon, P., *Back from the Brink* (London: HarperPress, 2010).

Spicer, M., *The Spicer Diaries* (London: Biteback, 2012).

Stark, L. P., *Choosing a Leader* (Basingstoke: Macmillan, 1996).

Stephenson, H., *Mrs Thatcher's First Year* (London: Jill Norman, 1980).

# Bibliography

Stewart, G., *Burying Caesar: Churchill, Chamberlain and the Battle for the Tory Party* (London: Phoenix, 2000).

Stuart, J., *Within the Fringe* (London: The Bodley Head, 1967).

Taylor, A. J. P., '1932–1945', in D. Butler (ed.), *Coalitions in British Politics* (London: Macmillan, 1978).

Templewood, Viscount, *Nine Troubled Years* (London: Collins, 1954).

Thatcher, M., *The Downing Street Years* (London: HarperCollins, 1993).

Theakston, K., *Winston Churchill and the British Constitution* (London: Politico's, 2003).

Thorpe, D. R., *Alec Douglas-Home* (London: Sinclair-Stevenson, 1996).

Waddington, D., *Memoirs* (London: Biteback, 2012).

Walters, D., *Not Always with the Pack* (London: Constable, 1989).

Wapshott, N. and Brock, G., *Thatcher* (London: MacDonald & Co., 1983).

Watkins, A., *A Conservative Coup* (London: Duckworth, 1991).

Watson, N., *Robin Chichester-Clark* (London: Profile Books, 2020).

Williams, C., *Harold Macmillan* (London: Phoenix, 2009).

Williams, H., *Guilty Men: Conservative Government, 1992–97* (London: Aurum Press, 1998).

Wilson, H. H., *Pressure Group* (London: Secker & Warburg, 1961).

Wilson, R., *5 Days to Power* (London: Biteback, 2010).

Winterton, Earl, *Orders of the Day* (London: Cassell, 1953).

Young, H., *One of Us* (London: Macmillan, 1989).

Young, K., *Sir Alec Douglas-Home* (London: J. M. Dent, 1970).

Ziegler, P., *Edward Heath* (London: HarperPress, 2010).

# Index

# Index

# Index

# Index

# Index

# Index

# Index

# Index

# Index

# Index

Milton Keynes UK
Ingram Content Group UK Ltd.
UKHW011415041023
429931UK00001B/1/J

9 781526 173300